The False Dawn: European Imperialism
in the Nineteenth Century

Europe and the World
in the Age of Expansion

edited by Boyd C. Shafer

THE
FALSE DAWN
European Imperialism
in the
Nineteenth
Century

by
RAYMOND F. BETTS

UNIVERSITY OF MINNESOTA PRESS □ MINNEAPOLIS

OXFORD UNIVERSITY PRESS

1976

Library of Congress Catalog Card Number 75-14683

ISBN 0-8166-0762-1

Europe and the World
in the Age of Expansion

SPONSORS

Department of History of the
University of Minnesota

James Ford Bell Library of the
University of Minnesota Library

SUPPORTING FOUNDATIONS

Northwest Area Foundation
(formerly Louis W. and Maud Hill
Family Foundation), St. Paul

James Ford Bell Foundation,
Minneapolis

ADVISORY COUNCIL

EDITORS

FOR SUSAN

Editor's Foreword

The expansion of Europe since the thirteenth century has had profound influences on peoples throughout the world. Encircling the globe, the expansion changed men's lives and goals and became one of the decisive movements in the history of mankind.

This series of ten volumes explores the nature and impact of the expansion. It attempts not so much to go over once more the familiar themes of "Gold, Glory, and the Gospel," as to describe, on the basis of new questions and interpretations, what appears to have happened insofar as modern historical scholarship can determine.

No work or works on so large a topic can include everything that happened or be definitive. This series, as it proceeds, emphasizes the discoveries, the explorations, and the territorial expansion of Europeans, the relationships between the colonized and the colonizers, the effects of the expansion on Asians, Africans, Americans, Indians, and the various "islanders," the emergence into nationhood and world history of many peoples that Europeans had known little or nothing about, and, to a lesser extent, the effects of the expansion on Europe.

The use of the word *discoveries*, of course, reveals European (and American) provincialism. The "new" lands were undiscovered only in the sense that they were unknown to Europeans. Peoples with developed cultures and civilizations already had long inhabited most of the huge areas to which Europeans sailed and over which they came to exercise their power and influence. Nevertheless, the political, economic, and social expansion that came with and after the discoveries affected the daily lives, the modes of producing and sharing, the ways of governing, the customs, and the values of peoples everywhere. Whatever their state of development, the expansion also brought, as is well known, tensions, conflicts, and much injustice. Perhaps most important in our own times, it led throughout the developing world to the rise of nationalism, to reform and revolt, and to demands (now largely realized) for national self-determination.

The early volumes in the series, naturally, stress the discoveries and explorations. The later emphasize the growing commercial and political involvements, the founding of new or different societies in the "new" worlds, the emergence of different varieties of nations and states in the often old and established societies of Asia, Africa, and the Americas, and the changes in the governmental structures and responsibilities of the European imperial nations.

The practices, ideas, and values the Europeans introduced continue, in differing ways and differing environments, not only to exist but to have consequences. But in the territorial sense the age of European expansion is over. Therefore the sponsors of this undertaking believe this is a propitious time to prepare and publish this multivolumed study. The era now appears in new perspective and new and more objective statements can be made about it. At the same time, its realities are still with us and we may now be able to understand intangibles that in the future could be overlooked.

The works in process, even though they number ten, cover only what the authors (and editors) consider to be important aspects of the expansion. Each of the authors had to confront vast masses of material and make choices in what he should include. Inevitably, subjects and details are omitted that some readers will think should have been covered. Inevitably, too, readers will note some duplication. This arises in large part because each author has been free, within the general themes of the series, to write his own book on the geographical area and chronological period allotted to him. Each author, as might be expected, has believed it necessary to give attention to the background of his topic and has also looked a bit ahead; hence he has touched upon the time periods of the immediately preceding and following volumes. This means that each of the studies can be read independently, without constant reference to the others. The books are being published as they are completed and will not appear in their originally planned order.

The authors have generally followed a pattern for spelling, capitalization, and other details of style set by the University of Minnesota Press in the interests of consistency and clarity. In accordance with the wishes of the Press and current usage, and after prolonged discussion, we have used the word *black* instead of *Negro* (except in quotations). For the most part American usages in spelling have been observed. The last is sometimes difficult for historians who must be concerned with the different spellings, especially of place names and proper nouns, at different times and in different languages. To help readers the authors have, in consequence, at times added the original (or the present) spelling of a name when identification might otherwise be difficult.

The discussions that led to this series began in 1964 during meetings of the Advisory Committee of the James Ford Bell Library at the University of Minnesota, a library particularly interested in exploration and discovery. Members of the university's Department of History and the University of Minnesota Press, and others, including the present editor, joined in the discussions. Then, after the promise of generous subsidies from the Bell Foundation of Minneapolis and the Northwest Area Foundation (formerly the Hill Family Foundation) of St. Paul, the project began to take form under the editorship of the distinguished historian Herbert Heaton. An Advisory Council of six scholars was appointed as the work began. Professor Heaton, who had agreed to serve as editor for three years, did most of the early planning and selected three authors. Professor Boyd C. Shafer of Macalester College (now at the University of Arizona) succeeded him in 1967. He selected eight authors and did further planning. He has been in constant touch with all the authors, doing preliminary editing in consultation with them, reading their drafts, and making suggestions. The Press editors, as is usual at the University of Minnesota Press, have made valuable contributions at all stages. Between Professor Shafer and the authors — from England, Canada, New Zealand, and the United States — there have been voluminous and amicable as well as critical exchanges. But it must be repeated, each author has been free to write his own work within the general scope of the series.

Raymond F. Betts, the author of volume VI in this series, is a specialist in French colonial history of the nineteenth century. The holder of doctorates from the University of Grenoble (France) and Columbia University, he has written and edited several books and many articles on the subject of European imperialism, including a recent contribution to the UNESCO *General History of Africa*. He has traveled in many of the countries that were former European colonies and has lectured at universities in England and France, as well as in the United States. Formerly on the faculty of Bryn Mawr College and Grinnell College, he is now professor of history at the University of Kentucky.

University of Arizona   Boyd C. Shafer

Preface

The false dawn that greeted and disappointed the visitors in E. M. Forster's *A Passage to India* is a literary image that might serve as a value judgment of modern overseas empire in general. The splendor about it rose only in the minds of its most ardent advocates and appeared in those brief moments of official pageantry that marked the occasion of a state visit, official holiday, or installation of a new governor. High talk about European cultural responsibility was never approached statistically by state aid or numbers of administrators sent to the colonies; dreams of global communities uniting diverse peoples on different continents were never fulfilled; anticipations of a glorious legacy once the colonial effort had ceased became in reality vexing political and economic problems.

The term *empire* is now badly tarnished, the human activity it defined everywhere subjected to the harshest of historical judgments. Yet no bright dawn of understanding has appeared on the academic horizon. And, perhaps, none should be expected. The contours of the historical problem are enormous. Indeed, no single theory will provide a meaningful explanation for the myriad of forms that imperialist activity took; no single model will allow for an integral reconstruction of its history.

The variety of usage of the word *imperialism* in recent years suggests the controversial nature of the subject and the tendency of that word to roam the wasteland of political polemics. If considered simply as an act of domination, imperialism could explain any asymmetrical power relationship — hence most human contacts, whatever their institutional form.

Thus, it could become a nonsense word, as totally lacking in content as in resonance.

Nevertheless, the process that explains modern Europe's overseas expansion has been traditionally and regularly labeled "imperialism." Coined in the last century and thereafter extended temporally in both directions, the word *imperialism* remains appropriately nineteenth century. At no other time was the disparity between European power — here defined as organizational, technological, and financial — and that of the other regions of the world, save the United States, so obvious because so immense.

However explained or justified, the acts of empire were directly controlled by the situation expressed in Hilaire Belloc's sardonic ditty, "Whatever else, we have got / the Maxim gun, and they have not." The machine gun did translate European power brutally and directly to many quarters of the world; and where it did not, the demonic industrial genius behind this destructive device generated other forms of domination. Colonial resistance was often reduced and colonial support enlarged by the iron and steel mechanisms that inspired awe and aroused excitement with the regular movement of their well-articulated parts. The "shock value" of western technology, as Prime Minister Nehru once remarked, was important;[1] in this instance it had an undeniable if unmeasurable effect on the success of the imperialist enterprise.

What distinguished empire in the nineteenth century from that of preceding centuries is found in the factory and the mentality that instituted it. Nineteenth-century theorists of imperialism appreciated this condition and frequently benefited from its deadly and impressive products. Twentieth-century critics have extended this theme of technological and organizational rationalization until it has reached that imposing power complex contained in Juan Bosch's term *Pentagonism*[2]— something of an indiscriminate and illicit commingling of the spirits of Euclid, Moltke the Elder, Lord Kitchener, and John D. Rockefeller.

Imperialism was power, a metaphysical extension of a cultural vision that discerned no confining frontiers. This says all and very little. It explains a mood and offers a general justification, but it provides no intelligence about the factors that urged a Charles Foucauld in the direction of North Africa, a Charles Gordon to China, or — to vary given

---

[1] Jawaharlal Nehru, *Toward Freedom* (New York: John Day, 1942), p. 278.
[2] Juan D. Bosch, "Pentagonism," *Evergreen Review*, 61:29–33, 85–87 (1968).

names — an Albert Schweitzer to Equatorial Africa. Nor does it inform much about the motives for the French annexation of Algeria or the British establishment of a protectorate over Borneo. Behind the grand generalization are found many particulars, some still ill defined historically. Until recently, the outward thrust of Europe was the dominant one in most interpretations, thereby assuring a Eurocentric approach to colonial history. Now that we know better the details of the relationship of the kingdom of Bonny to Great Britain or of Tanga to Germany, we are more willing to qualify and reconsider.

This book attempts to measure the vast dimensions of European empire in the nineteenth century. If the analysis appears "traditional" because it concentrates on European motives and actions, it does so principally to complement the other more regionally defined volumes in this series. Compressed as it is in these few hundred pages, the exciting and variegated history of that expansionist century is treated thematically and topically rather than chronologically. I will not plead the advantages of such an arrangement, any more than I will ignore the distortions it necessarily produces. But a topical approach should permit a focus on major issues that might be misplaced or unstressed in a general narrative sweep.

Therefore, I consider this to be an extended essay, not a general survey. The introductory chapter is, perhaps, a gossamerlike reconstruction of certain nineteenth-century ideals and purposes. Yet whatever the difficulties encountered in any historical attempt to capture the spirit of another age, an appreciation of both the indifference and the enthusiasm with which imperialism was greeted can only be gained through an awareness of the competitive expansion that was considered a desirable norm of social behavior by the prevailing middle classes — and which informed the thought of Karl Marx and Charles Darwin, as well as that of Cecil Rhodes. In brief, empire was not the subject of popular indignation or interest that it is today, and one must understand why.

The three major parts of the volume reflect the standard divisions of historical inquiry and will, I hope, suggest the major concerns seizing Europeans then engaged in empire building. Part I is the most traditional, a political history of expansion which describes how and why territory was acquired. Part II, a composite of intellectual and cultural history, concentrates on the ideology of imperialism. Part III is a form of social history stressing institutions and methods of domination and reactions to them.

The problem of definition has been a trying one. As a history of nineteenth-century European imperialist activity, this book begins with a cursory review of colonial affairs since the Treaty of Paris of 1763 and ends with a final glance toward the Western Front in August 1914. These dates, representative of diplomatic and political history, are little more than convenient to a study of this sort, which also embraces social and economic developments across the face of the globe. Although contemporary Europeans rhapsodized on the bridging of continents and the spanning of oceans — activities that briefly brought the world to Europe — the lines of historical development do not so nicely converge.

The complexity of the phenomenon — or, better, the phenomena — of modern imperialism has both annoyed and awed me, removed geographically so many hundreds of miles from the waters across which that history swept and removed so much further in spirit. In our age, when power seems invariably to imply abuse, it is exceedingly difficult to view imperialism dispassionately. For this reason, the imaginative "leap into the past" is, I believe, greater from our jumping-off place to the late nineteenth century than, say, to the sixteenth century. We understand, appreciate, and can empathize with Martin Luther more easily than we can with Frederick Lugard.

When I first observed the former palace of the French governor-general in Dakar, Senegal, I wondered what spirit such a structure could have been designed to contain. I confess I still do. The thoughts of the imperialists obviously rose to the monumental on occasion; yet today the results of their efforts are either in ruins or have been converted to new purposes. It is easy to dismiss the whole historical scene as politically ponderous, economically pretentious, and morally vacuous.

Nevertheless the historical significance of modern empire will not be denied. Imperialism was one of the most influential forces shaping the modern world. The formal empires, like the men who ruled them, may soon be forgotten, but the spirit that moved and structured them cannot be ignored. The pall of industrial smoke hanging over Mount Fujiyama or enshrouding the Golden Horn and the tricolors flying over the governmental buildings in Abidjan or New Delhi are visible symbols of the effects of imperialism. In all, it was quite a historical act, clumsy and uninspired as much as calculated and high-flung, but universally influential.

I would like to believe that the text which follows is in the tradition of what the French refer to as *haute vulgarisation*. It is a synthesis of the work of many minds, an attempt to place in contemporary perspective issues that the scholar must review and the introductory student should see. I willingly acknowledge my indebtedness to that international group of scholars who, in the last twenty years, has seriously reconsidered the history of modern empire and has made of it much more than an intellectual grand tour of European constitutional and political activities around the world.

More particularly I wish to thank Professors William Cohen of Indiana University, Wm. Roger Louis of the University of Texas, David Gardinier of Marquette University, and Jerry Calton of the University of Kentucky who have read with patience and critical concern all or part of this manuscript. The librarians of the Bibliothèque Nationale in Paris, the British Museum and the Commonwealth Institute in London, the Bibliothèque Africaine in Brussels, and the Africana Collection at Northwestern University have been most cooperative and tolerant of my many requests. Kenneth L. Betts and James W. Betts proved willing research assistants in ferreting out illustrative material and in the initial preparation of maps. The University of Kentucky Research Foundation generously made possible a brief but valuable trip to Paris for additional material. Carolyn Dock typed most of the manuscript with skill and good humor, and she was aided by Barbara Collins, both of whom deserve particular thanks.

Professor Boyd C. Shafer, editor of the series in which this volume appears, performed his duties with more than the usual diligence toward the manuscript and indulgence toward the author. I greatly appreciate his encouragement and sympathy.

My wife, whose own activities precluded any direct involvement in the preparation of this book, was a generous source of encouragement and of good humor when these sentiments were most needed and therefore deeply appreciated.

For the high quality of the production of the book all credit goes to the editorial staff of the University of Minnesota Press. Any errors in judgment or fact are my own.

R. F. B.

University of Kentucky
March 2, 1975

Contents

List of Illustrations

List of Maps

The False Dawn: European Imperialism
in the Nineteenth Century

They awaited the miracle. But at the supreme moment, when night should have died and day lived, nothing occurred. It was as if virtue had failed in the celestial fount. . . . The sun rose without splendour.

E. M. FORSTER, *A Passage to India*

CHAPTER 1

An Age of Expansion

Now surrounded by pejorative connotations and viewed as gaudy in its official trappings, imperialism was consonant with much of the spirit and aspiration of nineteenth-century Europe. Although the expansionist mood of the times cannot be considered the source of impulsion to empire, it did provide the cultural atmosphere in which such far-ranging activity could be carried on with expressions of public indifference, toleration, or occasional wholehearted support.

To the modern mind, disenchanted by the experience of two world wars and an ecological crisis of imposing dimensions, blatant displays of power and the rhetorical flourishes justifying them are disturbing. Yet only a few generations ago, general public response was rather different in tenor. This variation in attitudes suggests two ages quite apart in their world views. It further suggests that an introduction to the study of modern imperialism might well begin with a consideration of the multiple ideas and factors that conditioned the Europeans of this "century of progress" to overseas conquest and domination. Imperialism was not a curious aberration of that age; it was at one with it, perhaps the most exaggerated form in which the hyperbole of the moment was cast.

In all outward appearances western Europe was universally dominant during the second half of the nineteenth century. At no other time was any continent such a center for the dispersal of ideas, goods, political problems, and military operations. Power and expansion, causally related, were the subjects of considerable metaphysical concern and the accepted source of contemporary realities. The theories of the Manchester and Viennese schools of economics, the bridges of Isambard Kingdom Brunel, the concepts of the Social Darwinians, the Brussels Palace of Justice, and the Eiffel Tower, though apparently unrelated, are all expressions of civilization responding for the first time to the possibilities of power unleashed from nature and enslaved by man. Like the steam engine, which is the most obvious artifact of the age, technology and the spirit that informed it provided the dynamic thrust that temporarily created a Eurocentric world and propelled the significant vehicle of global domination — modern imperialism.

Overseas expansion was a constant, not an intermittent, factor in nineteenth-century European history, as any review of territorial acquisition or contemporary literature on the subject will attest. Although the most intensive activity occurred in the last quarter of the century and is frequently labeled the "New Imperialism," at no time during the century was there a lengthy period in which empire was ignored — or not extended. Yet while such expansion was a constant factor, only infrequently was it a pronounced one in public debates of major national issues. Never attaining the popularity that continental wars or sports enjoyed, colonial expansion generally remained extramural, both spatially and psychologically. It would be erroneous to conclude, however, that the European empires were acquired in "a fit of absence of mind," as has been said with exaggeration of the British. Whatever its particular causes, the activity was seldom unintentional, even if it was not always well planned, well directed, or well supported. As for its proponents, whether on the scene or in the ministries at home, they were most purposeful, thinking in terms of "God, gold, and glory."

In contrast with the relatively small number of persons involved as empire builders, the extent of the activity was enormous, reaching worldwide proportions by the turn of the century. Not a continent was without European influence, and few were the regions that did not succumb to some type of European domination. Formal empires were of staggering dimensions, enormously exceeding the geographical size of the metropolitan states that ruled them. The subcontinent of India and the vast reaches of North Africa were shadowed by European flags, but imperial territory also included flakes of land situated in the Pacific and the Caribbean. It was proudly stated that only in the British empire did the

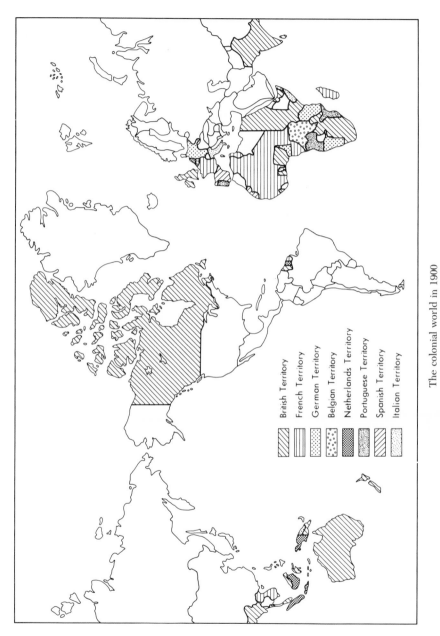

British Territory

French Territory

German Territory

Belgian Territory

Netherlands Territory

Portuguese Territory

Spanish Territory

Italian Territory

The colonial world in 1900

sun never set, yet at many latitudes Frenchmen, Germans, and others also basked in its rays.

As if in a condition of paradox, this age of political expansion was also the age of geographical contraction. The first stage of that elaborate grid system we describe with the words *telecommunications* and *mass transportation* was then designed and installed. Phineas Fogg, hero of Jules Verne's *Around the World in Eighty Days,* made his dashing trip in 1872 in unexpectedly brief time, proving that faraway lands, if not yet adjacent to everybody's backyard, were accessible by train and boat, with bookings arranged by Thomas Cook and through the agency of the telegraph. Appropriately, geography was labeled the "science of distances," and, accordingly, distance was considered to be a function of time. Such additional geographical definition was one more obvious indication of the steady encroachment of western societies upon the world beyond them.

Since the second Age of Exploration at the end of the eighteenth century, when Captain Cook and other navigators carefully plotted the Pacific Ocean, the areas of the world inscribed as terra incognita were rapidly being given place names.[1] The development, rather immodestly called the opening up of the world, was a source of keen interest to nineteenth-century Europeans. Motivated by scientific curiosity, commercial acquisitiveness, and a sense of high adventure, numerous explorers set out to "discover." The center stage was soon to be Africa, the "darkest Africa" of Mr. Stanley. But the Far East and Oceania received a large number of western visitors who opened economic doors, painted verbal and oil pictures of exotica, and reveled in what was romantically referred to as the "mysteries of the East."

The action was primarily set upon the seas. The maritime age, which found its confident philosopher in Captain Alfred Mahan, launched not only the imposingly structured battleship and the screw-driven ocean liner of palatial proportions, but also the less praised vessel of bulk commerce, the tramp steamer. The world was now awake. In the early years of the nineteenth century, New England whalers engaged the Pacific and fast clipper ships skirted the China coasts. By mid-century the ponderous Indiamen of the eighteenth century were replaced by P&O steamers, connecting England to India by way of swift service from Suez to Calcutta. Companies like the English Elder Dempster and the French Mes-

---

[1] See J. H. Parry, *Trade and Dominion: The European Overseas Empires in the Eighteenth Century* (London: Weidenfeld and Nicolson, 1971), notably chapter 3.

sageries Maritimes established shipping routes and wharves along the west coast of Africa. The Rubbatino Company of Genoa, maintaining a Red Sea route, in 1870 sought a coaling station on the east coast of Africa. Far removed from Europe proper, Hong Kong and Singapore rose to become entrepôts of worldwide fame.

As for nineteenth-century exploration, several historians have insisted that its distinctive aspect was fluvial. The major oceans were then known and trafficked, but continental penetration was still underway, and the river suggested the most attractive entry. Indeed, one of the most fascinating problems to European explorers was the form and commercial suitability of African and Asian river systems. In Africa the search for the headwaters of the Nile was matched by a search for an east-west network, flowing from the Senegal or Niger River, that might connect with the Nile at roughly right angles. Such a system would have allowed for the commercial penetration of Africa in a manner not dissimilar to that of North America by way of the St. Lawrence, the Great Lakes, and the Mississippi. The discovery of the entrance of the Niger at the Bight of Biafra by the Lander brothers in 1830 was widely acclaimed, but the Niger's southeastward flow denied it the role of an African St. Lawrence. A half-

Indo-European telegraph cable being laid, 1865. From *Illustrated London News*, July 8, 1865. (Reproduced by permission of *Illustrated London News*.)

Demonstration of the Maxim gun, 1889. From *Scientific
American Supplement*, October 5, 1889.

Armored train used in the British occupation of Egypt, 1882. From
Scientific American Supplement, September 23, 1882.

Ships of the naval forces sent to Chinese waters during the Boxer Rebellion, 1900. From *Scientific American Supplement*, September 15, 1900.

century later, Stanley made his monumental trip from the east to the west coast of Africa by way of the Zambezi to the Congo. He thereby proved the existence of a latitudinal river network, but it was neither fully connected nor susceptible to large-scale commerce. About the same time half a world away, both French and English explorers, with the imagined riches of China before them, sailed up the rivers of Southeast Asia in anticipation of finding wide waterways by which to bind the South China trade to their own national economic interests. The French expedition of 1866–68 up the Mekong in Indochina was described by the president of the Royal Geographical Society in London as the most important expedition of the nineteenth century — an exaggerated description not unusual for the age.[2]

What waterways could not provide, railways might. Exploratory missions, many sponsored by the French, were charged with determining convenient routes over which roadbeds might be laid. Often inspired by engineers and generally guided by them, these missions were occasionally seen as an opportunity to test pet schemes and plans for long-range communications systems. An interesting technology of imperialism, re-

[2] Stephen A. Roberts, *The History of French Colonial Policy, 1870–1925* (Hamden: Archon Press, 1963; first published, 1929), pp. 422–423.

moved only in time from the intentions and activities of some of the western planning accompanying today's foreign aid to developing countries, was then evident. Although the Cape-to-Cairo scheme, popularized by Cecil Rhodes, is the best known of these grand plans, it was neither the most imaginative nor the most daring. The Transsaharan, which had been a French dream from the 1870s onward, was enlarged to become the Transafrican, an elaborate but easily constructed railroad system — or so its promoters argued — with electric trains cutting swiftly and directly through French territories extending from Algeria to Chad.[3]

Throughout the world the movement was the same. Steamships frequented well-marked ocean lanes; transcontinental railroads bound coasts together, as in the United States, Canada, and Russia; north-south railroads joined hinterlands to seaports, as in India, Nigeria, and South Africa; canals, like the Suez and Panama, greatly reduced oceanic travel times. And farsighted observation revealed that moment in the not too distant future when airships would drone serenely over continents. Thus the earth was made one and compact. "The century that is just closing has brought with it great changes. There are no longer any far-off lands . . . Steam and electricity have well-nigh blotted out distance," rhapsodized an editorial in the *Baptist Union* in 1898. King Leopold II of Belgium, a man of fewer words, had offered the same thought many years before, when he had commented, "There are no longer any continents."[4]

This dramatic alteration of spatiotemporal relationships, perceived by so many Europeans in the 1800s, became heavily weighted with political significance by the last quarter of the century. Not since the creation of the state system in the sixteenth century did the international political pattern seem so susceptible to, and even needful of, modification. Then on the threshold of the age of global politics, late nineteenth-century imperialists crudely toyed with ideas of geopolitics and put together verbal constructs of fine resonance, like "Greater Britain," "La Plus Grande

[3] A persuasive treatment of the technology of imperialism is offered by Henri Brunschwig, "Notes sur les technocrats de l'impérialisme français en Afrique noire," *Revue française d'histoire d'outre-mer*, 54:171–187 (1957). On the Transafrican railroad, see Etienne Roumens, *L'impérialisme français et les chemins de fer transafricains* (Paris: Plon, 1914).

[4] *Baptist Union*, 8:338 (1898), quoted by Ernest May, *American Imperialism: A Speculative Essay* (New York: Atheneum, 1968), p. 193; Note from Duc de Brabant (Leopold II) to Jean LeJeune, dated May 20, 1865, printed in Leon LeFebvre de Vivy, *Documents de l'histoire précoloniale belge, 1861–1865* (Brussels: Académie Royale des Sciences Coloniales, 1959), p. 33.

France," and "Grossere Deutschland." The use of the comparative form of the adjective implied qualitative as well as quantitative change; in a new form of moral arithmetic the biggest was equated with the best.

Hardly surprising in an age when the millenary had already been replaced statistically and culturally by the millionary, the preoccupation with gross accumulation, whether of products or territory, was made the proper concern of imperialists. There were many, it is true, who were more interested in the political form and structure of empire than in its size. But none denied that without colonies the states in which they lived would be diminished — reduced perhaps to the status of Switzerland, Belgium, or Holland in the twentieth century. Lord Alfred Milner, one of the most renowned of the imperial proconsuls, voiced such sentiment in a speech he made in 1906: "Greatness is relative. Physical limitations forbid that these islands should retain the same importance among the vast Empires of the modern world they held in the days of smaller States . . . But Greater Britain may remain such a Power."[5]

There is no need to read between the lines to detect the ambivalence which had already begun to permeate the thought of men like Milner. The measured self-confidence which enabled Europe to assign itself the pivotal position in international politics and industrial economics appeared to be disrupted by this world newly appointed according to the latest dictates of technology. The assertion of the geographer Halford J. Mackinder that the European phase of history was passing away as the Mediterranean had done before it implied that the European state as a cultural as well as a political unit was diminishing with the rapid expansion of the political world. Indeed, much of the imperialistic rhetoric expressed a dreadful concern that the twentieth century would bring a new order in which the sea-to-shining-sea states of America and Russia would compete with and disturb the ocean-straddling European states, already jostled as their numbers had increased.[6]

The reality of the fear was apparent in production and population statistics, but the extent of it was conditioned by the ideologies that enshrined the ideas of competition and conflict.

The most popular and pervasive of these ideologies was nationalism. Originally conceived as the integer that would unite diverse peoples into a

[5] Speech delivered before the Manchester Conservative Club, December 14, 1906, reprinted in Lord Alfred Milner, *Imperial Unity* (London: National Review Office, 1907), pp. 18–19.

[6] H. J. Mackinder, *Britain and the British Seas* (London: Henry Froude, 1904), p. 350.

responsible community of citizens separate from, but complementary to, other like groups, nationalism by the second half of the century was becoming both exclusive and aggressive, primarily gaining political definition by the projection in time and space of national competition. Recent enemies like France and Germany were forced into historical attitudes of rivalry; Great Britain again became "Perfidious Albion," encircling the world with its money, navy, and diplomacy; Germany felt constrained and sought its "place in the sun"; and Italy revived dreams of mare nostrum. European states were anthropomorphized, endowed with the aggressive spirit and selfish disposition that late nineteenth-century social scientists and many of their twentieth-century descendants assumed to be the basis of human nature.

The use of the organic metaphor to describe state behavior was in keeping with the period's scientific attitude. Just as the seventeenth century had been the age of the inert sciences, like astronomy and physics, so the nineteenth was the era of the biological, in which change through time was the new dimension. The temporal factor was therefore all important, but nowhere more than in the rash of evolutionary theories that marked the thought of the century so profoundly. At midpoint, when Darwin published his *Origin of Species*, the ideas of competition, struggle for survival, and evolution through adaptation were familiar to the literate public. The creation and approval of a vocabulary of social behavior for Darwin's biological thesis were easily accomplished.

Social Darwinism complemented the laws of the marketplace and more than hinted at the idea that progress occurred through the aggressive play of natural forces. Here was a dialectic that could explain and justify Europe's ascendancy in the world, mute complaints of social injustice at home, lead to the acceptance of wars as historical necessities, and make selfishness a fact of life. Moreover, the stark alternatives of organic existence — growth or decay — were translated into the stark alternatives of national state existence. A succession of elaborate but brooding comments on this subject came from writers representing most of the nations of the Western World, and these opinions were treated with a seriousness that suggested both their contemporary respectability and the emergence of a form of national tribalism. One of the clearest expositions of such Social Darwinian imperialism was provided by Jules Harmand, a French theorist of empire who also had colonial service in Indochina. He wrote in 1910: "[Conquest] is immoral, but the truth is that it is a forced immoral-ity. Conquest is one of the manifestations of the law of struggle for existence, to which we are submitted not only by nature which condemns us to perish or to conquer, but also by our civilization."[7]

The characteristic of civilization that Harmand considered so compelling was its economic dynamism, which, he believed, necessitated the incorporation, as markets or sources of raw materials, of those areas of the world otherwise "lost" by the "incapacity" of the indigenous populations. This connection between sociobiological growth and economic development was imagined to impose on overseas expansion an inevitability to which men like Harmand happily or worriedly resigned themselves and their nations.[8]

Even before Harmand wrote, however, other thinkers with a vision grander than his apprehensively observed their shrinking globe. Between 1893, when Frederick Jackson Turner presented his now famous paper on the American frontier, and 1907, when Lord Curzon delivered his Romanes Lecture on the frontier, the cultural implications of the contraction of space were widely considered. The optimists and romantics, in the idyllic mood of Walt Whitman when he wrote A Passage to India, saw in "God's purpose from the first" — or in man's benign reason — "the lands to be welded together." Others with a scientific twist of mind developed theories of social velocity regulated by a sort of direct ratio between the intensification of communications and the extension of political consolidation. The well-known attempt of Brooks Adams to construct a Galilean theory of civilization — "the velocity of the social movement of any community is proportionate to its energy and mass" — simply overshadowed similar ideas of several French sociologists, but complemented the thought of Sir Charles P. Lucas of the British Colonial Office who observed that space in the colonial world was a "fluctuating and uncertain unit" which consequently complicated, because of undulating definition, colonial administration and social relations.[9]

[7] Jules Harmand, Domination et colonisation (Paris: Flammarion, 1910), p. 153.

[8] On the subject of imperialism and Social Darwinism, see Bernard Semmel, Imperialism and Social Reform: English Social-Imperial Thought, 1895–1914 (New York: Doubleday, 1968; first published, 1960), chapter 2; Walter LaFeber, The New Empire: An Interpretation of American Expansion, 1860–1898 (Ithaca, N.Y.: Cornell University Press, 1969; first published, 1963), chapter 2; Raymond F. Betts, Assimilation and Association in French Colonial Theory, 1890–1914 (New York: Columbia University Press, 1961), chapter 4.

[9] Adams's theory appears in The Law of Civilization and Decay (New York: Vintage Books, 1955; first published, 1895), p. 6; that of Charles Lucas in Greater Rome and Greater Britain (Oxford: Clarendon Press, 1912), p. 37. See also Jacques Novicow, "La croissance et la décroissance des sociétés en fonction du temps," Revue internationale de sociologie,

The new metaphysical principle that space was a prime factor in determining the quality of culture produced in the minds of some analysts the unpleasant corollary that a state of nonexpansion was equivalent to cultural atrophy. This was a thought gloomily consonant with the fin de siècle spirit and sufficiently expressed to stand as a fitting preface to the subsequent work of Oswald Spengler. The French in particular were seized with such ideas as early as the 1870s when memories of their military defeat by the Germans and worry over a falling birthrate made the theme of cultural decay a familiar one in arguments for a forceful policy of territorial expansion. In somewhat poetic form the thought was simplified as follows: "Every people which encloses itself . . . behind the wall of its mountains and the moat of its rivers without concern for spreading something of itself abroad . . . is a people ready for the tomb."[10] Yet the dismal hue that Social Darwinism often cast over such a scene was much less evident in French interpretations than in those advanced in English.

From the little band of despairing American and British prophets, two individuals merit some attention. The American Brooks Adams and the Englishman Charles H. Pearson separately but complementarily put together a rather detailed analysis of the impending decline of the West.

The urbane Adams surveyed the Western World in his *Law of Civilization and Decay*, published in 1895, and in a series of articles which appeared at the time of the Spanish-American War. As he looked eastward across the Atlantic, he saw nothing to excite: France was in the process of decay, while Great Britain suffered from social inertia. As he looked westward in 1898, he noticed that "the continent which, when Washington lived, gave a boundless field for the expansion of Americans has been filled." His chief concern, it is obvious, was with the environment, with the manner in which social energies were either mobilized and displaced or adapted to the ever-changing conditions and locales in which men live. Much of the appeal of Adams's thought, however, derived from the simple frontier thesis upon which it partially rested. Now cluttered and closed, continental America could find through expansion into the Pacific the route by which to escape submission to the law of

---

2:273–289 (1894); and Henri Decugis, "De l'influence de progrés des communications sur l'évolution des sociétés," *ibid.*, 3:496–523 (1894).
[10] Pierre Legendre, *Notre épopée coloniale* (Paris: Tallandier, 1901), pp. 597–598.

cultural decay that Adams had rigidly formulated and uncompromisingly imposed.[11]

Pearson's thoughts, publicly expressed but a few years before those of Adams, were of the same sort. In his *National Life and Character*, published in 1893 — and more than chronologically coincidental with Turner's initial work — Pearson spoke "of the filling up of the land" in the Temperate Zone, a subject of interest to him since 1868 when he had visited the United States and had noted the rapidity with which the land was being peopled. Pearson's general conclusion about the future of the Western World was even more fated than that of Adams. He saw the world approaching what he called "the stationary state," a condition characterized by the restriction of markets, places for immigration, and outlets for the ambitious and discontented. At a future time, he prophesied, westerners might awaken "to find ourselves elbowed, hustled and perhaps even thrust aside by peoples whom we looked down upon as servile." That these peoples might then be westernized was Pearson's sole comfort.[12]

The particular interpretations of Pearson and Adams were more dismal than those entertained by most European imperialist ideologues. Although some of them were willing to agree with Pearson that the narrowing confines of the Western World might force its inhabitants to suffer physical and social decline, others offered the colonial frontier as a fortuitous ameliorative. At the time when North Americans provided a corollary for the frontier thesis by contending that national extension into the Pacific would revitalize the economy, Europeans developed an interest in the frontier for those nonstatistical qualities that formed the mystique surrounding interpretations of Turner's thought. Put otherwise, as the American continental frontier closed, the European colonial frontier opened — and with the psychic riches earlier found in the American Far West.

Some European imperialists assessed the attractiveness of the far-flung regions of their empires by the degree of isolation from the metropolis and by the amount of open space they seemed to offer for dynamic action and personal fulfillment. This was the characteristic of the land that drew European attention to the American continental frontier. Lord Curzon in

[11] LaFeber, *New Empire*, pp. 84–85.

[12] Charles H. Pearson, *National Life and Character: A Forecast* (London: Macmillan, 1893), pp. 14, 28, 85.

his Romanes Lecture of 1907, one of the few European conceptual appraisals of frontiers, commented on the American school of frontier historians and then spoke of the types of men and activities determined by this frontier. He wrote, "From this tempestuous cauldron of human passion and privation, a new character, earnest, restless, exuberant, self-confident emerged; here an Andrew Jackson, there an Abraham Lincoln, flamed across the stage." In the British empire Curzon found the necessary counterpart to the American frontier and praised it unstintedly:

Outside the English universities no school of character exists to compare with the Frontier; and character there is molded, not by attrition with fellow men in the arts or studies of peace, but in the furnace of responsibility and on the anvil of self-reliance. Along many a thousand miles of remote border are to be found our twentieth century Marcher Lords. The breadth of the Frontier has entered into their nostrils and infused their being.[13]

While few wrote of this topic as Curzon did, a frontier psychology like that defined in American literature became a significant imperialist factor. The lure of open spaces, of star-canopied skies, and of struggling against primeval elements — this was the stuff of an extensive colonial literature, both fictional and autobiographical.

The growing interest in natural environment as a social determinant, found in the historical and geographical interpretations of the day, was positively emphasized in the literature of empire, which promised that the vast and unspoiled out of doors would enhance the characters of transplanted Europeans. The colonial personality — as described by admirers — was more free, noble, and energetic than the personality ensnared in an urban life of materialistic purpose.[14] As bourgeois existence appeared more stifling because more routinized, a variety of Europeans — from Gauguin to T. E. Lawrence — sought escape and perhaps themselves in barren desert and lush jungle. Hardy individualists, or at least nonconformists, they seemed to offer proof that the colonial frontier, like the American, could generously accommodate and satisfy those who were socially uncomfortable at home or ambitious beyond accepted restraint. When Marshal Lyautey spoke of Morocco and Algeria as the French "Far

---

[13] Lord George Curzon, "Frontiers": The Romanes Lecture for 1907 (Oxford: Clarendon Press, 1907), pp. 54–56.
[14] See Raymond F. Betts, "The French Colonial Frontier," in Charles Warner, ed., From the Ancien Régime to the Popular Front (New York: Columbia University Press, 1969), pp. 127–143.

West," he did so with the belief in their liberating influence on metropolitan Frenchmen.[15] And the heroes who emblazen the pages of French colonial novels are men of action and purpose, striking attitudes as large and as stark as the land in which they roam.[16]

Imperialists made spaciousness a national as well as personal concern in an effort to liberate thought and sentiment from old and limiting concerns. Sir Charles Dilke, author of the popular *Greater Britain*, suggested this mood as early as the 1860s. "The possession of India," he wrote, "offers to ourselves that element of vastness of domain which, in this age, is needed to secure width of thought and nobility of purpose." Two decades later, the conservative and militant German nationalist Heinrich von Treitschke equally extolled the grandness of scale that large countries enjoyed. "Their citizens' outlook upon the world will be freer and greater. The command of the sea especially promotes it. . . . The time may come when no State will be counted great unless it can boast of territories beyond the seas." Still another two decades later, Cecil Rhodes summed up all arguments in the homily, "Where there is space, there is hope."[17]

By the 1890s, this particular expansive mood was but one aspect of a shift in western thought from the positivist and the rational to the idealist and the romantic. The imperialist equivalent of Bergson's time-as-duration might well have been immensity-as-intimacy. Both were appreciations derived from perception, not observation; both were sensed in solitude, in a manner by which the mind reassembled measurement to give it personal and compacted form.[18]

Such an existence, however, was neither the reality nor the dream of a Tommy Atkins. Rather, this was a world created for and by an intellectual elite and latter-day mystics who found their native Europe dull and constraining. In entering a realm that appeared to be both infinite and intimate to them, they found the opportunity for a higher dedication to a greater destiny, whether that be Eternal France or God and Queen. The French romantic Ernest Psichari wrote a novel of contemporary colonial life enti-

[15] Louis Hubert Lyautey, *Paroles d'action* (Paris: A. Colin, 1927), pp. 52 and 104.

[16] On this subject see Roland Lebel, *Histoire de la littérature coloniale* (Paris: Larose, 1931).

[17] Charles Dilke, *Greater Britain* (Philadelphia: Lippincott, 1869), II, 104; Heinrich von Treitschke, *Politics*, trans. Blanche Dugdale and Torben de Bille (New York: Macmillan, 1916), I, 36; Rhodes cited by Paul Leroy-Beaulieu, *Le Sahara, le Soudan et les Transsahariens* (Paris: Guillaumin, 1904), p. xiv.

[18] A most interesting philosophical treatment of the general subject of personally perceived space is Gaston Bachelard, *The Poetics of Space*, trans. Maria Jolas (New York: Orion, 1964).

tled *Voyage of the Centurions*.[19] Almost any colonial officer, given to the
historically dramatic, would have delightedly acquiesced in the choice of
historical comparison found in the title.

The frontiers of empire that the modern centurions were guarding
were also the last regions of this world still unexposed to the harsh examination and regimentation of western civilization. But not for long. "The
retreat of mystery has been exposed to the full gaze of modern civilization," proclaimed the author of one of the many books commemorating
the new century. "Even the Polar regions are not regarded with awe."[20]
For the romantic adventurer and the colonial theorist the hitherto vast
world was contracting to that congested proximity and overall similarity
so aptly described in Buckminster Fuller's term *spaceship earth*.

The attitudes, sentiments, and thoughts just briefly described — all
responses to the excitement and anxieties generated by a technologically
oriented civilization — were the crude elements of an ideology of imperialism. All-encompassing, like the activity it was meant to explain and
justify, the ideology ranged across the century's intellectual landscape.
Lofty national purpose and individual duty were combined in the assumption of the "white man's burden"; the tooth-and-fang jungle of the Social
Darwinians compelled states to strengthen themselves by expansion; the
workings of the marketplace suggested colonies as sound business ventures. Vertically, the ideology of imperialism rose to the metaphysical and
was grounded in the pragmatic. There is, for instance, the rhetorical
flourish of the University of London historian J. A. Cramb: "Imperialism,
I should say, is patriotism, transfigured by a light from the aspirations of
universal humanity." And then there is the simply put commercial caveat
of the Frenchman Henri Mager: "Without colonies, no more exportation."[21]

In truth, the arguments for imperialism were frequently corollaries of
other ideologies, like nationalism, capitalism, racism.[22] The peripheral
relationship of imperialism to the other "isms" is in part due to the

[19] On the centurion guarding the borders of empire, he wrote, "Oh, exile, taste the joy of
being true to yourself. . . . You are alone here in the sweet thought of night, and, tomor-
row, in the frugal morning, you will be a man at grips with the land, a primitive planet, a
free man in open space." *Le voyage du centurion* (Paris: Conard, 1947; first published,
1915), pp. 127–128.

[20] John C. Wright, *Changes of a Century* (London: Stock, n.d.), p. 10.

[21] J. A. Cramb, *The Origins and Destiny of Imperial Britain* (London: John Murray,
1915), p. 20; Henri Mager, *Les cahiers coloniaux de 1889* (Paris: A. Colin, 1889), p. iii.

[22] Philip Curtin, ed., *Imperialism* (New York: Harper & Row, 1971), pp. xii–xiii.

obvious fact that empire was external to but dependent on the domestic politics and economics of the various European countries. To provide it with coherence and relevance, imperialists related expansion to those issues that appealed to the public as questions of "national interest."

But this dependent ideological relationship was also due in part to the gap — geographical as well as temporal — between policy and practice. What became matters of "national interest" were often defined far from the vaulted chancelleries at home by the man on the scene, the colonial adventurer, who was satisfying personal ambitions by enlarging them to fit national dimensions. There was more than an occasional disjunction between local activity overseas and national policy at home. Such a situation also made imperialism an ideological ex post facto justification for already acquired territory, or, put crudely, the publicity by which the real estate was to be sold.

There is no risk of exaggeration in stating that imperialism was a weak intellectual construct put together in the last decades of great system building in the Western World but assembled from strands of thought that stretched across the century. Seldom treated to profound or coherent analysis by its proponents, imperialism approached the ideological proximity of nationalism. Indeed, it can be argued that as doctrine imperialism was an expansion of nationalism in space, if not in content. Both were more sentiment than analytical thought, invocations of a communal spirit which was to assure historical purpose. Thus, they were something of a religious surrogate in a time when the *res publica christiana* had already fractured beyond repair, and, now along with it, its sustaining belief system.

The religio-historical idea of "manifest destiny," which assured Americans of the righteousness of their cause as they spread westward, is the most famous of such postulates, although it was closely complemented by expressions of faith intoned on the other side of the Atlantic. There, too, empire approached the spiritual whenever a common purpose or appealing general justification was sought for it. The English more than rivaled contemporary Americans in political sermonizing. Lord Curzon, an obvious example, offered a providential purpose when he asserted that imperialism "is a preordained dispensation, intended to be a source of strength and discipline to ourselves and of moral and material blessing to others." A hardly known but ardently enthusiastic imperialist, Ellis T. Powell, lectured the Royal Colonial Institute on "The Faith of an Imperialist" in 1912 and probably stirred his audience with these words: "In truth, both King and nation are bowed in reverent salutation before a supreme Imperial Intelligence which is greater than the King." A string of similar references to the providential nature of British involvement in the world is easily found.[23]

The French, perhaps because of the Third Republic's distinct policy of anticlericalism, seldom argued late in the century that the divinity guided the destiny of empire, but they never ceased to speak of history as the sponsor. The well-known concept of a *mission civilisatrice*, for instance, was traced back to Roman origins when the vocation of converting barbarians was supposedly first practiced. Transmuted by Christianity, rationalized by the universalism of the Enlightenment, imposed in part by the Revolution, and finally willed to the Third Republic as a national legacy, the civilizing mission became both right and obligation. Frenchmen posed their nation as the faithful heir of Rome, as the carrier of the torch of civilization. Imperialism, according to the French historian and politician Gabriel Hanotaux, "is a matter of extending overseas to regions only yesterday barbarian the principles of a civilization of which one of the oldest nations of the world has the right to be proud." Shortly after World War I, one sentimentalist went further in paean, but not beyond the limits of French colonial rhetoric: "There lives in the French heart," he asserted, "a spontaneous piety (in the nature of a spiritual instinct) for the civilizing mission to which France has ever dedicated herself."[24]

The selection of such comments on the metaphysics of empire need not be chronologically limited to the end of the century. Reaching back in time, the historian will touch upon similar thoughts in most any decade. Thomas Carlyle, for instance, assigned the English no mean place in the world in the year 1829. "World History," he insisted, had given two tasks to his countrymen: "The grand industrial task of conquering some half or more of this terraqueous planet for the use of man; then secondly, the grand Constitutional task of sharing in some pacific and endurable manner, the fruit of the conquest, and showing all people how it might be done." The French vice-consul in Shanghai wrote with Old Testament prophecy in 1855: "The moment has come for France . . . to play the

---

[23] Lord George Curzon, "The True Imperialism," *Nineteenth Century*, 63:161–162 (1908); Ellis T. Powell, "The Faith of an Imperialist," *United Empire*, 3:475 (1912).

[24] Gabriel Hanotaux, *L'énergie française* (Paris: Flammarion, 1902), p. 365; Charles Castre, *The Ideals of France* (New York: Abington Press, 1922), p. 34.

first role in the Far East. An occasion more favorable will never be offered us. Faithful to the mission that Divine Providence has confided to us, we will once again show ourselves [to be] the champions of humanity."[25]

All imperialist thought throughout the century was buoyed by the assumption of cultural ascendancy. Ranging from the humanitarian to the racist in interpretation, this assumption was seldom questioned; most often it was received as a historical if not a divine "given" — a principle as self-sufficient as it was nationally satisfying. Woven into national histories like Jules Michelet's romantic account of France or Thomas Buckle's "scientific" explanation of English civilization, progress was shown to lead to goodness. Put in the religio-nationalist poetry of the time, "God shed his grace on thee." And, consequently, "thou" — the organic collectivity described as State or Nation — would dutifully transmit it.

Such thoughts seem to be superficial and self-serving interpretations of the Hegelian Idea. If seen in this light they reveal the uses of history in the 1800s and therefore provide valuable reminders that the ideology of imperialism which appeared in the last years of the century had traceable antecedents. The general objective of that ideology was the glorification of the nation-state, both through the extension of its domains and in the elevation of its responsibilities. The combination of material possession and moral purpose is what, in the minds of the imperialists, conferred upon empire its grandeur and what assured that imperialism was, in Lord Milner's words, creed rather than cry.[26]

Yet imperialism was viewed in its own time by many observers as a practical necessity, not a metaphysical nicety. This particular idea was coincidental with, indeed conditional of, the "New Imperialism." The connection between industrialism and imperialism was discussed nearly as much in the 1800s as it is today by historians of the subject, but the concluding third of the century was the period in which industrial problems were disturbing older social relationships and pressing upon foreign affairs in a new and bothersome way.

The crux of the century's expansionism, as has been suggested earlier, was the industrial process which, like the force unleashed by the sor-

[25] Carlyle quoted by Richard Faber, *The Vision and the Need: Late Victorian Imperialist Aims* (London: Faber & Faber, 1966), p. 63; French vice-consul quoted by John F. Cady, *The Roots of French Imperialism in Eastern Asia* (Ithaca, N.Y.: Cornell University Press, 1967; first published, 1954), p. 107. Professor William B. Cohen of Indiana University is now working on a study of French imperialist thought in this early period.

[26] Milner, *Imperial Unity*, p. 15.

cerer's apprentice, appeared to be increasingly uncontrollable. Jules Ferry, frequently considered the political architect of the modern French empire, once described colonial policy as a safety valve for the steam-driven industrial machine. There was, as his metaphor indicates, grave concern about external restriction and possible resultant internal explosion. The so-called "Long Depression" of the 1870s and 1880s, the erection of defensive tariff walls in the same period, and the continuing migration of the laboring and peasant populations from Europe were events seriously considered by European politicians. The fear of diminishing areas available for economic exploitation was another aspect of the general concern at the end of the century when the contraction of space was ominously commented on. What later historians, following Frederick Jackson Turner, would call the "frontier of trade" was seemingly being pushed to its extremity at the time the frontier of space, previously described, was reaching its limits.[27]

Within Europe, conditions seemed to be dreadfully pressing. The domestic dislocation that industrialism necessitated — the obvious demographic shift from countryside to city, for instance — raised fears of extreme social discontent, if not revolution, as Pearson and others revealed in their writings. The impending internal crisis, imperialists argued, could only be averted abroad. Settlement colonies could absorb increasing populations; tropical dependencies could provide raw materials and might become brisk markets; the various segments of empire, as markets, might partly answer the "social question" by stimulating domestic production and hence relieving unemployment at home; finally, the far ends of empire might shelter firebrands and malcontents who threatened to tear the social fabric.

In summary, the faces of imperialism were numerous. The imperialism of prestige over which the flag majestically waved was joined by the imperialism of geopolitics in which strategy figured colorfully on large-scaled wall maps. This, too, was joined by the imperialism of trade which manipulated and added up statistics to justify colonies as outlets; and by social imperialism through which domestic social problems would be alleviated or diverted by a popular glance and a national thrust overseas. As there is no single theory of imperialism suitable for all conditions and all

[27] The first reference to the term in a colonial setting is that of W. K. Hancock, *Argument of Empire* (Harmondsworth: Penguin Books, 1943), p. 69. Particular reference was made to West Africa.

climes, so there was no single purpose animating the thoughts of the high-minded, or the calculations of the profit-seekers, or the decisions of the politically manipulative. Imperialism was like the mohair settee — a convenience of the age.

Yet, despite all the objectives it was called upon to serve and the needs it was required to satisfy, imperialism as doctrine and policy attracted no great number of serious adherents. Some idea of the extent of support can be gained by briefly considering the voluntary associations pledged to the furtherance of empire. They did appear in some profusion, but their memberships were never very numerous. By far the largest, but one with additional purposes, was the Primrose League in England, which numbered a million in 1891. On the Continent, the Deutsche Kolonialgesellschaft, an amalgam formed in 1887 of two earlier societies, had the highest membership, which reached 23,500 in 1887. No other national colonial society touched it in size. The Comité de l'Afrique Française, the most important of a cluster of French colonial associations, had a total of slightly less that 3000 dues payers in the first years of the twentieth century; and the Royal Colonial Institute, founded in 1868 and later with branches throughout the British empire, had about 4000 followers in 1892.

Most of these organizations performed the functions currently attributed to lobbies; they were designed primarily to arouse public interest in the imperialist cause. For instance, the first aim of the Deutsche Kolonialgesellschaft was "to turn the national ardor toward German colonization and to spread in ever-growing circles the knowledge of the necessity for it."[28] Although the associations included among their number the obvious interest groups of businessmen, naval expansionists, militarists, and financiers, no single group provided the leadership. Indeed, even the political tendencies of each organization were not restricted to one party or persuasion. However, most of the societies were directed either to activities in a particular geographical area or to a particular colonial problem. For example, the Union Coloniale Française sought to enhance French financial interest in Indochina; the short-lived Imperial Federation League bore a self-explanatory title, as did the Société Française d'Émigration des Femmes.

Expression of these varied efforts was given in the many periodicals

[28] Quoted by Pauline R. Anderson, *The Background of Anti-English Feeling in Germany, 1890–1902* (Washington, D.C.: American University Press, 1939), p. 181.

that proliferated at this time, some of which were house organs of the colonial associations, while others reached out to a wider audience. In England, as in the United States, a penny press, sometimes given to yellow journalism, held forth in exuberant prose. The *Pall Mall Gazette*, the *Daily Express*, and the *Daily Mail* all directed their efforts to the cause of empire, and with assertions not dissimilar to the *Daily Mail's* statement that it was "the embodiment and mouthpiece of the imperial idea."

The public at large responded heartily only on exceptional occasions. The return of the French explorer Savorgnan de Brazza from the Congo stimulated a press campaign that aroused Parisian and national fervor and urged the French parliament to ratify a treaty of protection that Brazza had signed with King Iloo. The British were seized with a virtual delirium of imperialism during the Diamond Jubilee of Queen Victoria when the panoply and exotic variety of the empire were displayed in solemn array along the streets of London. Stanley's explorations in Africa, the needless but dramatic death of General Gordon at Khartoum in 1885, the Fashoda incident of 1898 when France and England intersected in their African colonial efforts — events such as these generated keen public interest and precipitated considerable parliamentary debate.

Between these intermittent outbursts of enthusiasm and concern, the imperial cause kindled bright fires only in domestic hearths through the consumption of pulp fiction. The various works of G. A. Henty (for example, *With Kitchener in the Sudan*), Rider Haggard (*King Solomon's Mines*), and Pierre Loti (*Fantôme d'Orient*) entertained a wide reading public, offering a moment of enchantment to the Victorian family done with its supper. Diversion, not engagement, was the chief result.

Dedicated imperialists in the nineteenth century were proportionately few, and their audiences were not extensive. However, both formed an active minority which represented a number of interest groups. Aside from the jingoes — those strident and unclassifiable nationalists who furthered any cause cloaked in the flag — the promoters of imperialism were the educated and the prosperous. It was an affair of the upper and middle classes. If there was any distinction to be drawn in attitudes, it was probably the one Lord Milner discerned when he differentiated between imperialists of the "blood-red type" and those for whom imperialism was a "business proposition."[29]

[29] Lord Alfred Milner, "The Struggle for Imperial Unity," *British Empire Review*, 6(no. 6):128 (1909).

The blood-red types were, of course, the deeply dedicated zealots, who attempted to lift imperialism from the crass to the noble and to invest it with historical purpose. Most obvious among their ranks were members of the English aristocracy who, by social temperament and ideals inculcated at home and in school, found a calling in empire. The upper echelons of imperial administration were well served by noblemen; for instance, eleven of the fourteen viceroys of India in the sixty-year period from 1858 to 1918 had been peers by birth. If the spirit that moved such men eastward was not always nobility of purpose, it was for many an obligation to imperial trust. Lord Curzon vividly describes his own dedication first aroused at Eton when a visiting speaker declared that India in itself was a greater empire than Rome and that "the rulers of that great dominion were drawn from the men of our own people, that some of them might perhaps be taken from the ranks of the boys who were listening to his words. Ever since that day . . . the fascination and, if I may say so, the sacredness of India have grown upon me."[30]

The public school tradition, suggested in Curzon's statement, was an important factor in forming an imperial ideal. The "Muscular Christianity" of Rugby, for instance, was frequently embellished by an Oxbridge education to produce that "all-rounder," versed in the Classics and prepared to overcome by good taste, "playing the game" well, and other such qualities of the polished amateur what was lacking in specialized training and skills.[31] If there was a motto appropriate to this group, it certainly was to be found in Lord Rosebery's assertion that the British empire "was the greatest secular agency for good the world has seen."

Individuals of this elevated social station were joined at home and abroad by members of the middle class and, at least in France, by representatives of the provincial petty bourgeoisie who had "after their classical studies, a desire to escape toward a freer life and a higher ideal."[32] From these groups came some of the greatest exponents of empire: the self-

[30] Lord George Curzon, *Speeches of Lord Curzon of Kedleston, I: 1898–1900* (Calcutta: Office of the Superintendant of Government Printing, 1900), pp. iv–v. See Colin Cross, *The Fall of the British Empire* (London: Paladin, 1970; first published, 1968), p. 34, on the number of aristocratic viceroys in India.

[31] On this subject see A. P. Thornton, *The Imperial Idea and Its Enemies: A Study in Power* (London: Macmillan, 1959), pp. 84–94; Cross, *Fall of the British Empire*, pp. 34–37; and Rupert Wilkinson, *The Prefects: British Leadership and the Public School Tradition. A Comparative Study in the Making of Rulers* (London: Oxford University Press, 1964).

[32] Hubert Deschamps, "French Colonial Policy in Tropical Africa between the Two World Wars," in Prosser Gifford and William Roger Louis, eds., *France and Britain in Africa: Imperial Rivalry and Colonial Rule* (New Haven, Conn.: Yale University Press, 1971), p. 557.

made millionaire Cecil Rhodes; the Birmingham screw manufacturer Joseph Chamberlain; the Algerian landowner of peasant stock Eugène Etienne; and the journalist from Lorraine Jules Ferry. When asked about the alleged limitations of bourgeois French administrators, a well-placed colonial official remarked after World War I, "The middle classes have certain virtues which are well known. They make honest, reliable, and generally impartial agents of the State."[33]

The ideas and beliefs that shaped the sense of duty animating the imperialist mind were partly fashioned by that segment of the intelligentsia which was nationalist or *étatist* in disposition. This group was two-ply in composition. The upper was academic, stationed at the universities where its members either formed a historical and moral consciousness cast in a heroic mold or offered economic and social projections of what empire would mean for the nation-state. Gustav Schmoller at the University of Berlin, Alfred Girault at the University of Bordeaux, Halford Mackinder at Oxford, J. A. Cramb at the University of London are a sampling of these persons.

The thought of many of the academics inclined toward nationalism was bound together by one intellectual trend: the elevation of the state to a new ethical and/or worldly position. What the Germans call the *Kulturstaat* and *Machtstaat* formed the basis for a long series of university lectures and academic studies. In the tradition of Leopold von Ranke, a prewar generation of German historians was "generally agreed that it must be Germany's task in history to transform the balance of power in Europe into a balance embracing the whole world."[34] Such a *Weltpolitik* was bound to demonstrate that the principal obstacle to its realization was British naval power. Before this generation spoke out, the formidable person of Heinrich von Treitschke, that "fire-eating Pan-German,"[35] was already haranguing his students with the need for international struggle and war as the means by which to enhance the tensile strength of the nation. He produced no school, but many historians of the following generation were influenced by his praise of belligerent imperialism.[36]

[33] Quoted by William B. Cohen, *Rulers of Empire: The French Colonial Service in Africa* (Stanford: Hoover Institution Press, 1971), p. 91.

[34] Quoted from Walter Vogel, *Das neue Europa*, by Ludwig Dehio in *Germany and World Politics in the Twentieth Century*, trans. Dieter Pevsner (New York: Alfred A. Knopf, 1965), p. 60.

[35] W. E. B. DuBois, *Dusk of Dawn: An Essay toward an Autobiography of a Race Concept* (New York: Harcourt, Brace, 1940), p. 46.

[36] Dehio, *Germany and World Politics*, p. 60.

The Hegelian ideal had left its native Germany for England where it took new form in the Oxford neo-idealist movement of the late 1870s. Yet this Oxford school was not detached from the English romantic movement, and, in truth, found deep roots in Platonism. Its best known proponents were Thomas H. Green, who centered his attention on ethical politics, and Bernard Bosanquet, who devoted himself to logic and metaphysics. Green's thought is fittingly summed up in the statement that civil institutions allow the individual to realize "his reason, i.e., his idea of self-perfection, by acting as a member of a social organization in which each contributes to the better-being of all the rest." The "moral self-determination" by which freedom is gained, Bosanquet asserted, is captured in the homely phrase "being equal to the situation." Such notions of responsibility, service, and self-identification with a larger moral organism were easily assimilated into a noble conception of empire and thus appreciated by several outstanding British imperialists, of whom Lord Milner is the most obvious proconsul and J. A. Cramb the most obvious propagandist.[37]

Those individuals hawking empire at the more popular level were the journalists and lobbyists who had assigned themselves the task of alerting the general public to the importance of colonies. Appearing behind the lectern at the private club or the specialized society and writing in the small-circulation journals that propagandized the colonial cause, they displayed the widest range of arguments. Among their number the most famous was Henry Stanley, searcher after Livingstone and soon advertiser of the wonders of the Congo. He was matched in energy and rhetoric by Verney L. Cameron, who was the first to cross Equatorial Africa and who spoke of the region he had visited as if it were the end of the rainbow. More temperate but no less avid was the Frenchman Joseph Chailley-Bert, son-in-law of a governor of Indochina and thus inclined by disposition and marriage toward the value of empire. He wrote several short books, several dozen articles, and helped found the Comité de l'Afrique Française and its offshoot, the Comité du Maroc. These three men and others like them were of the blood-red type, who were, however, at-

[37] T. H. Green, *Lectures on the Principles of Political Obligation* (London: Longmans, Green, 1927; reprinted from *Philosophical Works*, II, 1886), p. 33; Bernard Bosanquet, "Life and Philosophy," in J. H. Muirhead, ed., *Contemporary British Philosophy* (New York: Macmillan, 1924), pp. 69–70. For general appreciations of the subject, see J. H. Muirhead, "Past and Present in Contemporary Philosophy," in *ibid.*, pp. 310–315; and Heinz Gollwitzer, *Europe in the Age of Imperialism, 1880–1914*, trans. David Adam and Stanley Baron (New York: Harcourt, Brace and World, 1969), pp. 154–156.

tempting to arouse indifferent citizens at least to the belief that imperialism was a good business proposition.

Like all other professional or economic groups, the European business community did not subscribe unanimously to the colonial cause. On the contrary, response was irregular and inadequate, at least in the opinion of the advocates of empire. On August 28, 1897, a writer in the *Kolonialzeitung* lamented, "What has our industry, which has long lived from the fleshpots, done for the development of our colonies?" And two years later, in a speech on the colonial budget, Eugène Etienne, leader of the *parti colonial* and second only to Ferry in significance as a French imperialist in this era, remarked that France was scarcely interested in colonial investment.[38]

Yet a number of businessmen did respond and some did invest. Shipping magnates were an obvious group, as were textile manufacturers, exemplified by the German cotton industry in Turkey and the Lancashire cotton interests in India. The merchants of Bordeaux and Marseilles, like those of Liverpool, were involved in West Africa. Moreover, certain entrepreneurs or financial schemers directly expanded empire — for instance, George Taubman Goldie, ambitious head of the Royal Niger Company, or Cecil Rhodes, who stated with real business acumen that philanthropy is good, but "philanthropy + 5%" is better. Nevertheless, businessmen as a national class or interest group did not collectively inaugurate or maintain empire, whatever and however they individually profited from its existence.

This particular point indicates that imperialism followed no neatly cleft economic or political lines. It was not simply the affair of conservatives or capitalists, but enjoyed acceptance from individuals in many sectors of society. Republicans in France, anxious to reaffirm national greatness after the resounding defeat Napoleon III received at the hands of Prussia, lauded the imperial effort. Their chief spokesman was Jules Ferry, a middle-class republican and ardent anticlerical. Monarchists in Italy considered their now unified nation expanding in the Mediterranean as part of a new era in which the glories of ancient Rome would again be burnished. The head of the Catholic party in Belgium, Jules Malou, rather contemptuously looked upon the efforts of Leopold II to create an em-

---

[38] *Kolonialzeitung* quoted by Anderson, *Background of Anti-English Feeling*, p. 191; speech of Etienne on colonial budget, March 6, 1899, in Eugène Etienne, *L'oeuvre coloniale, algérienne et politique* (Paris: Flammarion, 1907), I, 302–303.

pire. "It's not a bad thing," he remarked, "for a sovereign as enterprising as ours, to have his favorite hobbyhorse upon which he can work off his excess energy."[39] But the French Catholics Louis Hubert Lyautey and Ernest Psichari extolled the glories of empire.

From those political quarters where one might not expect to find ideological support, there was at times tolerance and even acceptance. In England, liberals, the proponents of individualism and democracy, were able to reconcile with no great intellectual effort the principles of *libertas et imperium*. They evoked the concept of trusteeship as proof of liberal responsibility, but, more importantly, they strived for some form of imperial unity that would strengthen the forces of liberalism in a world growing less respectful of them.[40] The historian W. F. Monypenny offered a good explanation of this position: "The [British] Empire, then, is obviously a middle term between the two other great Empire States [the United States and Russia] that are its contemporaries, holding the balance between them, free alike from the exaggerated nationalism of the one and the exaggerated imperialism of the other."[41]

Even socialists who never sang paeans to empire did not always shower it with contempt. The Marxist Left was opposed to empire in principle, yet some theorists recommended a general policy of aloofness, because they accepted the necessity of passing through this capitalist phase as through others. However, some Fabians responded differently, urging the restructuring of the imperial edifice rather than its dismantling. George Bernard Shaw, in his Fabian manifesto of 1900, aimed at "the effective social reorganization of the whole Empire" so that it would serve the nation and the populations of the colonies, not just the privileged groups. And the French socialist Jean Jaurès publicly upheld the cultural mission that his country pretended to fulfill in its possessions. He even contended, "I am convinced that France has, in Morocco, interests of the first order; I am convinced that these same interests create for her a kind of right."[42]

[39] Quoted by Pierre Daye, *Léopold II* (Paris: A. Fayard, 1934), p. 203.

[40] See J. E. Tyler, *The Struggle for Imperial Unity* (London: Longmans, Green, 1938), pp. 75–76; and Bernard Holland, *Imperium et Libertas: A Study in History and Politics* (London: Edward Arnold, 1901). A critical contemporary view is that of J. L. Hammond, "Colonial and Foreign Policy," in n.a., *Liberalism and the Century* (London: R. Brimley Johnson, 1900), notably p. 176.

[41] W. F. Monypenny, "The Imperial Ideal," in n.a., *The Empire and the Century* (London: John Murray, 1905), pp. 22–23.

[42] On the Marxist view, see particularly Arthur Ascher, "'Radical' Imperialists within

If, then, empire was not a cause that shaped or shook majority opinion in the nineteenth-century European nations, it was one that had a wide range of social appeal, primarily because it provided some assurance against an uncertain future. To the general public, however, empire was a fact of modern life. Like gas lighting or city slums, it was a by-product of the expansive industrial system.

Yet in the very last years of the nineteenth century and in the first few of the twentieth there was a truly popular mood of imperialism. "Today," wrote W. F. Monypenny, "power and dominion rather than freedom and independence are the ideas that appeal to the imagination of the masses — and the national ideal has given way to the Imperial."[43] Although he was referring to Great Britain, the proposition could have been extended to the entire Western World. Between Queen Victoria's Diamond Jubilee in 1897 and the end of the Russo-Japanese War in 1905, there was a flurry of imperialist excitement and activity. This was the time when Americans rejoiced in their military prowess and new significance in the world as a result of the Spanish-American War (1898–99); when Kaiser Wilhelm II made a pretentious trip to the Near East (1898), appearing in the guise of a latter-day Teutonic knight; when Sir Edward Elgar composed his imperialist march "Pomp and Circumstance" (1901); when Rudyard Kipling wrote his best known imperialist poem "The White Man's Burden" (1899); when the Greater Britain Exhibition was held in Earl's Court, London, with the official guide stating that "Greater Britain . . . is the synonym of the greatest nation which has become the greatest empire the world has ever seen" (1899); when a well-attended International Colonial Congress was held on the occasion of the International Universal Exposition in Paris (1900); and when the grand race for one of the last pieces of unclaimed territory, the North Pole, was started and completed (1906).

The imperial power of Europe was at its zenith. If the pessimistic philosophers and political theorists wondered how long the condition could last, the public at large perceived a long run ahead. Robert Owen, at mid-century, had compared European civilization to a railroad train

---

German Social Democracy," *Political Science Quarterly*, 76:555–575 (1961); Shaw quoted by Bernard Porter, *Critics of Empire: British Radical Attitudes to Colonialism in Africa, 1895–1914* (New York: St. Martin's Press, 1968), p. 114; Jaurès's statement given in parliamentary debate, *Journal Officiel*, Deputés, November 20, 1903, p. 2312.
[43] Monypenny, "The Imperial Ideal," p. 6.

moving swiftly and comfortably toward the future. Most people would still have agreed with him. The century's emphasis on power, both industrial and metaphysical, seemed well placed, and empire therefore fit in effectively, if not perfectly. Few, however, imagined how fragile and artificial the European imperial systems were. Like the bronze statues of rulers standing in colonial squares around the world, empire was much larger than life, but it also rang hollow.

PART I

Annexation and Accumulation

I would annex the planets if I could.

Cecil Rhodes

"Seek ye first the political kingdom," prophetically advised President Kwame Nkrumah of Ghana some years back. The primacy of politics he then enunciated has long been maintained in historical analyses of empire. The *Primat der Aussenpolitik* accounts for the assiduous attention given to nineteenth-century diplomatic maneuvering in the Mediterranean; treaty negotiations in the Far East; and war or threats of war in South Africa, the Sudan, and the Pacific. But economic factors have seldom lingered far behind in the colonial reckoning. The industrializing nineteenth-century states undertook the partial measurement of political power in steel indices and export trade statistics.

The process of acquisition of empire was one in which economic and political factors mingled — in a manner that has been as much complicated as it has been clarified by the historiographical debate over the causal patterns of imperialism. To some Marxists and to some diplomatic historians the issue is readily and strongly joined; to most others, the only certainty is the plurality of causes, the confusion of activity, and the asymmetry of the resulting imperial structures. To reduce to a simple or singular explanation a series of actions that caused such a vast and varied collection of territories to revolve around Europe is to invite distortion.

Yet to reassemble European empires historically is to recognize the imposing dimensions they acquired in contemporary world politics. Empire was an important, if generally disturbing, concern in the European chancelleries at the end of the nineteenth century, even though the subject had previously occupied the official attention of only a few personnel. It is true that many of the greatest statesmen of the era scarcely gave a fig about the matter, but, as has already been demonstrated in chapter 1, there were dedicated imperialists who equated political grandeur with territorial extensiveness. Although some historians are now willing to discount the fact, there is no denying the political significance of overseas empire.

To state the obvious, empire is one of the oldest and most frequently imposed forms of government. If, therefore, there was little that was new under the nineteenth-century tropical sun, the imperialism of world politics was nonetheless distinctive and, moreover, a historical occurrence of monumental proportions.

CHAPTER 2

Old Problems
and New Directions

The nineteenth century began in the middle years of the greatest continental empire the Western World had yet supported and ended shortly before the clash of imperial systems in World War I. The politics of empire thereby define the century, but neither continental nor overseas imperial issues were ever so preoccupying or so extensive as in the beginning and concluding years of this century. Unlike the eighteenth century, when the coastlines of the New World and India reverberated with the sounds of contending military forces, the nineteenth century witnessed few occasions of acute European tension over colonial possessions, and these occurred primarily at the turn of that century. Politically and militarily the Continent dominated. Bismarck once commented, "My map of Africa lies in Europe." The French argued that the "fate of our colonies will be decided on the Rhine." Overseas expansion did not shift the center of power; it produced concentric circles of involvement.

Yet from most perspectives outside Europe, the activity was not as well figured. Military forays into North and West Africa, border skirmishes in Afghanistan and South Africa, punitive expeditions to China and Mexico, and hesitant island hopping in the Pacific are the sorts of engagements that made up the so-called pattern of imperialism. Often precipitated locally and reluctantly supported at home, the acquisition of territory continued throughout the century, yet no obvious political unity or bold causal pattern can be discerned. Indeed, these general characteristics explain the difficulty in assigning a meaningful structure to the

35

phenomenon of imperialism, just as they form the basis for the debate over its causes.

Before the late nineteenth century, when activity was so intense and far-reaching that the term *New Imperialism* has been affixed to it, expansion was characterized by the persistence of old problems and the probing in new directions. The Americas, despite the independence of the United States, remained an important center of colonial interest. Settler colonies from Australia to Algeria were politically the most vexing and governmentally the most demanding. Trade relations with Africa continued to follow the "middle passage" as the traffic in slaves persisted and intensified. The plantation system, one of the most remarkable colonial institutions, not only remained dominant in the New World but was also tried on African soil where, for instance, the French in Senegal attempted variations, although without much success. Finally, the southern Mediterranean, where the Christian West and Islamic East had joined in combat for centuries, lost none of its significance. From Napoleon's brief tour to Egypt in 1798 until the English bombardment of Alexandria in 1882, the French and the English often glanced antagonistically at one another as they looked apprehensively on the gateway to India and the Far East.

The scale of empire was now approaching global proportions. Areas previously touched but left unmarred by the European presence — because the effort of occupation exceeded available resources, or the possible results promised too little in return, or the territory had been insufficiently explored — were now intruded upon and pried open economically and politically. Such extension of interest did not lead to an immediate shift in the centers of activity. The suggestion that British imperialism "made a swing to the East" in the late eighteenth century cannot be supported historically,[1] but it is true that the new exigencies of naval strategy and international security — concerns heightened by the Napoleonic wars — were beginning to add a new geographical dimension to empire early in the nineteenth century.

Shortly after the American War for Independence, what has been called the "age of the strategic post" emerged.[2] Then, the settlement col-

---

[1] This particular idea was proposed by Vincent T. Harlow in *The Founding of the British Empire, 1763–1793*, 2 vols. (London: Longmans, Green, 1959 and 1964), vol. I: *Discovery and Revolution*, notably pp. 5–11. A critical appraisal of the work is that of Ronald Hyam, "British Imperial Expansion in the Late Eighteenth Century," *Historical Journal*, 10:113–124 (1967).

[2] Helen Taft Manning, *British Colonial Government after the American Revolution*,

ony was rivalled in consideration by the naval base, which might shelter a squadron of ships, reprovision and repair them, and thus serve as a point of defense against the enemy — notably the French. This new factor was clearly indicated in the comment of the directors of the East India Company in 1781 that "we must consider the Cape of Good Hope as the Gibraltar of India."[3] As the nineteenth century witnessed the substitution of steam for the sail (the use of a steamboat in colonial naval battle had occurred as early as 1825–26 in the Burmese river war), the search for coaling stations also entered the designs of empire. Thus, matters of strategy attached to trade but not solely dependent on it complicated the politics of imperialism.

Finally, traditional periodization has been disrupted by new theoretical constructs. Since the introduction of the complementary concepts of "formal" and "informal" empire into historical accounts two decades ago, the question of the continuity of expansion through commerce has been a begging one. "Informal empire" is a term employed in discussions of British expansion to suggest that the overseas trade of that island of shopkeepers was the persistent and dominant factor.[4] Trade without dominion where possible, trade with dominion where necessary is the maxim supporting the theory. Continuity, not change, is therefore seen as epitomizing the nature of British expansion; it was an ongoing process, not an erratic set of occurrences.

The importance of overseas trade to Great Britain in the nineteenth century cannot be gainsaid; its influence on British world politics and colonial history is not to be doubted. "The big changes in British expansion stemmed from the industrial revolution, not the American Revolution," one historian has pithily remarked.[5] But whether such a hypothesis will support the concept of informal empire as a past reality rather than as an academic construct is an issue now much debated.[6]

1782–1820 (New Haven, Conn.: Yale University Press, 1931), p. 289. On this subject, see also David K. Fieldhouse, "British Imperialism in the Late Eighteenth Century," in Kenneth Robinson and Frederick Madden, eds., *Essays in Imperial Government, Presented to Margery Perham* (London: Blackwell, 1963), pp. 26–34.

[3] Quoted in Gerald S. Graham, *Great Britain in the Indian Ocean: A Study of Maritime Enterprise, 1810–1850* (Oxford: Clarendon Press, 1967), p. 24.

[4] The classical statement on "informal empire" is Ronald Robinson and John Gallagher, "The Imperialism of Free Trade," *Economic History Review*, 6:1–15 (1953).

[5] Hyam, "British Imperial Expansion," p. 124.

[6] On this subject, see, for instance, Roger Owen and Bob Sutcliffe, eds., *Studies in the Theory of Imperialism* (London: Longman, 1972), and William Roger Louis, ed., *Robinson and Gallagher and Their Critics* (New York: Frederick Watts, 1975).

This economic thesis of an "imperialism of free trade," briefly explained above, has boldly contradicted the political thesis of nationally competitive states engaged in the "diplomacy of imperialism" and has provoked a serious reconsideration of the imagined hiatus in colonial activity during the mid-Victorian era. Although the concept of informal empire has recently been applied by some historians to situations of doubtful merit, as will be later shown, it has helped to reinforce the argument that expansion during the nineteenth century was going on constantly, even if unevenly. The "New Imperialism" of the late century, though distinctive in many ways, must henceforth be considered as an intensified and aggravated phase of a century-long occurrence.

This said and accepted, the possibility of providing sharp periodization to the history of nineteenth-century European imperialism is considerably diminished. It can now be seen that there were no obvious turning points at which the entire enterprise shifted from one mode or motive to another. Consistent with the expansionism that characterized many contemporary aspects of European life, imperialism runs through the century, but definitely accelerates toward the end. Perhaps the best approach to the subject, therefore, would be to consider first the old problems, then assess the new directions taken, and finally concentrate on the dimensions of the "New Imperialism."

Before such a survey, the major actors should be introduced. They appear in the political guise of great powers, but they are properly social collectivities bearing the name of nation-states. The history of nineteenth-century imperialism could well be written, from a European perspective, as the competition and conflict among a few such states, of which the pivotal two were Great Britain and France. Indeed, the "one hundred years of colonial rivalry" between these two countries is both a convenient and a meaningful theme by which to approach the politics of nineteenth-century overseas empire.[7]

Above all, this was the age of Pax Britannica. The term was an international fact as well as a grand historical allusion. In the first half of the century Great Britain enjoyed a preeminent position in world affairs because of the mediating functions of its navy and its wealth. The capitalist disposition of its growing industrial economy placed profit above plunder so that domination of markets and sources of raw material was a peaceful

---

[7] Such a theme was suggested seventy years ago by Jean Darcy, *France et Angleterre: Cent années de rivalité coloniale* (Paris: Perrin, 1904).

more than a military activity. Geography seemed to have treated the country kindly by allowing the main island quick and compact political and economic development conducive to initial leadership in the modern age.

The insularity that distinguished Great Britain from its continental rivals was multibeneficial. National unity had occurred earlier than it had in most other countries; the military was neither a financial drain nor a political problem in the way it frequently was on the Continent; the proximity of the centers of raw materials and industrial production to the sea made trade development easier than it was in most other places. While those nations that were to emerge as serious rivals to British supremacy at the end of the nineteenth century were consolidating through revolution, war, and constitutional reform, Great Britain presented a picture of relative domestic equilibrium through international dynamism.

Moreover, unlike any other state, Great Britain began the century with an impressive and viable imperial structure. Only Spain possessed more territory, but the Spanish colonial system was in decline and approached virtual disintegration by the 1820s. Portugal and Holland among the earlier colonial empires had already been overpowered and were to find their colonies moved about like pawns in a new round of the game of politics started by the French revolutionaries, intensified by Napoleon, and completed to English satisfaction at Waterloo.

Yet there was still France. It was a fitful century for that nation, beset and inspired by domestic upheaval, given to the pursuit of awesome empire under Napoleon, reduced to political boredom under Louis Philippe, defeated roundly by the Prussians in 1870, and relieved by an alliance of convenience with autocratic Russia at the end of the century. The Continent was the central field of French activity, much in the manner that the colonial world was that of the British, but oceanic urges about empire occasionally swept over high-placed French minds.

The emergence of France as the world's second colonial empire was at least historically consistent. Since the twilight years of the reign of the Sun King, Louis XIV, France had stood against England in fort and swamp. Its world position was later dramatically reduced in circumference and weakened in defensive strength, but it managed to cross into the nineteenth century as a colonial power of some consequence.

Although the British forcefully deprived the French of their remaining colonies during the Napoleonic era, most were returned according to decisions of the Congress of Vienna; thus France remained continentally fixed for only a short time. This sequence of events indicates that some continuity in overseas empire, even if momentarily fragmented, was as characteristic of modern French history as it was of British.

These general statements concerning the political situation of the two major empires will gather more meaning with a chronological survey of the changing conditions that sustained these empires and generated further rivalry between them.

Continuing Colonial Problems in the Early Nineteenth Century

Since the early eighteenth century, the contest for imperial primacy centered on Great Britain and France. Some historians have described this time as the "Second Hundred Years War," which concluded with the Congress of Vienna in 1815 but was preceded by a number of petty wars fought abroad in which politics and commerce were inextricably linked.[8] In the Caribbean, on the North American continent, and on the subcontinent of India, each of these two monarchies, then the two major states of the Western World, sought to extend and consolidate its authority principally by reducing and dislocating that of the other.

This authority had, by the eighteenth century, been assembled into an "old colonial" system, based on a simple economic principle of necessary colonial dependency and a similar axiom of metropolitan political ascendancy. Both notions were combined in the descriptive term *mother country*. The theory that the colonies existed for the economic well-being of the founding state justified the practice of restricting trade to bilateral movement between colony and mother country; the idea that all power emanated from the crown justified the royally chartered stock companies and autocratic colonial administrators.

The struggle between the two major "old colonial" systems seemed to have been arrested in 1763. France was then defeated in India and Canada, and its colonial ambitions checked to the extent that the peace treaty ending the Seven Years War began the thalassocracy of modern Britain. Now possessing a huge territorial empire on the American conti-

---

[8] The first such assertion was made in 1883 by J. R. Seeley, *Expansion of England* (1st ed.; London: Macmillan, 1883), p. 24.

nent and enjoying mastery of the seas, Great Britain was without political peers. Even the disintegrative effects of the American Revolution in the following decade did not seriously alter the British position, for the maintenance of Canada and the settlement of Australia were ample territorial compensations, while the naval successes after the embarrassment of Yorktown were proof of continued maritime dominion.

This British preponderance in the colonial world was, however, soon disturbed by the turbulence generated by the French Revolution and Napoleon. France again entered a period of active expansionism on the Continent and abroad, which was now charged with a revolutionary ideology that threatened the social as well as the political order. Waging war in the name of liberty and against traditional monarchy, France included England in its growing list of enemies on February 1, 1793. From that date until the abdication of Napoleon on April 4, 1814, these two nations remained in a state of conflict, stayed only briefly by the Treaty of Amiens (1802–3). Again they disputed territory around the world and again they met on two fronts and employed two modes of warfare: armies on the Continent; fleets in the colonies.

This double approach was in keeping with Britain's previous belligerent response to France's aggressiveness and consistent with Prime Minister Pitt's desire to retain a maximum of options — or with his tendency toward vacillation.[9] Even after Pitt's death in 1806 and because of Napoleon's outstanding victories in Europe, British policy continued to emphasize the colonies as much as the Continent. Victories seemed more promising in the colonies, and the highly vocal mercantile element, deprived of continental markets by Napoleon's policy of exclusion, insisted upon new areas for the deposit of accumulated goods.[10]

The military encounters of both states were indecisive until Waterloo, but the general historical result for the nineteenth century essentially confirmed the assertion made by a British diplomat to the French at the beginning of the century: "You are destined to be the most powerful nation on the continent, as we are on the sea."[11]

Overseas they frequently met, though rarely in agreement. Their

[9] See William W. Kaufmann, *British Policy and the Independence of Latin America, 1804–1828* (New Haven, Conn.: Yale University Press, 1951), pp. 4–5.

[10] *Ibid.*, notably chapter 1.

[11] Quoted in Herbert I. Priestley, *France Overseas through the Old Regime: A Study of European Expansion* (New York: Appleton-Century, 1939), p. 344.

eighteenth-century encounters concluded with nineteenth-century conflict renewed in the Caribbean and newly undertaken in the Mediterranean, but directed mainly toward India.

If India was later to become the jewel of empire, the Caribbean consisted of a string of islands poetically described as pearls — hence plunder worth the struggle. Richly providing Europe with such staples as sugar and cotton, these islands had made empire a paying proposition and continued to hold European attention, even though their economic worth was in relative decline by the end of the century. As continental problems spilled into the Caribbean again, the English returned to the strategy of the Seven Years War, which was, as one historian wryly put it, implemented with forces that were "as is customary . . . dispersed in ill-contrived expeditions without sufficient preparation or clear objectives."[12]

The French responded in complementary fashion. The revolutionary government had debated the issue of the emancipation of slaves and colonial representation in parliament. The latter had been granted in 1790, the former in 1794; but the planter class, worried about the extent of revolutionary political zeal, welcomed the British as restorers of order. British military success was immediate, but short-lived. Even though the islands of Martinique, Guadeloupe, and Tobago had been overwhelmed as early as 1794, and the major French territory of St.-Domingue seriously invested in the same year, indigenous resistance and rampant disease — the two persistent enemies of European imperialism — conspired to check British efforts. These two anti-imperialist agents were equally effective against France's attempts under Napoleon to reassert its sovereignty.

The central territory of political contention was St.-Domingue, and the chief difficulties were yellow fever and the skillful mobilization of the oppressed population by Toussaint L'Ouverture. Thousands of whites died from the one; many more thousands of blacks were inspired by the other. It was Toussaint L'Ouverture, more than any other force or factor, who altered and, indeed, dominated the political situation.

Toussaint has recently been described as the precursor of those leaders of national liberation movements familiar in the decolonizing contemporary world.[13] A lifetime slave and a figure of uninspiring physical appear-

---

[12] C. E. Carrington, *The British Overseas, Exploits of a Nation of Shopkeepers* (Cambridge: At the University Press, 1968; first published, 1950), I, 235.

[13] Aimé Césaire, *Toussaint L'Ouverture* (Paris: Présence Africaine, 1961), p. 310.

ance, he nevertheless forged his leadership in the torrid confusion following the French Revolution when social relationships were severely revised in law and in fact. What he might have done for St.-Domingue can only be guessed at; time was not his. Officially appointed French governor, he ruled without restrictions on his authority. Toussaint's free rein became a source not only of local opportunity for reform and economic improvement but also of growing irritation to the French. Most important, he mustered an army of fifteen thousand slaves which was strong enough to chasten the English and to frustrate French imperial designs. By 1798, English attempts to control the island were abandoned by treaty; French efforts were soon to begin again with force.

The Treaty of Amiens gave Napoleon sufficient respite from continental affairs to allow him to indulge in thoughts of a restored French empire centered in the Caribbean and extending northward to Louisiana and southward to Guiana. With Martinique and Guadeloupe returned as part of the peace negotiations and with Louisiana previously acquired from the Spanish, only St.-Domingue remained to be reintegrated, and that island was now approached militarily. An expeditionary force of twenty thousand invaded in 1802. Toussaint was defeated, captured, and deported to France where he died the following year. However, Napoleon had not reckoned intelligently with the untoward effects of his reactionary colonial policy, which included the reintroduction of slavery in Martinique and Guadeloupe in 1802. The prospects of reenslavement kept the spirit of resistance alive, and it was forcefully directed against the French by new indigenous leadership. Napoleon's victory was Pyrrhic. His legions decimated, his commander succumbing both to self-doubt and to yellow fever, and his attention again forced to Europe where war had resumed, the emperor abandoned St.-Domingue and, with the island, grand dreams of a New World empire.

In that same year, 1803, Louisiana was negotiated out of the French imperial system for the last time. Acquired from Spain in 1713 by France, Louisiana was divided at the time of the Peace of Paris in 1763 between England and Spain. The Spanish, or western, portion again became French in 1801, and, on that occasion, old illusions were revived. Since the appearance in the early eighteenth century of overlush descriptions in brochures fabricated by John Law's Mississippi Company, Louisiana had enthralled the French. Now Napoleon saw it as the hinterland that would supply the Caribbean island colonies, notably St.-Domingue, with foodstuffs and raw materials necessary to make the hoped-for empire self-sufficient and economically profitable. However, failure on St.-Domingue, combined with the realization of possible British seizure of Louisiana, convinced Napoleon of the impossibility of his colonial aspirations and of the need for negotiation with the new American Republic as the least unsatisfactory of available solutions. The resultant history is familiar. The Louisiana Purchase of 1803 was one of those rare land buys; it cost the United States little, and it has returned much.

For a brief period, then, the French empire in the New World was nearly reextended to its previous proportions. As meteoric as the career of the man who coveted it, this empire quickly disappeared from the political scene, marked thereafter only by French place names, the use of the French language, and the retention, after 1815, of the small islands of Martinique and Guadeloupe and of Guiana on the South American mainland.

Elsewhere and earlier Napoleon had allowed his imagination to roam about other continents. Of all the French imperialist projects cast across the five centuries since the sailors of Dieppe first put out to sea, the Egyptian campaign was the most grandiose and fascinating. The object was India, the precedent — if not the exact route — was provided by Alexander the Great, and the purpose was the reinstallation of authority in a part of the world where the French had recently been excluded by the British.

Leaving Toulon on May 28, 1798, a substantial fleet conveyed French savants, sailors, and a commander in chief whose stomach was not able to support his seaborne plans. The Mediterranean was then as much a French as an English sea, but the intrepid activities of Lord Nelson were soon to alter that situation. Initially, the French eluded English naval pursuit and disembarked successfully at Alexandria. From there Napoleon moved quickly overland, defeating the Egyptian Mameluke cavalry in the Battle of the Pyramids and arriving triumphantly in Cairo in July. Egypt was to be the French base of operations; beyond it lay India and the fulfillment of Napoleonic ambitions. It was Nelson who scuttled such plans when he finally caught up with the anchored French fleet and resoundingly defeated it in the Battle of Aboukir Bay. Without naval support Napoleon was compelled to proceed eastward on land. Again his intentions were frustrated, this time when he encountered severe Turkish resistance reinforced by active British support. Thus deprived of attractive alternatives and deeply concerned about his reputation, Napoleon pursued expediency: he removed himself from the scene. In October 1799 he unceremoniously departed from North Africa for France, leaving behind a military force which capitulated to the English in 1801. However, Napoleonic imperialism did not end then; its most impressive form would be revealed in Europe and in the eastward thrust that would rend Russia.

The colonial world at the end of the Napoleonic era was in a state of political disarray, over which fluttered the Union Jack. Starting in 1795, at which time the French occupied Holland and established the satellite Batavian Republic, the British turned to long-coveted Dutch colonies in the Far East and South Africa and handily invested them with a minimal display of military force. The island possessions of France in the Caribbean and in the Indian and Atlantic oceans were occupied by British troops, as was the small coastal colony of Senegal in West Africa. By 1815 Britain dominated the Far East, arbitrated in the Mediterranean, and was secure in the Caribbean. All that remained on a large scale of the old rival empires was Spanish America, and for over a decade that land mass had been fracturing.

The decolonization of Latin America was dramatic, romantic, and confusing. Napoleon's invasion of Spain and the abdication of the Spanish monarch Ferdinand VII precipitated it, but the rivalry between Spanish administrators and the colonial population, the ideology of the Enlightenment, and the example of the American Revolution had prepared the way. British foreign policy, through which Latin America was viewed as a possible commercial if not a colonial dependency, also encouraged — even provoked — decolonization. The theoretical debate around which early revolutionary action in Latin America revolved was a constitutional one: the colonies asserted that political loyalty was to the monarch, not to the state, while Spain contended that the empire was one with the mother country. When Napoleon forced his imperialism south of the Pyrenees, he also engineered the abdication of the legitimate Bourbon monarch and the installation of his brother Joseph in the royal office. Neither the Bonapartist rule nor the revolutionary Spanish regime that reacted against it was accepted wholly or wholeheartedly by the colonial elite in the Americas. Arguing for equality in the national state proposed by the revolutionary Cortes in Spain and for the retention of local sovereignty until the Bourbon was reinstalled, the dissenters in South America quickly became a national revolutionary force. The rebel movements of 1809–10 were not far removed from their northern counterpart in emphasis on representation and in the locus of sovereignty. In the person of Simón Bolívar the thought of the Enlightenment was translated into far-reaching action.[14]

Britain observed all this with the combined commercial and political interest that characterized its foreign policy at the time. In colonial terms, the issue was, however, quite clear. When Napoleon installed Joseph, he revealed his hope that Spanish America would be included in the still expanding Napoleonic realm. Of course, this desire was greeted with horror in England, where the politically active mercantile class regarded the Spanish empire as a possible dumping ground for goods shut out of traditional European markets. But the issue went further. There was even some talk of incorporating parts of Spanish America into the British empire. One swashbuckling attempt to seize Buenos Aires was peremptorily and privately undertaken by Sir Home Popham; the action succeeded but for a brief span in the summer of 1806. When the citizens rose to subdue the British land force, the possibilities of self-action for independence were demonstrated for other colonial populations to emulate and for the British government to consider soberly. Indirect involvement, conducive to the growing concerns of a nation of shopkeepers, henceforth became British policy.[15]

The revolutions of 1809–10 were not successful, but neither was the attempt by Spain to quell them. For another decade the Spanish-American empire was in political ferment, settled only with the independence of the colonies led by Bolívar and reluctantly acceded to by the Spanish king. United States recognition of the new republican states in 1822 assisted the outcome, as did British diplomacy in discouraging any Spanish attempt at political reassertion.

France initially complicated the situation. Immediately after the political revolution in Spain, French troops, forcefully endorsing the conservative policies of the newly formed Holy Alliance, restabilized the throne of Ferdinand VII by occupying most of Spain in 1823. Its physical presence, combined with a political affinity with Spain, prompted France's intense interest in the Spanish colonial question. The French foreign minister

[14] Victor A. Belaunde, *Bolivar and the Political Thought of the Spanish American Revolution* (Baltimore, Md.: Johns Hopkins Press, 1938), chapter 10.
[15] Kaufmann, *British Policy*, notably p. 53.

Chateaubriand contemplated a plan whereby the old Spanish empire might be converted into separate monarchies under crowns worn by chosen European princes. The scheme was double pronged. It could pierce the republican movements disturbing monarchical Europe and, at the same time, extend French influence into Latin America. Canning, then British foreign minister, remonstrated verbally against French intentions and sought cooperation from the United States. Seriously suspecting Canning's motives, Secretary of State John Quincy Adams followed his own Anglophobic tendencies and urged that the United States reject cooperation and issue instead a unilateral statement, which was to be the famous Monroe Doctrine. The French, nevertheless, were sufficiently disconcerted by Canning's threat to offer a memorandum in October 1823 by which they agreed to subscribe to the British position of nonintervention. The first phase of modern European overseas expansion thus ended, as it had been earlier intensified, by a manifestation of French-British rivalry.

With the dissolution of the Spanish-American empire, European colonial efforts in the New World were virtually expended. Great Britain alone still commanded much territory and many people on a long seaboard that had earlier harbored subjects of half a dozen European states. Yet France would briefly try at empire here again with the military occupation of Mexico in 1861 and the establishment of a client state ruled by the emperor Maximilian.

In the eighteenth century the New World had become the major center of colonial attraction, not only providing a variety of colonial governments but also sharply reflecting European rivalries, the latter so well evinced in the French and Indian Wars. The termination of empire in the Americas meant the conclusion of the largest and most successful experience with settlement colonies. Partly an accident of religious and political persecution and, retrospectively, a curiosity of an age when demographic pressures to emigrate were not very strong, the settlement colony had come to define empire as well as to disrupt it. The revolutionary movements succeeded in reducing empire to a bitter memory in the minds of many politicians in Europe, but not to such an extent that the general enterprise was foresworn. Even before the rebellious reaction of the British and Spanish colonies, Europeans were actively engaged elsewhere, producing new forms of empire and consequent rivalry.

New Territorial Expansion

The period extending from the conclusion of the Congress of Vienna to the scramble for Africa in the last quarter of the century is one in which European activity was most varied and about which recent historical discussion is most lively. Again, neither single cause nor simple theme will explain it well.

Yet even at a cursory glance, one characteristic is evident: the extension of geographical involvement. The independent Americas continued to figure in European designs, particularly as trade areas of primary importance to Great Britain. But now something like a slow "swing to the East" occurred with the development there of Anglo-French commercial and political rivalry. In other regions, imperialist activity was also easily discernible, such as in the Mediterranean and along the west coast of Africa. As scattered and haphazard as the results may have appeared if charted on a map, they were the foundations of extensive territorial empires and, at this time, the main lines of Anglo-French colonial rivalry.

It seems that Great Britain and France proceeded abroad for quite different reasons. The Pax Britannica was chiefly for commercial purposes. "It is the business of Government," averred Lord Palmerston, "to open and secure the roads for the merchant." Palmerstonian principles, which directed so much of British foreign policy in this period, combined trade with politics to secure, in the words of the Earl of Clarendon, "the honour and advantage of England."[16] There was a certain amount of national bluster in all of this — flag waving and the commencement of "gunboat diplomacy" — but there was also a keen realization of Great Britain's preeminent position and the advantages that international peace provided it.

Empire and commerce frequently grew symbiotically, but their relationship was never rigidly and regularly fixed. It is therefore historically dangerous to assert that an "imperialism of free trade" directed mid-Victorian affairs, in which the home government exerted its influence overtly by force and covertly by diplomatic pressure to assure that the many markets of the world would welcome British goods. The vicissitudes

[16] Palmerston quoted in Charles Webster, *The Foreign Policy of Palmerston, 1830–41: Britain, the Liberal Movement and the Eastern Question* (London: Bell, 1951), II, 751; Clarendon quoted in Ronald Robinson and John Gallagher with Alice Denny, *Africa and the Victorians: The Climax of Imperialism in the Dark Continent* (New York: St. Martin's Press, 1961), p. 4. Both quotations are particularly stressed in *ibid.*, pp. 4–5.

of trade were not usually the concern of Whitehall. At times, as will be seen with respect to China, doors were forced open; yet on other occasions, as in Latin America where British trade was of great importance, the government very seldom remonstrated, even when severe commercial imbalance or unfriendly treatment worked to the disadvantage of its nationals. If, then, chief interest overseas was in trade and not territory, no simple, direct correlation can be drawn between the two.

France was not a workshop of the world in this era, and French imperialism accordingly has supported no theory of "informal empire." Granted French industry was proficient, in comparison with the British it was rather restricted in scope. It is generally agreed that the dominant factor accounting for French overseas interest at this time was political. In a period following a decade of Napoleonic grandeur, colonial activity allowed France to reassert itself internationally and to realize a new national prestige. On more than one occasion, it also performed another political function, that of diverting attention to successful involvement abroad so as to counter discontent at home.

Interestingly, efforts at expansion were less regularly initiated or endorsed by the foreign office than they were by the navy and the missionaries — two disparate groups zealously bound together in promoting French authority abroad. Naval officers, generally afflicted with Anglophobia, viewed England as the arch colonial rival and sought *points d'appui* in Africa and Madagascar to counter British influence there. In the Far East, high ranking officers urged occupation of harbors in Indochina and were anticipating, along with their counterparts in the United States, the opening of Japan to foreign influence. Even more obvious was the missionary imperialism that prevailed around the globe. Joining naval efforts in Japan and Madagascar and enjoying prior claim and greater involvement in Indochina, Catholic missionaries sought the double objective — often fused into one — of extending their religion and the French national culture which supported it.[17]

Yet such factors were never combined in a coherent national policy of

---

[17] The literature on the motives for French imperialist expansion in this era has become quite extensive in the last twenty years. See, particularly, Henri Brunschwig, "Anglophobia and French African Policy," in Prosser Gifford and William Roger Louis, eds., *France and Britain in Africa: Imperial Rivalry and Colonial Rule* (New Haven, Conn.: Yale University Press, 1971), pp. 3–34; John F. Cady, *The Roots of French Imperialism in Eastern Asia* (Ithaca, N.Y.: Cornell University Press, 1967; first published, 1954); and Meron Medzini, *French Policy in Japan during the Closing Years of the Tokugawa Regime* (Cambridge, Mass.: Harvard University Press, 1971), chapter 1.

expansion. In both Britain and France few of the personnel in the foreign ministries openly championed the cause of empire, and parliamentary chambers did not resound with colonial debates. Such a political situation did not mean, as was once said with particular reference to Great Britain, that an era of anti-imperialism was at hand. If few politicians ardently upheld empire and if some contested it, virtually no one insisted that his nation be divested of its colonies. Indeed, new theories of imperialism were deliberated, some of which anticipated the ideological arguments of the end of the century. Yet none of these stimulated a general mood of expansionism, even if some did affect colonial policy. The one notable exception to this — the ill-starred effort of Napoleon III to install and maintain Maximilian in Mexico — was described in its day as pure adventurism.

Frequently, isolated individuals precipitated "accidents" of acquisition, acting out of concern for the nation or themselves and upon reasons consonant with nineteenth-century political behavior. For instance, the ambitious and talented Englishman Sir Stamford Raffles had on his own initiative, but with the approval of the governor of India, negotiated with the sultan of Johore in 1819 to obtain the island of Singapore, originally unrequested by any English government. In like manner, the freebooting and heroic James Brooke gained personal control of Sarawak on North Borneo, which soon thereafter became a British protectorate. Of French endeavors, Victor Regis, a Marseilles merchant trading on the west coast of Africa, manipulated the government of Napoleon III into establishing a protectorate over Porto Novo, the first French political step toward intrusion in Dahomey. Less successful, the Duc de Brabant (the future Leopold II) sent one of his father's ministers a piece of granite with the words "Belgium needs colonies" carved on it — a befitting monument to his personal aspirations and future accomplishments. But neither in Belgium nor elsewhere in western Europe was there an active colonial party or a popular call for empire building. This general domestic condition was, however, no deterrent to the addition of territory.

Again, but more so than before, regional problems conditioned the motives and determined the degree of antagonism or cooperation between the two major contenders. On the European Continent, England and France engaged in a preliminary Entente Cordiale, fostered initially by Palmerston, but appearing thereafter in several cooperative international ventures down through the Crimean War. "England and France have many interests, commercial and political, all over the world, which are perpetually coming into contact," stated Palmerston, "and a good understanding between Paris and London is necessary."[18] Despite the general parity of the two powers hinted at in Palmerston's statement, Great Britain remained predominant abroad, and France was forced on more than one occasion to accommodate its policy to this condition.

The particulars can be assembled along two extended lines of international encounter. Historically, the first runs back to Napoleon's interest in the East. Geographically, it runs from naval contact in the Mediterranean overland to India, where the British political presence was in part disturbed by fear of a possible French military appearance there during the Napoleonic era; then it proceeds to the Pacific shores where interest in China brought England and France together in both a policy of cooperation and a condition of rivalry. By the end of the century, this line of encounter would be described by the British as a "lifeline of empire," which concept suggests an interoceanic naval policy assuring the trade routes to India.

While the intentions of France on this vast part of the globe were often as vague as they were grandiose, there was no serious effort to emulate Great Britain. French politicians, looking eastward, made historical reference to the crusading activities of St. Louis as indication of cultural priority, especially in the middle of the century when Napoleon III appeared in the guise of protector of Christian religious sites against Turkish policies. Before then, other political designs had been sketched. The Prince de Polignac, foreign minister of France in 1830, remarked that, through the French occupation of Algiers, he hoped to speed the disintegration of the Ottoman empire and thereby, "despite England," extend "French influence into the heart of Asia."[19] With the reconstruction of a significant navy during the reign of Louis Philippe and with the evolution of an active Chinese and Japanese policy, French efforts were pushed beyond the heart of Asia to its very periphery. Yet grand intentions were never matched by political realities; it is safe to assert that British diplomacy regularly contained France in the Near and Far East.

The second line of encounter, more knotted geographically, was re-

[18] Quoted in René Albrecht-Carrié, *Britain and France: Adaptations to a Changing Context of Power* (New York: Doubleday, 1970), pp. 82–83.

[19] Quoted in Charles-André Julien, *Histoire de l'Algérie contemporaine*, vol. I: *La conquête et les débuts de la colonisation, 1827–1871* (Paris: Presses Universitaires de France, 1964), p. 35.

stricted primarily to the west coast of Africa. Here Great Britain and France were originally proximate because of the slave trade, their activities represented by chartered companies. In the nineteenth century the trafficking in human kind was gradually replaced by commercial interest in palm oil and gums, the chartered company being replaced by small groups of merchants trading on their own, and not on national, account. West Africa was then a "traders' frontier,"[20] with a minimum amount of political involvement and few noticeable diplomatic anxieties from a continental European perspective. The one exception to this condition was found off the east coast on the island of Madagascar where English and French missionary rivalry led to political intrigue. The seesaw responses of the Hova monarchy finally tipped in favor of the French through a treaty of protectorate signed under duress in 1885.

These two lines of encounter were also the two major channels along which later imperialism, the scramble for Africa and Oceania, was communicated. A brief survey of the major aspects of European expansion in this early period should heighten an appreciation of Anglo-French overseas rivalry as well as endorse the thesis of continuity in nineteenth-century imperialism.

Initial focus on the Mediterranean area reveals the history of one empire yielding important components for the creation of two new ones. The weakness of the Ottoman empire was the source of general European concern and intervention and the basis for Anglo-French contention and territorial acquisition. From without, Russia was pressing into the region of the Black Sea. From within, the political activities of Mehemet Ali were a major source of local disturbance in the first third of the century and the focal point of Anglo-French opposition. Mehemet Ali was an indirect legacy of the Napoleonic invasion of Egypt. Albanian born, former soldier in the service of the sultan against Napoleon, he made himself pasha of Egypt by force and ability. Despot and modernizer, Mehemet Ali looked to the engineers and military advisers of France for technical assistance and turned to the Ottoman provinces about him as areas for military conquest. However, the new European colonial activities in which he figured began west of his original base of power.

The French expedition against Algiers in 1830, which initially appeared to be a minor incident in the Mediterranean situation, was to become

[20] This idea was first offered by W. K. Hancock, *Argument of Empire* (Harmondsworth: Penguin Books, 1943), p. 68.

one of the most important in modern imperialism. Even though only nominally part of the Ottoman empire, Algiers was the first major unit to be removed by a European power. Yet French intentions in 1830 were neither clear nor far-reaching, and, if anything, France entered Algiers with as much hesitation as force. Since 1827, when the French government had responded to a diplomatic insult by a naval blockade of Algiers, the situation confronting that North African city was confusing. The blockade was unsuccessful, albeit costly, but plans for a land-sea invasion were put aside for fear of disturbing Great Britain's stance as a Mediterranean power. Further antagonism developed in 1829 when the Algerians massacred the French sailors of a grounded blockade ship and even more when they fired on a French naval officer sent to attempt negotiation.

Aggressive action replaced these indecisive efforts shortly after Polignac assumed the foreign ministry in 1829. At the time, he was devising a grand scheme for the total dismemberment of the Ottoman empire, then engaged in a disastrous war with Russia. More restricted, yet still ambitious, was a North African plan presented to him by a consular officer, which he seized as if it were his own. According to it, Mehemet Ali would be equipped by France to invade and subdue the Barbary coast, which included Algiers. The idea was appealing because of the possible extension of French influence through Mehemet and the potential acquisition of military installations along the conquered shore. This plan, too, was never realized, because the French failed to provide the ships Mehemet Ali demanded. On a different scale, the Algerian expedition was undertaken solely by French troops which were supposed to return victoriously after ten weeks in the field. Polignac, in an unpopular domestic situation, also hoped the expedition would add a little luster to the reign of Charles X. Unfortunately for him the government fell in the July Revolution, while the occupation of Algiers continued in earnest.[21]

Ironically, the first and one of the last large colonial possessions of modern France was approached amid confusion, without meaningful justification, and for ill-defined purposes. A long history of military activity was yet to follow, as the "limited" occupation was extended in time, space, and degree of domination.

East of Algeria, European political activity was brisker, set in motion principally by the military ambitions of Mehemet Ali. In disputing with the sultan, he seized Lebanon and Syria and even threatened Turkey in

[21] The best account of Polignac's activities is that of Julien, *Histoire de l'Algérie*, chapter 1.

1833. He was momentarily contained as a result of Russian support to Turkey, but again posed an international problem in 1838 when he roundly defeated an invading Turkish force sent into Syria. Thus the Egyptian ruler appeared poised to destroy the Turkish empire itself. For the obvious reason that the empire was a political buffer as well as a center of rival European influence, Britain and Russia reluctantly had to agree to maintain it. France, although cooperating with them, viewed Mehemet Ali as a potential ally, not a present threat to order in the Near East.

The issue came to a diplomatic climax in 1840, when the entente between England and France was replaced by overt antagonism. Adolphe Thiers, then premier of France and a staunch supporter of Mehemet Ali, desired that the pasha have hereditary possession of both Egypt and Syria. Palmerston objected and maneuvered Austria, Russia, and Prussia into a treaty in 1840 that allowed Mehemet Ali hereditary rights to Egypt but only lifelong possession of Syria. The pasha ignored the time schedule provided for his response to the treaty's conditions; Palmerston therefore brought the matter to his attention by a display of military force. British naval support of Turkish efforts in Lebanon and Syria obviously strengthened the Ottoman empire's internal situation — and had an inverse effect on the resolve of the French cabinet. Therefore, Mehemet Ali accepted only hereditary control of Egypt.

The Near Eastern question at this time centered on Mehemet Ali, but it had much broader and more persistent ramifications. As is evident, Great Britain and France were vying for political authority in the area, each trying to extend its sphere of influence. But British concern went beyond Egypt deep into Asia. Hence, Mehemet Ali's possession of Syria would have threatened to disrupt British trade lines to India, both over land and across the Isthmus of Suez and on to the Red Sea. The concept of a "lifeline of empire" was now developing, with the containment of Egypt an important part of its maintenance. The French, in turn, were trying to exploit and extend their cultural advantages in Egypt. French financial investment, the missionary work of French Catholics, and, finally, the realization in 1869 of Ferdinand de Lesseps's scheme for an isthmian canal more than suggest the directions of French penetration. In colonial terms, the Near Eastern question was really the Egyptian question, one for which there was no satisfactory European answer, even after the British occupied the country in 1882.

Ferdinand de Lesseps lecturing on the canal at the Parisian Universal Exposition of 1867. From *L'Illustration*, September 28, 1867.

View of work on the Suez Canal, near Kantara. From *Illustrated London News*, March 20, 1869. (Reproduced by permission of *Illustrated London News*.)

Proposed monument, entitled "Temple of Peace," to be erected upon the completion of the canal. From *L'Illustration*, November 23, 1867.

Colonial Developments East of Suez

Mediterranean imperial rivalry can be considered the most enduring and frequently the most intense in the nineteenth century, but it can also be said that it was more than matched in scope and historical effect in the Far East. Older colonial rivalries and their territorial results were intensified with new interest in the Pacific and Indochina. China was the territory most susceptible to annexation; India was to become a colonial empire unto itself. Although France, Holland, and Portugal maintained scattered possessions in the Indian Ocean, this body of water was in effect a British sea; and although the United States and Japan were to contest British naval superiority in the western portion of the Pacific before the century was out, British ships effectively imposed naval authority in that region as well.

Everything British centered on India. Market and fortress, it was the most important dependency of the British empire and its chief source of political grandeur and expected wealth after the revolt of the American colonies. British presence there had been marked in the late seventeenth century by the trade of the East India Company; in the eighteenth century the politics of trade predominated, with the rival French maintaining only a few coastal trading posts as the century expired. Parliamentary concern over the direction of the East India Company's economic and political activities was well expressed at this time and was institutionalized in Pitt's India Act of 1784, which severely circumscribed the company's authority. However, the company continued to rule through governmental discretion until the Sepoy Revolt of 1857. That famous uprising, generated by religious and political discontent among soldiers in Bengal, forced the British crown to assume direct political control.

This intensified political involvement was matched by worry over the "turbulent frontiers" created by the potential intrusion of France and then Russia and by the disruptive energies of border peoples.[22] So vast was the territory over which England held sway and yet so removed from political concourse with London that at times two foreign policies seemed to exist.[23] For India, if not for the British Isles, the most pressing problem was that posed by the Russians on the northwestern frontier, a concern which had troubled the minds of governors-general since the Napoleonic era. The local situation was not uniquely Indian, but in part derived from the Near East, where Anglo-Russian contention had existed for some time. By 1828, the Russian drive to the East had gained considerable political ground; the successful conclusion of a war against Persia placed that country under Russian domination. The results suggested to the anxious British the possibility of further Russian penetration into Afghanistan through Persia and thus to the frontiers of India. When Persia began an aggressive policy toward Afghanistan, British fears seemed near realization.

The upshot of all this was the first Afghan War of 1838–42, which was premised on the obvious proposition that Afghanistan would be either British or Russian. As inept as it was drawn out, the war has been deemed foolish and unfortunate by many historians, but at the time it seemed understandable as part of the extensive state of affairs just briefly described.[24] After initial success and then protracted confusion and

[22] John S. Galbraith, "The 'Turbulent Frontier' as a Factor in British Expansion," *Comparative Studies in Society and History*, 2:156 (1960).

[23] J. A. Norris, *The First Afghan War, 1838–1842* (Cambridge: At the University Press, 1967), p. 7.

[24] *Ibid.*, pp. xiii–xvi.

humiliating losses, the British ultimately rallied. Prompted by thoughts of revenge and by the new field commander Sir Charles Napier, they concluded the war with a successful campaign in the autumn of 1842.

Although the war enlarged British India with the addition of two provinces now ruled as the Sind, it did not solve the problem of the turbulent frontier. Further military activity was required against the able and well-organized Sikhs, who responded to Britain's presence on the border by a show of strength directed toward Delhi in 1846. The first of two Sikh wars ended by treaty in 1846 which granted to the British the right to place a resident in the Sikh capital of Lahore. The second war broke out a few years later after the murder of a British agent and a general uprising. Bloodier and harder to win than the first, it ultimately led to imperial control over the Punjab and, therefore, a further extension of the frontier.

A similar but less belligerent piecing together of empire was in progress still farther east, where the British operated in conjunction with, and in opposition to, other European states. As befits the immense waters in which they took place, these pursuits in and adjacent to the Pacific Ocean were varied and complicated. Yet the trade element dominated, and much of the naval and political action directed against local governments, piratism, and rival Europeans was undertaken to secure commercial advantages or to protect trade routes.

The intense Anglo-Dutch rivalry localized around the archipelago must be explained in these terms. Having lost Ceylon as a result of the Napoleonic wars, the Dutch wished to uphold their commercial preponderance in the cluster of islands that today forms the state of Indonesia. Their economic penetration caused Britain considerable consternation, particularly since the British, desirous of maintaining Holland as a buffer state overseas and in Europe against French aggression, had acted with diplomatic generosity by returning to the Dutch most of their possessions. The Dutch response of commercial exclusiveness proved disadvantageous to both the British East India Company and the country trade, a condition made worse by the British lack of bases in the region as a result of earlier diplomatic settlement with Holland. This was the situation that aroused Raffles to search for a base and that finally led to a treaty in 1824 between the two countries whereby spheres of influence were delineated, with the Dutch accepting British priority in Malaya.[25]

British expansion continued apace. Movement into Malaya, which

[25] See particularly Graham, *Great Britain in the Indian Ocean*, p. 343–344.

eventually ended in a series of protectorates, was essentially the result of local trade interests, primarily in tin mining, but was confounded by indigenous political disputes and coastal piracy. West of the peninsula, the British altered their relations with the Burmese in 1825 by undertaking a war initiated in behalf of the East India Company to protect its territory bordering on Burma. Here again, in geographically altered form, was the frontier problem, finally resolved to Great Britain's advantage in a second Burmese War in 1852 when all of Lower Burma fell under British control. Considering that the activities in this region were matched by the growing colonization of Australia and, after 1840, of New Zealand, it appeared that all Southeast Asia well into the Pacific was about to fall under European, particularly British, domination.

Even though general conditions in China, that famous Far Eastern trading emporium, were not, in European eyes, strikingly different from those in other countries on the Asian continent, the political results were. An imperial power of grand dimensions in previous centuries, China had been connected with British interests by the East India Company and through two commodities of great consumption, tea and opium. Traffic in both increased tremendously at the turn of the eighteenth century. Tea imports to England were ten times more than they were at mid-century, which intensified the search for other suitable items of trade. Previously, precious silver bullion lay heavily in the bottoms of English ships, because the obvious English article of export, woolens, had little market in China.[26]

Some compensation for England's trade imbalance was made by the "country" trade, that movement of goods from India to China by private merchants under license to the company. They transported a wide variety of products from cotton to bird nests and opium. Strikingly, opium, whose popular use in China dates only from the early nineteenth century, was soon in enough demand to become the major element in the country trade. The company managed to regulate India's opium production and exportation, but it engaged only very briefly in the trade, leaving this enterprise to its licensees. Officially, all this trade centered in the city of Canton, the only port allowed open by the self-sufficient and haughtily isolated Manchu (Ch'ing) dynasty. There the "hong" merchants, those

---

[26] John K. Fairbank, *Trade and Diplomacy on the China Coast*, vol. I: *The Opening of Treaty Ports, 1842–1854* (Cambridge, Mass.: Harvard University Press, 1953), p. 59; and Hsin-pao Chang, *Commissioner Lin and the Opium War* (Cambridge, Mass.: Harvard University Press, 1964), pp. 3–4.

alone permitted to deal with foreigners, negotiated briskly and cordially with the British. Until 1833 the East India Company and its licensees enjoyed the British monopoly with China, which was in fact the predominant trade since the Napoleonic era. At the time of the expiration of the company's monopoly, the opium trade had extended illicitly along the coasts, encouraged by increased production and by the profit motives of other foreigners present, among whom figured Americans.

Chinese governmental concern over the trade and British governmental irritation over the treatment of its merchants and representatives both intensified. The dispatch of an English naval official, Lord William Napier, to represent his country's interests in Canton was deemed most inappropriate by the Chinese, since it violated precedent.[27] The emperor's appointment of Commissioner Lin to terminate the opium trade particularly troubled the commercial waters, for Lin seized and destroyed large quantities of opium and restricted the British in Canton. The Opium War of 1839–42 was the dismal outcome of this confusion and distrust, which were compounded by squabbles and litigation between British sailors and Cantonese officials. In this first Sino-British War, the Chinese handled themselves as poorly militarily as the British handled them diplomatically. By the Peace of Nanking in 1842 five "treaty ports" were opened to British trade with guaranteed extraterritoriality; Hong Kong was ceded to Great Britain; and China moreover had to pay an indemnity. The war was a cultural shock for the Chinese and particularly for the Manchu leadership. It proved the superiority of western arms, confirmed in the first of the "unequal" treaties China was forced to sign during the century. Moreover, the outcome was the clear beginning of what ultimately became the grand principle of Pacific trade — the Open Door policy. For the Americans and the French soon obtained concessions similar to those reluctantly granted the British.

Indeed, foreign demands increased as the effectiveness of Manchu rule diminished. An alien dynasty, the Manchus had dominated China since the middle of the seventeenth century, but in the nineteenth they were beset by political forces they could scarcely contain. The Taiping Rebellion, one of the most interesting and significant revolts in modern history, was the source of immediate disorder. Religious as well as political in inspiration, it was directed not only against the Manchus but also toward an earthly heavenly empire rudely constructed on Protestant principles.

[27] Fairbank, *Trade and Diplomacy*, p. 78.

With strength and conviction, the Taiping rebels moved from the southern province of Kwangsi north to victory in Nanking in 1853.[28]

What was primarily an eruption in the internal history of China greatly affected external relations and, consequently, the incipient imperialism spreading along the coast. The situation provides a meaningful example of the catalytic effects occasionally produced by local political events on imperialist development. In this particular instance, the British were ardently joined in their response by the French who now lingered in hopeful anticipation along the China coast.

It was largely missionary and patriotic zeal that propelled the French into Chinese waters during the reign of Louis Philippe.[29] A lackluster foreign policy was the cause of some French diplomatic concern. Not only was the regime of Louis Philippe regarded as arriviste in conservative Europe, but also it was forced, because of its weakness, to respond almost abjectly to the foreign policy of Great Britain. The setback France received by supporting Mehemet Ali in Egypt was diplomatically humiliating and just one of several international frustrations. The new premier François Guizot, although Protestant, sanctioned the old but continually ambitious missionary effort of the Catholics in the Far East because it was the only chance of success left to a government intent upon propping itself up at home by disembarking politically on other shores.

French interest in China was more than casual when Guizot first sent a diplomatic mission there in 1841 with the purpose of sizing up the political and commercial possibilities. A French missionary arranged a meeting near Canton in late 1841 between the French representatives and Chinese officials, at which the Chinese requested military aid against the British in the Opium War in return for ill-defined but apparently promising concessions. Nothing significant came from this and subsequent discussions, and the Treaty of Nanking foreclosed the Chinese need for further negotiation. But the French continued their pursuit, and now in more impressive form. Another mission set sail in 1843, larger than the first and with a more ambitious task. Guizot hoped it would emulate the British by reaching a favorable trade agreement with the Chinese, and he also wanted it to explore the possibilities of a naval base by which to support future commercial activities. The former was obtained but the latter was not, even though the French made a few tentative forays, to the

---

[28] Ten years later, the Taipings were checked under the direction of Sir Charles Gordon, thereafter "Chinese" Gordon.

[29] On this subject, see Cady, *Roots of French Imperialism*, chapter 2.

consternation of the Spanish and the British in the region. A French admiral's suggestion to occupy Tonkin in Indochina was ignored by his government because of complicating problems in Europe at the time. In sum, the most successful part of French imperialist effort during the reign of Louis Philippe was the missionary involvement in China, assured and accelerated by an edict of religious toleration which the Manchu emperor issued in 1845.

Anglo-French involvement in China was sustained by the Taiping Rebellion, the missionary activities of the French, and the probability of further commercial advantage for both countries. Significantly, the Taiping Rebellion brought about a momentary alliance between England and the France of Napoleon III. The success of the Taipings and the concomitant weakness of the Manchus argued for European intervention, which obviously would have been advantageous to European commercial interests. Of the several nations invited by the British to join, only France was willing to do so. But the proposed intervention was never realized, chiefly because the Taiping march northward was arrested by the Chinese government. Anglo-French relations remained of a cooperative nature and finally led to joint intervention when the second Sino-British conflict, the Arrow War, took place.

Without profound cause, the war was as much a matter of political vengeance as anything else. It derived from two incidents in 1856: the execution of a French missionary and the Chinese seizure of the *Arrow*, a ship flying the British flag, although its official registry had expired a few days before. Initially, the British undertook military action alone, with the French on the scene hesitant to participate. But both powers occupied the city of Canton in 1857 and were able to force through the favorable treaties of Tientsin in 1858. By these two new agreements, European influence in China was greatly increased. Six new ports were added to the original five and diplomatic representation was accorded by Peking.

Military tension did not end, however, for a haughty British delegation en route to Peking met opposition from Chinese forces on the river, with the loss of English life. In 1860, Great Britain and France together occupied Peking, an event notable for the wanton destruction of the emperor's summer palace by the British. From the new treaties negotiated with the Chinese, the French received financial indemnity, the British obtained the Kowloon peninsula behind Hong Kong, and both countries were granted joint occupation of the island of Chusan, which the French had previously coveted.

China was not colonized by the Europeans, nor were Anglo-French relations greatly improved by the Chinese wars. A basic discrepancy in purpose and policy denied any serious cooperation. For the British, trade was the dominant consideration; for the French, prestige.[30] With these same concerns, France focused attention on Indochina, which would become its prime colonial possession during the Third Republic.

The French presence in Indochina was of long duration, extending back to 1624 when the Catholic missionary Alexandre de Rhodes, unable to enter Japan, carried his work there. Through the remainder of the *ancien régime*, the Catholic efforts were sanctioned by the emperor of Annam, thus assuring France a primacy that helped to thwart commercial attempts by the British East India Company. The political situation changed rapidly after 1815 when, during the Restoration government of Louis XVIII, French missionary efforts in Annam were attacked by three successive emperors, culminating in the vigorous assertions of Tu-Duc to extirpate Christianity in his land.

In support of Napoleon III's Chinese policy, the French responded with naval force, employing units cruising the South Pacific. A joint Franco-Spanish bombardment and occupation of Da Nang (Tourane), near the city of Hué, took place in 1858 as a reply to the execution of a Spanish bishop. Saigon endured a similar attack from the French, but neither resulted in French demands for territorial advantage. However, a garrison of predominantly Senegalese troops left at Saigon was under fire for eight months until naval support, then diverted to China, could return to rescue it. The end of the siege marked the first step toward territorial acquisition: Admiral Bonnard annexed three of the provinces of Cochin China, the southernmost portion of Annam. Contiguity once again proved itself to be the physical law of imperialism, for in 1878 the French added the neighboring three provinces, which had also been causes of disturbances. In the same year the Second Empire established a protectorate over Cambodia and began explorations northward, which, in another decade, were to enmesh France even more seriously in Sino-Annamite affairs.

[30] *Ibid.*, p. 295.

Toward the Partition of Africa

Contrasted with the Far East, the large continent of Africa in the early decades of the century was still unencumbered by Europeans and their military apparatus. Activity was restricted instead to a small number of explorers, missionaries, and local merchants. Although Africa would become the primary political field for the late nineteenth-century imperialist scramble, from the contemporary European perspective that continent remained poorly observed and, hence, was easily dismissed. However, recent scholarship, in correcting earlier ethnocentric notions, not only has raised African history to the dignity it merits but also has demonstrated that the scramble was preceded by more than a flutter of European activity.

Aside from the French penetration into Algeria and the Anglo-French diplomatic encounters over Mehemet Ali — as much parts of African as of Mediterranean history — the Europeans were most visible at the southern tip of Africa, where the British had successfully seized the Dutch Cape settlement during the Napoleonic wars. Thereupon began a century of discord involving the native populations, the British, and the Boers, as the Dutch settlers styled themselves. Although the British occupied the Cape, which had great strategic possibilities as a major route to India, they were rather reluctant imperialists. Indeed, they moved inland not out of greed for land but with the intention of assuring a regional Pax Britannica between the Boers and the Bantus and at the urging of humanitarian and missionary groups, like the influential London Missionary Society, which were gravely disturbed by the Boers' ill treatment and virtual enslavement of the Hottentots.[31] With the abolition of slavery in the British empire in 1833, the political issue was noticeably aggravated. Efforts to maintain a political line of demarcation for the colony were to no avail, for the slaveholding Boers began in 1834 their trek north to escape British policy and land taxes and to seek the tremendous quantities of land they needed as pastoralists.

Subsequent history can be summarized in two words: encounter and conflict. As the Boers moved northeastward, a demographic shift of indigenous Africans was also occurring, spurred on chiefly by the military accomplishments of Shaka, leader of the Zulus, a group within the Nguni peoples. Shaka was a ruthless military genius of epic proportions who

---

[31] See John S. Galbraith, *Reluctant Empire: British Policy on the South African Frontier, 1834–1854* (Berkeley: University of California Press, 1963).

organized his troops into well-disciplined regiments and courageous fighters. By the time of his murder in 1828 his advance had resulted in the occupation of the better part of Natal — a territory east of the Cape Colony — and the flight of large numbers of the Natal population out and across the Drakensberg to the pastureland of the Veld, toward which the Boers were heading.

The period that follows in Boer history is analogous in many respects to the opening of the Far West in America. For the native Africans, however, it was an era of grave turmoil. The strong-willed and self-reliant Boers fought the Bantus and established a republic in Natal which lasted six years until the British, in 1845, took over that territory on the Indian Ocean and hence important to the protection of the water route to India. Disgusted but undismayed, the Boers moved inland from Natal to join other of their kinsmen; both groups formed two internal non-African states, the South African Republic of Transvaal and the Orange Free State. Yet like Franco-Algerian history, Anglo-Boer history was to be a drawn-out military affair, erupting several times again and climaxing only near the end of the colonial era.

Elsewhere, Eurafrican relations were not so pronounced. It is true that previously determined trade outlines slowly began to acquire political configurations, but disruptive intrusion into the hinterlands of Africa did not come until later in the century. Previous to the era of the scramble, European activity in black Africa was concentrated on the west coast. A most important market region even before the appearance of Europeans, the coast was tragically conditioned by the slave trade. With this trade, which forced Africa into the Caribbean colonial pattern, forts and factories came to dot the coast, and littoral states, like Dahomey and Bonny, grew as suppliers and political buffers.

The slave trade was abolished by the Congress of Vienna, at which time the English provided a naval squadron to enforce the act. But until the abolition of slavery in the Americas, the infamous practice continued and actually increased in volume through the 1830s. Alongside it, however, grew new sources of trade. Industrializing Europe had ample need for palm oil, which, as a commodity for exportation, was seconded only by the much less significant peanut cultivated by the French in Senegal. The amount of trade, though erratic from year to year, had developed by 1860 to the point where political authority to regulate relations between European traders, their African middlemen, and general African clientele became a matter of concern, yet essentially of local concern.[32] At the time neither the metropolitan French nor the British were enthusiastic about the possibilities of empire in this region. The French attitude appeared to be as inconsistent as the succession of home governments, whereas the British ministries maintained a policy of constant, if not always successful, opposition to intervention. Local merchants of both nations occasionally forced policy along unexpected lines as they extended trade and thereby created entanglements. France's first political arrival on the Ivory Coast was in this way unintended, as was Britain's on the Gold Coast. What domestic interest there was in Africa came from evangelical hopes, wafted from England, for a noble combination of Christianity and commerce leading to subsequent African cultural reform. From France the chagrins of the navy, so often caused by engagements with the British, were given vent in Senegal where naval officers were "bizarrely seeking on land the dominion they could not hold over the high seas . . ."[33]

As the second half of the century unfolded, the relationship between trade and politics drew closer, but not because government so desired. Palmerston, in acceding to the request of one English merchant based on the west coast, summed up the changing attitude thusly in 1860: "It may be true in one sense that trade ought not to be enforced by cannon balls, but on the other hand trade cannot flourish without security, and that security may often be unattainable without the exhibition of military force."[34] At the time Palmerston was speaking, the British had taken over the Danish and Dutch forts along the Gold Coast and in the next year established a protectorate over Lagos. The French were already extending inland into Senegal. Under Louis Faidherbe, one of the major French colonial figures, and then governor of Senegal, French merchant interests were receiving protection against the aggressive incursions of El-Hadj Omar, a dynamic Tukulör leader engaged in his own empire building. By the time of his recall from Africa in 1865, Faidherbe had carved out a large portion of the hump of West Africa for France and placed it under a vaguely defined protectorate. But his action was an unusual deviation from the European political norm at that time and in that place.

---

[32] Colin W. Newbury, "Trade and Authority in West Africa from 1850 to 1880," in L. H. Gann and Peter Duignan, eds., *Colonialism in Africa* (Cambridge: At the University Press, 1969), I, 84.

[33] Michael Crowder, *West Africa under Colonial Rule* (Evanston, Ill.: Northwestern University Press, 1968), p. 52.

[34] Quoted in John D. Hargreaves, *Prelude to the Partition of West Africa* (London: Macmillan, 1963), pp. 36–37.

This rapid *tour d'horizon* of the pre-1870 colonial world has revealed the increasing extent of European expansion and the hesitant national policy that frequently accompanied it. Local and regional activities, running the gamut from the commercial to the religious, were controlled by European cabinet decisions that were often as precipitate as they were carefully weighed. Still unencumbered by suggestions or demands for extensive political domination, European governments primarily freighted what interests they had abroad in the cargo crates of national firms.

Yet the disposition of world political power was changing just as European industrial control was increasing. By mid-century, several eastern empires were collapsing, and out of their ruins would emerge some of the major territories of the western colonial empires.[35] Incursions into both the Near and the Far East were made possible and attractive by the decline of the Ottoman empire in the one region and of the Manchu in the other. To a lesser degree, the disrupted internal stability of the Egyptian empire a few decades after the death of Mehemet Ali attracted European political attention.

For a moment there was a precarious balance, partly the result of European indecision and political disinterest, partly the result of the ability of these declining empires to hold off the Europeans and to quell the internal disorder that would later act as a provocation for European intervention. This confused and brief state of affairs changed rapidly in the forty-year period preceding World War I, when Europe fumbled to seize the world until then outside of its military grasp or beyond its political vision.

[35] One of the first assertions of this general relationship was made by A. J. P. Taylor, *Germany's First Bid for Colonies* (London: Macmillan, 1938), p. 1.

CHAPTER 3

The International Politics
of Empire since 1870

Far off, beyond the best nineteenth-century schemes mapped out in the
chancelleries of Europe, Fashoda suddenly took on great political significance and aroused general public interest in 1898. It would have been
considered a most unlikely center of Anglo-French confrontation even a
dozen years before, yet in the autumn of 1898 it appeared to be the
precipitant of war between these two nations. Queen Victoria lamented
this possibility and was scarcely willing to consider "a war for so miserable
and small an object."[1] Fashoda was deep in Africa, a military point in
territory as uninviting to European tastes and interests as the mountains
of the moon, but it was now deemed valuable enough to create major
European tension, an acute colonial situation which had few equals in the
preceding years of the century.

Although Fashoda was not the end of European expansion, it was a high
point, perhaps even the climax. That Europeans had reached the very
core of a continent they had hitherto practically ignored in their grand
political deliberations is, to say the least, suggestive of changes almost
bordering on a state of political frenzy. It is this quickened tempo which
immediately distinguishes the international politics of the "New Imperialism" and permits its most important manifestation to be described
as the "scramble for Africa."

The political confusion thrust upon the world by this multiple expan-

[1] Letter from the queen to Salisbury, October 30, 1898, quoted in G. N. Sanderson,
England, Europe and the Upper Nile, 1882–1899 (Edinburgh: University Press, 1965), p. 1.

sion finds its complement, but more modestly scaled, in the scholarly search for its causes. Few aspects of modern imperialism have engendered more concern, and, accordingly, historians for generations have tried to find the primum mobile or, in more contemporary academic vocabulary, the independent variable responsible for its occurrence.

Individuals have often been elected for responsibility. Blame and honor have been showered on Henry Stanley, the famous explorer, and Leopold II, the infamous entrepreneur who was his sponsor as well as the king of the Belgians. Otto von Bismarck is even more regularly raised above historical footnote and allowed to occupy pages as the shrewd *Realpolitiker* without whom Africa and the Pacific would not have been so seriously invested. And Benjamin Disraeli has been regarded as the herald of modern imperialism, his famous Crystal Palace speech of 1872 belatedly heard as an open declaration for expansion.

Forces more than personalities have dominated the causal pattern right from the start. Among these none has held such attraction as that which is strongly Marxist in derivation. According to this view, industrial capitalism, expanding to new markets and seeking new places of capital investment, promoted imperialism as a means to greater profits. Whether such profits were in actuality obtained and whether even anticipation of them was based upon real or mythical evaluations of the potential economic worth of the territories to be acquired does not distract from the basic premise of the argument: economic intention. Recently, a compelling variation of the economic argument considers imperialism to be a temporary regulator of the economic and social dysfunctions which the irregular growth of the industrial economy caused in Germany and Great Britain. The notion of a "social imperialism" designed to alleviate domestic apprehension over markets and possible class conflicts, problems reflected in bothersome unemployment statistics, is one that does respond to this interpretation of dysfunction.[2]

In opposition to the economically oriented theses, historians persuaded by the idea of the *Primat der Aussenpolitik* have found the generator of imperialism to be the dynamism of the European state system. New *champs de manoeuvre* were sought or found in Africa, the Near and Far

[2] On this subject see in particular Hans-Ulrich Wehler, "Industrial Growth and Early German Imperialism," in Roger Owen and Bob Sutcliffe, eds., *Studies in the Theory of Imperialism* (London: Longman, 1972), pp. 71–90; Bernard Semmel, *Imperialism and Social Reform: English Social-Imperial Thought, 1895–1914* (New York: Doubleday, 1968; first published, 1960).

East, as power politics were extended out from a small continent where the unification of Italy and of Germany had removed traditional centers of conflict and territorial parceling. Anglo-French and Franco-German national rivalries figure into the working of this hypothesis, which relies primarily on analyses of diplomatic activity and an appreciation of the concept of balance of power.[3]

Against these interpretations, which are joined at least in their general acceptance of the existence of the "New Imperialism," stands the most influential of recent theories, that which posits the existence of "informal" (market-dominated) and "formal" (politically annexed) empire, both of which were directed toward economic expansion. By asserting that British imperialism persisted as a continuing function of domestic economic development, and by demonstrating that political annexation in the mid-Victorian period was as significant as it was later, the thesis denies the uniqueness, suddenness, and intensity of the "New Imperialism."[4]

Finally, recent scholarship of the "inside out" sort, which has investigated incidents of imperialism particularly in Africa, has sought to modify the Eurocentric bias present in most causal analyses of imperialism. Local factors are here shown to have provoked political involvement, sometimes both unintended and undesired in the capitals of Europe. Therefore, colonialism, that is, local colonial activity, preceded imperialism, that is, national policy. From the same general perspective and in line with the informal-formal empire thesis, it has been argued that the response of local rulers and elites — that is, the degree of their cooperation or resistance — severely regulated the extent of direct European political involvement. The same is true of certain aspects of indigenous politics, such as the proto-nationalist movements that sought local reform and hence disturbed the stability of existing regimes, with the consequent threat to local European interests inducing political intrusion.[5]

[3] The outstanding diplomatic study remains William L. Langer, *The Diplomacy of Imperialism, 1890–1902*, 2 vols. (New York: Alfred A. Knopf, 1935). One of the most recent statements emphasizing the political nature of imperialism is David K. Fieldhouse, "'Imperialism': An Historiographical Revision," *Economic History Review*, 14:187–209 (1961).

[4] Ronald Robinson and John Gallagher, "The Imperialism of Free Trade," *Economic History Review*, 6:1–15 (1953).

[5] Among the many studies approaching this aspect of the causal problem, see in particular Ronald Robinson, "Non-European Foundations of European Imperialism: Sketch for a Theory of Collaboration," in *Studies in the Theory of Imperialism*, pp. 117–140; and John D. Hargreaves, "West African States and the European Conquest," in L. H. Gann and Peter

This brief review of what is a voluminous literature effectively hints at the complexity and contentious nature of the scholarly debate over causes. If no general resolution of this issue is apparent, not much is gained by only arguing that various factors operated in each historical instance of territorial acquistion. No one would deny the uniqueness of every historical act, but the chronological clustering of these occurrences of European political involvement around the world does beg the question of the similarity of general causes. Now that the thesis of the "New Imperialism" is being seriously rehabilitated, it is all the more desirable to consider those unusual qualities of action and intent which set it apart from the expansion that preceded it in the century.

Were the term not wearily overworked in contemporary historical analysis, "crisis" might well summarize that sudden confluence of domestic conditions and diplomatic activities which caused European politicians and theorists to bring together the many and far-spread colonial acts into a nationally enunciated policy and an ideology of imperialism. The imperialism of anxiety, it might also be called, the worrisome response to socioeconomic pressures which seemed to threaten both European world primacy and the domestic position of the governing elites. It is interesting and important to note that many later critics, as well as earlier sponsors, of imperialism saw it as an outlet: a safety valve for the industrial steam engine, according to Jules Ferry; a last stage for a self-destroying capitalism, according to Lenin; a solution to the "social question" of the underemployment of the urban poor, according to Cecil Rhodes, Lord Milner, and several modern historians; a source of opportunity for the military, no longer so grandly employable in bourgeois Europe, according to Joseph Schumpeter.[6]

Europe, as a collection of competing states and of economically disturbed societies, was being conditioned to an age of imperialism. Attitudes do not directly cause major political events, it may be true, but they do mold and regulate them. In a mutually supporting way, imperialism-of-the-act, that performed by the individual on the spot and in accordance

Duignan, eds., *Colonialism in Africa*, vol. 1: *The History and Politics of Colonialism, 1870–1914* (Cambridge: At the University Press, 1969), pp. 190–219; and the introductory chapter of David K. Fieldhouse, *Economics and Empire, 1830–1914* (Ithaca, N.Y.: Cornell University Press, 1973).

[6] The ideas of most of these individuals will be explained in the following chapters. See, notably, chapter 4.

PUNCH, OR THE LONDON CHARIVARI—JANUARY 19, 1884.

THE BEAST OF BURDEN.

MESSOO. "IF YOU CANNOT LEAD HIM, MON CHER, LET *ME!*"
JOHN BULL. "NO, THANK YE. IF I CAN'T *LEAD* HIM, I'LL *RIDE* HIM!!"

Egypt, 1884. From *Punch*, January 19, 1884. (Reproduced by permission of *Punch*.)

with local conditions, was combined with imperialism-of-the-mood, that which made statesmen and citizens alike receptive to what occurred outside of their national boundaries — and often outside of their immediate control.

An appreciation of this interrelationship can be gained most effectively from a review of the global implications of the "New Imperialism." In traditional fashion, this review will begin on the European Continent and will pay particular attention to the arch colonial rivals of the nineteenth century: Great Britain and France.

The "Calm" in Europe

In international relations the decade of 1870 might be described as a transitional one, the period in which the inner-directed era of European nation building gave way to the outer-directed age of global conflict. The American authority on seapower Captain Alfred Mahan tried his hand at

MARCHEZ! MARCHAND!

GENERAL JOHN BULL (to MAJOR MARCHAND). "COME, PROFESSOR, YOU'VE HAD A NICE LITTLE
SCIENTIFIC TRIP! I'VE SMASHED THE DERVISHES—LUCKILY FOR *YOU*—AND NOW I RECOMMEND
YOU TO PACK UP YOUR FLAGS, AND GO HOME!!"

Fashoda incident of 1898. From *Punch*, October 8, 1898.
(Reproduced by permission of *Punch*.)

L'AMITIE OBLIGE.

Madame La France. "YOU'LL COME AND SEE ME THROUGH THIS RATHER DULL FUNCTION, WON'T YOU?"
Mrs. Britannia. "WELL, IT'S NOT MUCH IN MY LINE; BUT ANYTHING TO PLEASE YOU, MY DEAR."

First Moroccan crisis, 1905. From *Punch*, July 19, 1905.
(Reproduced by permission of *Punch*.)

depicting this state of affairs which was contemporary with his writing. He observed that there was "an equilibrium on the Continent, and, in connection with the calm thus resulting, an immense colonizing movement in which all the great powers were concerned."[7] The word *calm* was really a poor euphemism for tension, and a complicated tension at that, considerably determined by a series of entangling alliances — and anticipated revisions. Yet what Mahan was getting at was correct enough; after 1870, with the unification of Germany and of Italy, the major cockpits of the Continent were gone, covered over by sovereign states.

The realignment of European power was to be to the disadvantage of both France and Great Britain, and it also was a factor in their intensifying concern over colonial empire. For France, the new alignment had been achieved at its expense, through military defeat. Some supporters of overseas expansion therefore introduced the argument that national strength might be replenished and national prestige regilded abroad. For Great Britain, the new alignment was to become a source of anxiety, for French expansion was viewed as a threat to the imperial Pax Britannica, while German economic and military prowess soon became a reminder of the importance of the empire to the home islands.

In the last three decades of the century the major political problem for France was that it was no longer the major political problem of Europe. The age of French hegemony had ended with the Franco-Prussian War. Henceforth Germany dominated the European scene and would do so for the next three-quarters of a century. This unwanted condition divided French politicians into two broad schools of international thought: those led by Clemenceau who focused their attention "on the blue line of the Vosges" and warned against distractions from that site; those led by Jules Ferry who turned their attention abroad and assumed that in empire France would find its continental strength again. As before, the principal theme was national prestige. However, "what had hitherto been a trait confined to sailors or soldiers, for whom national prestige was associated with professional success, now became national in character."[8] This is

---

[7] Alfred Mahan, *Naval Strategy, Compared and Contrasted with the Principles and Practices of Military Operations on Land* (Boston: Little, Brown, 1911), p. 104.

[8] Henri Brunschwig, "French Exploration and Conquest in Tropical Africa 1865–1898," in *Colonialism in Africa*, I, 139. A most recent statement which underlies the nationalistic aspects of French imperialism during the Third Republic is Raoul Girardet, *L'idée coloniale en France de 1871 à 1914* (Paris: Table Ronde, 1972). Also see Boyd C. Shafer, *The Faces of Nationalism: New Realities and Old Myths* (New York: Harcout Brace Jovanovich, 1972), pp. 260–313.

not to argue that the majority of the people were seized with the desire to transport the tricolor to tropical climes, but it is to say that imperialism became an important adjunct of contemporary French nationalist politics. In this relationship lies the explanation for the outbursts of public opinion which occasionally cheered expansion as well as the general parliamentary acquiescence which supported it with funds, however limited. More specifically, the popularity of French colonial endeavors was directly contingent upon public and parliamentary perception of European rivalry. Anglo-French rivalry in the early 1890s and Franco-German rivalry after 1904 made imperialists of continentally oriented nationalists.[9]

Even though public support of expansion was largely an erratic function of nationalism, there was nonetheless a small body of ardent advocates whose enthusiasm was in no way contingent. In 1894 a *parti colonial* appeared, a little coterie of parliamentarians and publicists, generally of republican persuasion, who joined together in a loosely formed phalanx to defend and to encourage extension of the colonial cause. As the *groupe colonial* in the Chamber of Deputies, parliamentary members of the *parti colonial* sought to influence legislation; as the sponsors of a number of colonial associations outside of parliament, members engaged in propaganda for their cause and backed a number of exploratory missions, notably to Africa.[10]

Before the decade of the nineties, the French national effort was diffuse and haphazard. No well-articulated program and no individual pointed the way. Indeed, the credit given to Jules Ferry as the guiding genius of French colonialism before 1890 was then and still remains exaggerated. Ferry arrived at his honorific post of founder of the second colonial empire both belatedly and accidentally. Not until he was appointed premier in 1881 did this republican, concerned essentially with domestic issues, become politically aware of the meaning of empire. He then inherited a foreign policy which involved the imminent occupation of Tunis. Initially surprised that such an action would be considered in an election year, he nevertheless accepted the policy, allowed the dispatch of troops, and thereafter became convinced that imperialism merited vindication. When

[9] C. M. Andrew and A. S. Kanya-Forstner, "The French 'Colonial Party': Its Composition, Aims and Influence, 1885–1914," *Historical Journal*, 14:101 (1971).
[10] On the role of the various committees, see *ibid.*, pp. 99–128; Henri Brunschwig, *Mythes et réalités de l'impérialisme colonial français, 1871–1914* (Paris: A. Colin, 1960), chapter 8; and Roger G. Brown, *Fashoda Reconsidered: The Impact of Domestic Politics on French Policy in Africa, 1893–1898* (Baltimore, Md.: Johns Hopkins University Press, 1969), pt. I.

he was again premier between 1883 and 1885, he followed as much as he initiated the continued pursuit of empire in Indochina, on Madagascar, and along the coast of West Africa.[11]

Ferry's most famous utterance — "colonial policy is the daughter of industrial policy" — would have made better economic sense if it had been expressed in English. French economic interests had to be aroused to colonial enterprise, not placated by it. Economic arguments were mostly ex post facto justifications or preliminary assurances, designed to mollify if not to inspire a conservatively bourgeois population which was interested in matters of the pocketbook even if it did not possess a large industrial complex belching out smoke and goods. Public initiative, then, was essentially nationalist and is best understood in light of France's recent defeat and contemporary worry about political status. Even so, there was as much local as national initiative until the 1890s. The army in the Sudan involved France as had previously the navy in Indochina. Not for the aristocratic classes — described in a famous aphorism about the English — but for the military was empire a "gigantic form of outdoor relief."

France in defeat was contrasted with Great Britain in political opulence. As the decade of the 1870s opened, the Pax Britannica appeared solid enough; financial investments were as sound as the pound and in evidence all over the world; the navy was without dangerous rivals; and the Foreign Office was able to stand above alliance in what has been grandly termed "Splendid Isolation." But this privileged position, one which very few modern nations have ever enjoyed, was not so firm after another two decades. By then the United States and Germany had become industrial and political powers of the first order, both seeking their respective place in the sun, soon to be observed from the decks of their newly formed navies. Politically, Anglo-American relations entered a new era of disturbance in Central and Latin America. Politically, Anglo-German relations continued to have the appearance of serenity, but in a short time they would be agitated by the scepter-thrashing of Wilhelm II. Industrially, however, there was no doubt, even among contemporary Englishmen, that the nation's situation was deteriorating relative to that of these two other countries. Although nearly another century would pass

[11] See Thomas F. Power, *Jules Ferry and the Renaissance of French Imperialism* (New York: King's Crown Press, 1944). An example of recent criticism of Ferry is found in Gordon Wright, *France in Modern Times, 1760 to the Present* (Chicago: Rand McNally, 1960), pp. 309–310.

before coals were carried to Newcastle, Solingen steel was seen in the shops of Sheffield before the century was out. Industrial stagnation and attendant labor problems made the "state of England" question a touchy one in the 1890s, and the specter of French, and German, protectionism loomed menacingly before English eyes, aware of the importance of world markets. Lastly, the placid moments in adjacent European seas were at an end. Renewed French naval construction in the eighties and nineties and the joint Franco-Russian naval display at Toulon in 1893 preceded by little the Tirpitz Plan for German naval might. The Naval Defense Act of 1888 and the "naval scare" of 1893 were fearful British reactions. The extent of worry can be ascertained from the suggestion of one naval critic that the navy and its stores be removed from the Mediterranean altogether.[12]

In the center of the British empire the era of Palmerston was over in mood as well as in fact. The spirit of expansionist confidence — a concert of commerce, Christianity, and culture — had ebbed by the early 1880s. Nevertheless, it was not replaced immediately by any popular compensatory urge to further colonial conquest. Instead, the one idea that predominated in colonial affairs was that of imperial consolidation. Schemes of imperial federation — Great Britain and the white-settler colonies joined economically, perhaps even politically in some form of close community — were loudly advertised. Of the lot assembled, that which came closest to realization in the late 1890s was Lord Salisbury's, a proposed *Kriegsverein*, imitative of Germany's successful continental model. Imperial defense was a pressing issue at the close of the century and was briefly inspired by the support the dominions offered Great Britain in the Boer War.[13]

This growing, defensive spirit, and not an articulated ideology of imperialism galvanizing the population, principally explains Britain's participation in the annexation of much of the remaining "free" land of the world. Preexisting colonial territories necessitated further territorial

[12] The opinion was that of a naval authority, W. Laird Cowles, who was part of the "scuttlers," those critics suggesting British withdrawal from the Mediterranean in the event of war. See Alfred J. Marder, *The Anatomy of Sea Power: A History of British Naval Policy in the Pre-Dreadnought Era, 1880–1908* (Hamden, Conn.: Archon Press, 1964; first published, 1940), pp. 209–214.

[13] On Salisbury, see J. E. Tyler, *The Struggle for Imperial Unity* (London: Longmans, Green, 1938), pp. 184–185. On the general subject, see Richard Koebner and Helmut D. Schmidt, *Imperialism: The Story and Significance of a Political Word, 1840–1960* (Cambridge: At the University Press, 1964), chapter 7.

safeguards — to prevent the occupation of contiguous lands by ambitious and aggressive rival states. As Africa was being scrambled for in 1883, the head of the African Department of the British Foreign Office, Percy Anderson, commented: "If there is one thing clearer than another, it seems to be that the French have a settled policy in Africa, both on the East and West Coast, and that policy is antagonistic to us. The progress of this policy is sometimes sluggish, sometimes feverish, but it never ceases."[14]

Many French perceived the same situation with the antagonists reversed. France was known for its political and cultural fits of Anglomania, and the end of the century was a fitful age in this respect. Paul Démolins's slight and popular study *A quoi tient la supériorité des Anglo-Saxons?* varied in tone between dirge and invective, but left no doubts in its readers' minds about the nature and causes of power generated across the Channel. Jean Darcy's *France et Angleterre: Cent années de rivalité coloniale*, published in 1904 when the Entente Cordiale was effected, suggested a colonial relationship which most Frenchmen woefully accepted. The failure of the earlier French effort and the apparent success of the English gave pause to speculation and to lament. As has been said many times, nothing succeeds less than success in foreign affairs; the British empire was loathed with admiration on the other side of the Channel by both France and Germany.[15]

The German factor suggests the interest in imperialism manifested by the leadership of that newly formed state, hitherto a "geographical expression." More than in any other country, the move toward imperialism was the decision of one man, Otto von Bismarck, who turned away from exclusive attention to continental European matters. The question "why?" has induced a variety of answers. The traditional literature on the subject would have it that Bismarck used the colonial issue, particularly as developed in Subsaharan Africa, to engage in complicated diplomatic maneuvers whereby an entente would be reached with France which, to

[14] Memorandum by Anderson, "On the French Occupation of Porto Novo," quoted by William Roger Louis, "The Berlin Conference," in Prosser Gifford and William Roger Louis, eds., *France and Britain in Africa: Imperial Rivalry and Colonial Rule* (New Haven, Conn.: Yale University Press, 1971), pp. 189–190.

[15] On the French attitude, see Raymond F. Betts, *Assimilation and Association in French Colonial Theory, 1890–1914* (New York: Columbia University Press, 1961), pp. 38–58. On the German attitude, see Pauline R. Anderson, *The Background of Anti-English Feeling in Germany, 1890–1902* (Washington, D.C.: American University Press, 1939).

be successful, would necessarily involve antagonizing England abroad. Certainly, Bismarck never lost sight of European affairs and he did attempt to soothe a France still suspicious and embittered as a result of the Franco-Prussian War. However, the selection of such a consideration as the motivating factor in Bismarck's acceptance of imperialism has of late been discounted by historians.[16]

Despite the new shadings of interpretation, there is general agreement that domestic rather than international concerns urged Bismarck to action. The recently created Reich did not rest on firm historical foundations or on a broad political consensus. The economic difficulties the new nation encountered almost immediately as a result of the beginning of the "Long Depression" seemed ready to threaten the old and somewhat brittle social order in which aristocrat and landowner held political power, while the working classes were kept from direct political intervention through the device of a complex governmental system. Furthermore, the need for a coalition of parties in the Reichstag to assure the success of his political program caused Bismarck to weigh the influence of popular imperialist sentiment on and in parliament.[17]

Neither politically nor economically, then, was the Reich a well-instituted social community, and Bismarck and his cohorts realized this. Overseas imperialism was thus viewed as one way to achieve national integration. In 1894 the then chancellor Prince Hohenlohe publicly acknowledged this argument. "The colonial movement," he told the Reichstag, "has bolstered up the feeling of unity and no government can and will miss this new and firm element which links the different tribes of the nation as well as the different social classes of the population."[18]

Part of the problem was the country's new industrial capacity, causing uneven economic and social development, with an abundance of goods and of workers susceptible to the vicissitudes of the domestic market. The

[16] The most criticized view is that of A. J. P. Taylor. See notably his *Germany's First Bid for Colonies, 1884–1885* (London: Macmillan, 1938), but also *The Struggle for Mastery in Europe, 1848–1918* (Oxford: Clarendon Press, 1954), chapter 13.

[17] The most important monographs in this new literature, upon which the following argument is based, are Henry C. Turner, Jr., "Bismarck's Imperialist Venture: Anti-British in Origin?" in Prosser Gifford and William Roger Louis, eds., *Britain and Germany in Africa: Imperial Rivalry and Colonial Rule* (New Haven, Conn.: Yale University Press, 1967), pp. 47–82; Hartmut Pogge von Strandmann, "Domestic Origins of Germany's Colonial Expansion under Bismarck," *Past and Present*, 42:140–159 (1969); and Hans-Ulrich Wehler, "Bismarck's Imperialism 1862–1890," *Past and Present*, 48:119–155 (1970). The last is a brief recapitulation of *Bismarck und der Imperialismus* (Cologne: Klepenheuer and Witsch, 1969).

[18] Reichstagverhandlungen, December 11, 1894, quoted by von Strandmann, "Domestic Origins of Germany's Colonial Expansion," p. 143.

issue of foreign trade therefore became a considerable factor in contemporary politics. Again, there is some agreement that Bismarck was seriously concerned about overseas markets and that, with the growing competition for colonies, he felt obliged, if not inspired, to assure Germany its share. Bismarck therefore appears historically as a reluctant imperialist, but an imperialist nonetheless, supporting the colonial enthusiasts and guaranteeing Germany a place in the sun because he was an intelligent realist, not a driven convert.[19]

A brief historical recapitulation of such sentiments at best explains only the domestic atmosphere of the European states in which the "New Imperialism" was generated. The question remains, What form did this all-too-old Anglo-French rivalry, with its new complications, take in the rush for still available territory? The answer to the question is twofold, for which the key words are preemption and contiguity.

There is ample reason to believe that the general European stimulant of the expansionism of the 1880s and particularly the 1890s, when the activity was at its most intense, was a type of national fear. The earth's "free" space was obviously limited insofar as European politics were concerned, and an awareness of this fact took on acute importance in this age of giantism and geopolitical thought. The "New Imperialism" was thus preemptive imperialism.[20] "Pegging out claims to the future," as Lord Rosebery advised, seemed a timely endeavor for many nations. This was an underlying reason why Germany, Italy, Japan, and the United States, along with an awakened Portugal, acquired imperial anxieties — and some amount of territory to relieve them. Even Australia, suddenly convinced that Germany was going to seize New Guinea in 1883, hastily laid claim to the territory, only to be disavowed by a less concerned English government. What the Germans described as *Torschlusspanik* — apprehension that the gate was closing on colonial empire — ran around the world.[21] Lord Carnarvon, the British colonial secretary, reportedly stated with respect to the Fiji Islands in 1874 that "the waste places of the earth were being filled up . . . and there were few outlying properties left."[22]

No longer, therefore, were England and France permitted to regulate

[19] See Wehler, "Bismarck's Imperialism," pp. 131–133.

[20] The term was suggested to me in a letter from Professor William L. Langer dated January 1, 1972.

[21] Turner, "Bismarck's Imperialist Venture," p. 51.

[22] Quoted by W. David McIntyre, *The Imperial Frontier in the Tropics, 1867–75* (London: Macmillan, 1967), p. 212.

their colonial affairs exclusively to each other's disadvantage. The new worldwide involvement not surprisingly aroused their concern. In 1893 the then foreign minister Lord Rosebery, in his famous "pegging" speech before the Royal Colonial Institute, remarked: "We should in my opinion greatly fail in the task that has been laid upon us did we shrink from responsibilities and decline to take our share in a partition of the world which we have not forced but which has been forced on us." Note how closely these words echo the sentiments expressed collectively by the Comité de l'Afrique Française in its founding year, 1890: "We are witnessing something that has never been seen in history: the veritable partition of an unknown continent by certain European countries. In this partition France is entitled to the largest share."[23]

Despite the "scramble," the "pegging" was not random. The geographical factor of contiguity was operative almost everywhere. It seems that international politics, at least in the last several centuries, like nature, abhors a vacuum. The proximity of unsubmitted lands was a provocation to worry and a source of temptation. A comparison of the maps of the colonized world in 1870 and again in 1900 reveals that the "New Imperialism" spread from the littoral regions inland, an expansion that moved generally in directions predetermined by the location of previously established colonial bases.[24]

An obvious problem of this intensified expansion was that of frontiers. For Great Britain, the "trade frontier" had been replaced in part by the "frontier of fear." For France, the political frontier was being extended along lines of an advancing military frontier. This condition was especially evident in Africa where, for instance, the growing importance of Egypt to England after the occupation of 1882 caused official concern over the southern boundaries of that state, a concern later motivating British involvement in the Sudan. The French "moving" colonial frontier in West Africa, for an additional instance, was pushed by the military as much as by the metropolitan government. As one recent critic has asserted, "The course of Sudanese expansion was to depend as much upon the attitudes

[23] Rosebery quoted by Langer, *Diplomacy of Imperialism*, p. 78; Comité de l'Afrique Française quoted by Brown, *Fashoda*, p. 20.

[24] This line of political development is most easily traced in Africa. See, for instance, the maps in J. P. Fage, *An Atlas of African History* (London: E. Arnold, 1958), pp. 41–44. On the idea of the effects of political contiguity, much has been written. See, for instance, G. Valmor, *Les problèmes de la colonisation* (Paris: Marcel Rivière, 1909), pp. 22–23, for a contemporary justificatory assessment.

and aspirations of the *officier soudanais* as it did upon those of the policy-makers."[25]

Combine all the conditions previously described, include missionary activity and particular economic stimulants such as newly discovered gold in the Transvaal, consider also the expansionist mood, and then it is possible to understand the complex pattern of late nineteenth-century expansion. Still predominantly a continuation of Anglo-French colonial rivalry, yet intensified by the political machinations of other countries and by obvious spatial limitations, the "New Imperialism" was distinguished in practice by its increased tempo and by its greater number of points of friction.

The Scramble for Africa

The "scramble for Africa" is the vast historical proof of these assertions. Swiftly moved from the periphery to the very center of European imperialism, this continent was deeply invested by European arms and policies; made the subject of diplomatic debate; and affected by these occurrences, as was no other part of the world, in a very short period of time.

As there is no single cause to explain this political situation, so there is no simple pattern by which to follow it historically. Just a half-century ago one of the first French historians genuinely interested in African history stated that the first serious penetration of the continent was by white settlers attracted to both those northerly and southerly regions in which climatic conditions were conducive to easy colonization.[26] Indeed, North and South Africa had, by the time of the scramble, been partly subjected to European rule.

The French presence in North Africa was certainly pronounced. Indirect influence in the Egypt of Pasha Mehemet Ali and political domination of Algeria were well advanced by the time France turned toward Tunis. There, contiguity played at least a justificatory role, for the immediate cause of French military action was tribal disturbance along the Algerian border, "one of the coincidences that abound in imperialist an-

---

[25] A. S. Kanya-Forstner, *The Conquest of the Western Sudan: A Study in French Military Imperialism* (Cambridge: At the University Press, 1969), p. 15.

[26] Georges Hardy, *Vue générale de l'histoire d'Afrique* (2nd ed., Paris: Colin, 1930; first published, 1923), pp. 124–125.

Africa: European territory in 1884

nals."[27] But before the French troops crossed eastward into new territory in March 1881, several preliminary conditions had been weighed. The finances of the Bey of Tunis were worrisome, certainly to the bondholders in Europe who wished the rapidly increasing state debt refunded. The quest for concessions aroused concern, particularly after the Italian shipping firm of Rubattino acquired the rights to an English-held railroad company that the French had also bid on. These two economic matters indicate the extent of European involvement in what today would be called the "modernization" of Tunis, and they also suggest, however anachronistically, a form of "neo-colonialism." However, the real pre-

[27] Parker T. Moon, *Imperialism and World Politics* (New York: Macmillan, 1961; first published, 1926), p. 194.

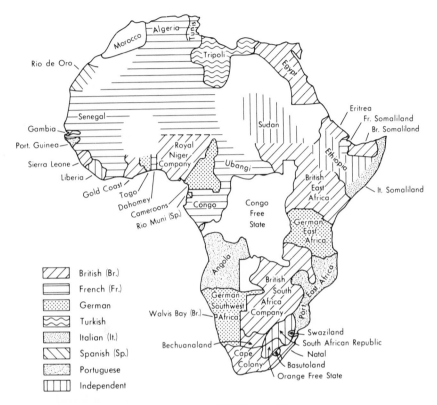

Africa: European territory in 1895

Legend:
- British (Br.)
- French (Fr.)
- German
- Turkish
- Italian (It.)
- Spanish (Sp.)
- Portuguese
- Independent

cipitant, and perhaps the dominant cause, of French action in 1881 was not economic but political. Fear of Italian imperialist intentions — for Tunis was a geographical and historical extension of old Carthage, and the Bey favored Italian business interests over French — disturbed the French Foreign Office and thereby involved Jules Ferry, the newly installed premier. Although Ferry announced that his action was to be strictly punitive, by 1883 and through a treaty signed with the Bey, France established a protectorate and thus greatly increased its North African empire.

In a not dissimilar way the British came to occupy more land in South Africa. There the demographic dislocation provoked by the treking Boers and the earlier military actions of Shaka continued to disturb the political situation. The Zulu War along the South African frontier occurred just before the French began to spread further their type of imperialism in North Africa. The major issue to the south persisted throughout the century: land disputes. The result was a continuously turbulent frontier, ever unfixed but moving northward as Bantu lands were encroached upon by the Boers living in the two white republics founded in the middle of the century. The most important political element, though used erratically, was the "imperial factor" — the British government. It was conditioned by domestic politics in England, missionary activity in South Africa, and broad concerns over imperial strategy — the naval lines of empire which ran down the eastern coast of Africa. There was never to be a satisfactory solution to the difficulties raised by the three different and opposed communities in motion in this region. Coincidental with, in part responsible for the scramble for Africa, the discovery of diamonds in the Orange River region in 1867 and the rush for gold in the Witwatersrand region in 1886 did nothing for the politics of the South African area save make them more abrasive.

This brief account of conditions at both ends of the continent as the partition of Africa was to begin in earnest lends credence to the assertion that these two points of penetration were initial and initiatory. The British were to continue to move northward into Africa, not quite realizing Cecil Rhodes's dream of a longitudinal empire reaching from the Cape to Cairo, but nearly so; and the French, settled in Algeria and already present on the west coast, were conjuring up schemes for a Transsaharan empire bound by iron rails. This symmetrical thrust seemed to acquire even further support with the British occupation of Egypt which has recently been the focus of debates about the causes of the scramble.

The Egyptian Question

Since the days of Mehemet Ali, Egypt had been a center of Anglo-French confrontation in an area of frequent Anglo-French cooperation. French cultural influence predominated and was, as is well known, greatly enhanced when Ferdinand de Lesseps proved that his plan to build a vast ditch was not a violation of French logic. The canal's success, however, went beyond British expectations and, for that reason, was in no way conditioned by British finances. This failure to invest in the Suez Canal Company was only corrected in 1875 when the financially distraught

Egyptian khedive Ismail Pasha sold his bonds in the canal. Disraeli, then prime minister, needed no prompting to purchase them. As he remarked of his action: "I have always and do now recommend it [the purchase of shares] to the country as a political transaction, and one which I believe is calculated to strengthen the empire."[28] Thus the financial difficulties created by Ismail's expensive public projects and private follies provided the means by which Great Britain acquired a political *cum* financial interest in Egypt. By the late 1870s there was no surcease for the khedive and little interest returned to the European bondholders. Attempts at financial reform, including an international debt commission, were not greeted with success; the truculence of Ismail seemed to be the only result.

Anglo-French impatience reached the point where Ismail was forced from power and was succeeded by his son Tewfik. Results were still not happy from the European, or the Egyptian, perspective. The government imposed financial stringencies upon the army, already discontent and nationalistic in its opposition to the now more obvious European presence. A military uprising, the first of what were to be the "colonels revolts" which characterized the decolonizing world, was led by a nationalist, Ahmed Arabi.

Under these conditions Britain and France again had to cooperate with each other temporarily. French Premier Gambetta saw Egypt as the means by which to refurbish not only French colonial policy but also the Anglo-French entente; he therefore drew up a diplomatic note which he hoped would express the potential nature of this cooperative spirit by threatening Egypt with concerted action.[29] Although Gambetta fell from office shortly after the note was issued, his proposed policy lingered on. By the late spring of 1882 both nations had sent a combined naval force to Egypt to demonstrate their support of the Tewfik government and their opposition to the supposed political chaos engendered by Colonel Arabi. Nevertheless, no further joint action was pursued by the two European governments. Instead, the French ships withdrew just before the British admiral responded to warlike activities, about which he had previously voiced his disapproval, by bombarding the fortifications of Alexandria on July 11.

This dramatic shift in events was further defined four days later when

[28] Quoted by William L. Langer, *European Alliances and Alignments* (New York: Alfred A. Knopf, 1931), p. 256.
[29] Charles-Robert Ageron, "Gambetta et la reprise de l'expansion coloniale," *Revue française d'histoire d'outre-mer*, 59:179 (1972).

Great Britain invited France to assist in the protection of the Suez Canal. This request prompted the French government to engage in parliamentary debate on the matter. Charles de Freycinet, Gambetta's successor, favored cooperation and therefore requested the funds to make it possible. On July 18 the issue was considered in the Chamber of Deputies, where Gambetta contributed the most significant words of the discussion. "It is not for the sake of the Egyptian national party that we ought to go to Egypt," he argued, "it is for the sake of the French nation. What I dread more than anything else is that you may hand over to England, for good and all, territories, rivers, and rights of way where your title to live and to trade is no less valid than hers."[30] This new expression of old French colonial fears did not move all the parliamentarians, however. The funds were voted by the Senate, but refused by the Chamber of Deputies. Thus France did not come to help occupy the canal zone, nor did Freycinet any longer occupy the premiership.

The English went in alone, for the "sake" of their nation. Even though the decision to occupy Egypt was reached after the bombardment of Alexandria, subsequent military action was brisk. Arabi's forces were defeated in the battle of Tell el Kebir, and Arabi was thereupon deported. The canal zone was protected by British troops, and the country was, in effect, occupied. The English found themselves the somewhat embarrassed masters of Egypt; the foreign minister Lord Granville assured the European powers that the occupation would be temporary, lasting only until order had been restored. "This promise was repeated sixty-two times between 1882 and 1922."[31] Financial matters, as with the French in Tunis, provoked the British action; political considerations fixed it. Not for the bondholders, but for the strategic importance of Egypt, better, the Suez Canal, did the English remain. It is true that the issue of the Straits was of greater significance than that of the canal during the century, even down to 1882, for the fear of Russia approaching India never diminished. Yet by the 1890s the Straits had declined to the canal in importance, and so Egypt became the right angle of the main route of British imperial concern which ran attentively through the Mediterranean, down the Red Sea, and into the Indian Ocean.[32]

[30] Quoted in A. W. Ward and G. P. Gooch, eds., *Cambridge History of British Foreign Policy* (Cambridge: At the University Press, 1923), III, 171.

[31] Taylor, *Struggle for Mastery*, p. 289.

[32] See C. J. Lowe, *Salisbury and the Mediterranean, 1886–1896* (London: Routledge, 1965), p. 118.

British occupancy was, however, no solution to the international implications of the Egyptian question. By assuming a seat of power there,
the British dislodged the French from a comfortable sphere of influence
and consequently aggravated them, a condition that endured through the
Fashoda incident. Moreover, England-in-Egypt required English interest in the southern border problems of the Sudan, hence a further intrusion into African affairs. Even in view of this development, it would be
simplistic to assert that Egypt provoked the scramble for Africa. Activity
south of the Sahara, where indeed most of the diplomatic maneuvering
took place, had its own sources of generation.

Tropical Africa

Consider once again the era of exploration that familiarized the scientifically minded with the natural contours of Africa and exaggerated the
hopes of those more interested in the potential yield of the resources.
Subsaharan Africa was, in a phrase of the late Victorian period, being
"opened up." And so were the eyes of one ruler who had earlier looked to
the Far East for colonial territory. Leopold II was a rich and ambitious
man, too large to be contained within the small confines of Belgium. He
posed as a philanthropist before he acquired a large share of Africa; he
acted like a robber baron thereafter. In words expressive of his gourmand
tastes, he stated in 1877 that he did not want "to allow slip by the
opportunity of obtaining for ourselves a piece of this magnificent African
cake."[33] Such possible consumption, however, was considered first in
economic rather than political terms.

Leopold's earlier desire for colonies had been dampened by the Belgian parliament's lack of interest. Realizing the political limitations of any
project that depended solely on his resources and wiles, he altered his
intentions at least momentarily and thought of trading concessions, not
territorial possessions.[34] But he approached the matter tangentially. In
1876, he called together a geographical conference at Brussels which had
the official purpose of determining how the vast areas of the Congo might
be closed to slavery and opened to "civilization." From this conference

[33] Letter from Leopold II to Baron Solvyns, dated March 1877, quoted by Baron van
Zuyler, *L'échequier congolais où le secret du roi* (Brussels: Dessart, 1959), p. 43.
[34] Jean Stengers, "King Leopold and Anglo-French Rivalry, 1882–1884," in *France and
Britain in Africa*, pp. 123–125. The argument which follows is largely based on Stengers and
Roger Anstey, *Britain and the Congo in the Nineteenth Century* (Oxford: Clarendon Press,
1962), notably chapters 5 and 6.

evolved a permanent organization, the Association Internationale Africaine, of which Leopold was president. As parent body it was to spawn a series of national committees, all of which would work together in the grandly defined task. Little of a cooperative nature resulted, however, for the British and French groups established no such internationally oriented committees, but contented themselves with activities solely in behalf of their national interests. Somewhat ironically, the chief rival of Stanley, who was soon to be in Leopold's employ, was sponsored by the French committee: he was Savorgnan de Brazza.

In a process of metamorphosis determined by Leopold, the Comité d'Études du Haut Congo emerged out of the association as an organization economic in objective but short of life. Under its aegis Stanley, just recently returned from Africa in 1878, departed again to explore the economic possibilities of the Lower Congo. Between 1879 and 1882, he signed a number of treaties granting Leopold sovereignty over chieftaincies in the Congo region. Beneath the appearances — a good place to look in the affairs of this king — resided a plan for an international economic enterprise which would exploit the wealth of the Congo. By now, 1882, another institutional metamorphosis had occurred and the Association Internationale du Congo appeared, out of which would emerge in final form the Congo Free State. The realization of this last structure, not originally anticipated by Leopold, was contingent upon more than just quickly negotiated treaties with African peoples; it involved first the hostility and then the consent of other European powers interested in the region.

To the fore, as usual, were Great Britain and France. The mouth of the Congo had long received British ships and had ingested small amounts of British trade. More recently, it had attracted French attention when the naval officer Savorgnan de Brazza, an ardent nationalist, explored the Lower Congo. His efforts yielded a treaty with King Iloo who thereby assigned France political rights over a large region on the northern bank of Stanley Pool. The French presence, vastly greater than that previously evident in the small trading station of Gabon, disturbed the English, irritated King Leopold, awakened the Portuguese, and aroused genuine nationalist enthusiasm in France.

The British Foreign Office now took the initiative, spurred by the thought that a French protectionist policy would descend the Congo. Portugal laid claim to the mouth of the Congo River and then began negotiations with Britain for a treaty which would recognize Portuguese sovereignty and guarantee British navigational and trade rights in the area. In 1884 the English Parliament refused to ratify the finally signed treaty, but in the meantime a concerned and adroit Leopold moved to save his investment. The possibility of being denied access to oceanic ports, should the Anglo-Portuguese treaty be approved, forced him to declare his stations or "states" in the Congo as guarantors of free trade. The maneuver was designed to win British support.

In a turn toward France, his immediate political rival at Stanley Pool, Leopold entered into negotiations to remove French objection to his claims to sovereignty there. The result of the "king's own initiative and improvisation" was a solution beyond any French expectations — preemption. France was given first acquisition rights to Leopold's possessions should he ever sell.[35] Certainly this allayed French fears and disposed the French favorably toward Leopold's proposed sovereignty. The English reaction was, as might well be expected, one of displeasure, while the German reaction was that of acquiescence. Yet the matter was not formally settled by all concerned until the Berlin West African Conference, which was held between November 1884 and March 1885.

That resplendent gathering of representatives from all the nations of western Europe, except Switzerland, and from the United States as well, played the game of division-of-spoils at its diplomatic best. Resounding statements were made about the obligations of civilization and the need for free trade; well-articulated legalistic phrases like "spheres of influence" and the "rights of previous occupation" now entered the vocabulary of international law. Yet the only significant political action taken was recognition of the Congo Free State as a sovereign nation. For the rest, the pronouncements were never communicated to Africa with any degree of clarity. What the Berlin Conference therefore revealed was not the good intentions of the European powers but their severe apprehension over conflicting national interests.

Indications of that apprehension were even evident in Africa. Diplomatic scurryings and local maneuvering of the sort found in the Congo were occurring elsewhere. The Congo situation may enjoy the dubious historical honor of being the first of such political developments; it was, however, rivaled in intensity and complexity in nearly every other quarter of Subsaharan Africa now disturbed by Europe.

[35] Stengers, "King Leopold and Anglo-French Rivalry," p. 160.

Trade concessions were transformed into political possessions; that, briefly, is the general history. The details are exquisitely complicated, fabricated by the activities of the imperialist-on-the-spot and shaded by the confusion frequently passing for official policy at home. Before scrambling about these details, the reader is invited to view the preexisting African political landscape.

Terra incognita to the ignorant European, Subsaharan Africa was already undergoing considerable political change at the time the Europeans arrived in number. Mention has been made of Shaka's activities in the southeast, but these were matched by a series of Moslem-inspired maneuvers elsewhere. It may well be the case that two-thirds of Africa would have been Islamic if European domination had been held off for another half-century.[36] Jihadic movements — religiously reformist, militarily directed Islamic crusades — had swept across much of West Africa in the late eighteenth and early nineteenth centuries, creating in their sweep political empires of sufficient magnitude to cause the later invading Europeans considerable difficulties. Particularly, the French penetration into the Sudan conflicted with and was severely delayed by two such empires established by the Tukulör. The Mahdist movement in the Sudan, which flourished in the 1880s and was not arrested until the end of the 1890s, totally disrupted Egyptian rule in that area and was one provocation for English intrusion when General Charles "Chinese" Gordon, who served under the Egyptian khedive as governor of the region, was killed by the Mahdists at Khartoum in 1885.

On the east coast similarly proportioned expansion had occurred. The sultan of Zanzibar was a member of an Arab dynasty which had extended its power along and across the Red Sea during the early part of the nineteenth century. In 1840 the center of that state was moved from Oman on the Arabian peninsula to Zanzibar and increased in both political and economic strength as the Arab merchants, in search of slaves and ivory, penetrated into Africa; meanwhile the sultan held sway over hundreds of miles of its coastline. This lateral action was met by another Arab thrust, from the north. The ruling progeny of Mehemet Ali seemed to have inherited his expansionist urges. During his lifetime, his son Ibrahim had penetrated into the Sudan and founded the major city of Khartoum. Under the khedive Ismail, further expansion took place, in part to

[36] Roland Oliver and J. D. Fage, *A Short History of Africa* (Baltimore, Md.: Penguin Books, 1962), p. 180.

repulse the slave trade, but also to benefit Egypt politically. Through these efforts Egypt became the major imperialist power in nineteenth-century Africa before the scramble and was matched in kind though not in scope only by Ethiopia. For that ancient country, resting high on a plateau and long on a tradition reaching back to the queen of Sheba, was politically remassed in the late nineteenth century to the extent that it was the dominant force in the Horn of Africa.

No historian today would disagree that the indigenous African political situation affected the pattern of European involvement. Intervention was encouraged both by the assertion of newly formed power and by the dissipation of the old. The effect of this condition is one of the most eagerly pursued investigations in contemporary African historical research, but it can only be touched on in a study such as this.

On the European side of the activity, the transformation from informal to formal control of trade through territorial acquisition took place first on the west coast. Here, as has been mentioned before, Anglo-French trading was performed on a small scale in commercial spheres of influence, which overlapped, but did not provoke any serious political problems. Under George Taubman Goldie's leadership the English traders in the Lower Niger were grouped together and thereafter were able to manipulate prices so that the French were in a disadvantageous commercial position and soon forced out. Then, in 1886, the English traders, still under Goldie's aegis, were formed into the Royal Niger Company, which enjoyed an administrative and commercial function in the region until the British government took it over in 1899. Shortly after, the government joined the company's former territory with the Lagos and southern protectorates into the vast colony of Nigeria.

The forward-moving British were pushing beyond the French traders in the area, for which reason they were the subject of French governmental concern. The French, situated on the Senegal River, soon sought to extend their influence beyond the Senegal to the northern reaches of the Niger. Not the energy of the merchants, but "le go-ahead des Américains," first expressed between 1876 and 1881 by the new governor, Brière de l'Isle, started the colony in motion in the form of railroad construction. Consequent activity involved France deeply in Sudanese affairs, a change of condition further emphasized by the establishment of a new military district in Upper Senegal, which was entrusted to the hardened and battle-tempted Colonel Borgnis-Desbordes. "This marked a

new stage in the attempt to push a military frontier ahead of the unenter-
prising Senegalese traders."[37] The military frontier was particularly
pushed in the 1890s when a number of French officers of high caliber
engaged the indigenous rulers in combat and submitted them and their
territory to French control. By 1898 the French had reached the fabled
city of Timbuktu and had carved out a vast West African empire which,
joined with coastal territories acquired by treaty of protectorate, was a
dozen times larger than the metropolis.

The change of policy that precipitated this military action in the first
place has recently occupied the attention of several historians who have
tried to relate it to the larger issue of the "scramble." Earlier interpretations which had seen this action in the broad light of European diplomacy
were later refocused geographically so that the British occupation of
Egypt was considered as the catalyst. Thus viewed, the French moves in
West Africa were seen as expressions of diplomatic chagrin and political
retaliation for France's peremptory elimination from Egypt. Although the
chronology lends support to the Egyptocentric thesis, the situation on the
west coast had been altered — and along with it policy — well before
England entered Egypt. A most recent analysis relocates the cause once
again, but this time in Paris.[38]

French thought and action had descended from Algeria into the Sudan
with the translation of the military policy initiated in the North by Commandant Louis Faidherbe. His suggestion for the military extension and
protection of French trade frontiers was acted upon, with some modification, in 1879–80. Then, the French foreign minister, who was Freycinet,
and the minister of the marine, who was the former governor of Senegal,
Admiral Jean Jauréguiberry, concerted their expansionist interests and
used their positions of authority to introduce these interests as policy.
Both men desired further French penetration into the interior. Anticipating intensified foreign competition in the region and hopeful of uncover-
ing some of its imagined wealth, they "made political control the basis
for economic development, and they set out to win their empire by
military means."[39]

The assertion that this French decision is the root cause of the West

[37] John D. Hargreaves, *Prelude to the Partition of West Africa* (London: Macmillan,
1963), p. 262.
[38] C. W. Newbury and A. S. Kanya-Forstner, "French Policy and the Origins of the
Scramble for West Africa," *Journal of African History*, 10:260–264 (1969).
[39] *Ibid.*, p. 275.

African scramble is plausible, but historical debate will probably no more rest there than did the French and the British imperialists who were responsible for the action so described. By the end of the nineteenth century, the previously sketched spheres of trade had been converted into well-delineated political protectorates and colonies, running along the coast from the Sahara to the Bight of Benin, thence down to the Congo and inland to the point where French aspirations to some control of the Upper Nile valley approached realization. That aspect of Subsaharan expansion was the last of the dramatic encounters, preceded by a myriad of negotiations in East Africa into which Germany and Italy suddenly intruded.

Germany and Italy in Africa

Germany's interest in Africa was quickly defined, appearing almost simultaneously on the southwestern and eastern coasts within the crowded time span of one year. The initial acquisition of territory by Germany was generally unexpected, certainly in the thoughts of the British Foreign Office and also in those of the German ambassador to the Court of St. James. Even Bismarck was at first doubtful. Worried about the possibility of German merchants being excluded from tropical markets which had fallen under the shadow of European flags, and pressed by his adviser on colonial affairs to act, he finally gave his support to the establishment of a protectorate over Angra Pequena in 1884.[40]

The southwestern coastal base for the trading operations of F. A. E. Luderitz, a Hamburg tobacco merchant, Angra Pequena was described by most contemporaries as a desolate area. Luderitz wished some assurance of governmental protection for his activities, but Bismarck initially refused because he assumed that England would provide such a service in the region. A delay of many months in a reply to a diplomatic note about the matter was the period during which Bismarck, more seriously pondering the problem of markets and his colonial adviser's arguments, changed his mind. He was further spurred by rumors that the British in Cape Colony were considering a lien on Angra Pequena, rumors which lent an ominous quality to Whitehall's delay.

In the meantime, feeling domestic commercial pressures, Bismarck had

[40] The most significant recent account of this activity is Turner, "Bismarck's Imperialist Venture."

appointed Gustave Nachtigal as commercial commissioner for the west coast of Africa. At first he was sent only to conclude trade agreements with local rulers, but his orders were altered to include treaties of protectorate with the rulers in the Cameroons and Togoland. The sum of all this was an outbreak of political activity in the spring and summer of 1884, whereby Germany acquired a West African empire initially consisting of Angra Pequena, the Cameroons, and Togoland.

Across the continent the results were of the same order, the pattern of procedure somewhat different, however. There, Karl Peters was dynamically present. Founder of the German Colonial Society and chief sponsor of the German East Africa Company, which was suddenly and busily engaged in the African territorial parcel business, Peters was the closest German personality to Cecil Rhodes: a nearly insatiable empire builder. Peters was in and out of Africa, first negotiating a clutch of treaties at the time of the Berlin West African Conference. These agreements netted him about sixty thousand square miles of territory which were placed under company jurisdiction, but soon thereafter were granted the protection of the German Imperial Government by a somewhat reluctant Bismarck. Back in East Africa between 1888 and 1890, Peters traveled through Uganda and Tanganyika, with other than the tourist's intentions. His activities and the governmental support they were receiving finally aroused Lord Salisbury, though long after other British officials had expressed concern. Earlier demands to support William Mackinnon's East Africa Company as a British counterweight were now met; the company received a royal charter in 1888 and thus the aura of governmental authority. Now Mackinnon and the Germans faced each other with mutual suspicion, while their governments briefly assumed the attitude of unwilling imperialists in this part of Africa.

Through these jumbled commercial and political activities, Great Britain and Germany were drawn together, but in serious opposition. The major problem emerging clearly in the British official mind was Germany's inward thrust toward the Nile. After a period of little attention to the area, Lord Salisbury formulated a new Nile policy, in part a result of his observation of German activity to the east and French motions from the west. The valley of the Nile was now considered crucial to the British imperial realm, another incident of the age's hydraulic politics and another effect of the decline of khedival power in Egypt.

The pressing differences between the two nations were peacefully resolved by an agreement in 1890, an elaborate settlement of a variety of is-

sues. The hinterland beyond the coast into which both countries were in-
truding was divided into spheres of influence, with the Germans effectively
restricted from the Nile. Ultimate control over the sultanate of Zanzibar
fell to the British in the form of a protectorate. German agreement to this
settlement was assured by the British relinquishing of Heligoland, an island off the coast of Germany and a British speck in the German naval eye.
This arrangement is another reminder of how negotiable so much of the
colonial territory was when considered in terms of European continental
exigencies.

Immediately after these negotiations, Great Britain brought under control the less important but still bothersome Anglo-Italian confrontation
farther south and consequently farther up the Nile.

Italy was nearly the last and certainly the least successful of the European nations participating in the colonial race. Premier Crispi, while not
the only voice cheering for colonies, was hardly joined by a choir.
Moreover, Italy's general political weakness in international affairs —
Bismarck ungraciously said it was a country with a big appetite and bad
teeth — made it dependent on Great Britain in both the Mediterranean
and the Red seas. It was William Mackinnon who, fearing German incursions along the coast, suggested to the Italians that they negotiate with
the sultan of Zanzibar for the concession of ports in the region of
Somalia.[41] The cordiality seemingly extended by the head of the Imperial
British East Africa Company was not repeated by the British government
when Premier Crispi ambitiously lay claim to Kassala, as part of the extending Italian empire above the Horn of Africa, in what became the
colony of Eritrea in 1889. Kassala was proximate to Khartoum in the
Sudan and therefore not a matter of indifference to Great Britain.
However, Crispi fell from office, and the successor government, which
was less solicitous of colonial affairs, arranged with Great Britain to establish spheres of influence. Thereupon, Italy, like Germany before it, was diplomatically removed from the region of the Nile.

Any new dreams of tropical empire expanding in the mind of Premier
Crispi, when he returned to power in 1893, vanished. Italian colonial activities along the western coast of the Red Sea had extended from the port
of Massawa in the north to that of Assab in the south and inland to the point
that they were a growing irritant to Menelik II, emperor of Ethiopia in 1889

[41] Robert Hess, "Germany and the Anglo-Italian Colonial Entente," in *Britain and Germany in Africa*, pp. 161–162.

and former Italian protégé when he had been ruler of the province of Shoa. By 1893 the relations between the two parties had erupted into warfare which the Italians intended to pursue in force. Some twenty thousand troops, operating in the northern Ethiopian province of Tigre, marched upon the city of Adowa in 1896. The resulting battle against superior numbers of Ethiopian soldiers was as ignominious for the Italians as it was glorious for the Ethiopians. One of the first significant proofs of the vulnerability of white imperialists, the Battle of Adowa spelled a major defeat for Italian empire in tropical Africa.

Confrontation at Fashoda

After 1896, the field of conflict was again dominated by England and France: the Sudan was the object; Fashoda was the outcome. The chief cause was the "imperialism of prestige," France's longed-for opportunity to twist the Lion's tail, to overcome some of the chagrin felt by many French politicians since the occupation of Egypt. In brief, interest in the Sudan was territorial and psychological. The unfolding of French intentions produced a scenario bold in inspiration and arduous in execution. Retold many times since its principal agent, Captain Jean-Baptiste Marchand, first related his experiences, the history of the expedition from the French Congo across Africa to the Sudan needs no recounting again. Its sponsors and its defined purposes, however, do merit immediate attention.[42]

Here again important preexisting African conditions prefaced the Anglo-French action. The establishment of a Mahdist state in the Sudan in the 1880s had effectively excluded the British-through-Egyptian influence there. Indeed, the death of Gordon at Khartoum was dramatic proof of the altered situation. The political chaos that resulted led the French to assume that, because the British had done nothing to reassert their authority in the region, the Upper Nile was, at least from the European perspective, *res nullius*. Its attraction to the French came by way of its initial attraction to the Comité de l'Afrique Française.[43] This organization, keenly interested in exploration, was to sponsor three missions to the area under question. Through its connections with the undersecretary and then minister of colonies Theophile Delcassé, the committee extended its concerns to gov-

[42] See G. N. Sanderson, "The Origins and Significance of the Anglo-French Confrontation at Fashoda, 1898," in *ibid.*, p. 287. On the expedition itself, see Pierre Renouvin, "Les origines de l'expédition de Fashoda," *Revue historique*, 200:180–197 (1948).
[43] See Brown, *Fashoda*, notably chapter 1.

ernmental proportions. Delcassé himself also became intrigued by the Egyptian question and slowly concluded that peaceful negotiation would not budge the English; more forceful action was needed.[44]

The vicissitudes of French politics — in this instance a strong difference of opinion between Delcassé and Foreign Minister Gabriel Hanotaux about African policy — complicate the history. However, the internal French situation, still to be further confused by the Dreyfus Case, was momentarily overshadowed by international complications, when verbal bombast about the Upper Nile was exchanged between French parliamentarians and their *outre-Manche* equivalents. The stiff British reaction to French fulminations took the form of a statement by Earl Grey in 1895 that any French movement in the Upper Nile would be considered an "unfriendly act."

Out of this charged atmosphere came Captain Marchand, a true believer in empire, an ambitious adventurer, and an outspoken Anglophobe. Marchand, desirous of heading a mission to the Upper Nile, made his wish known to Hanotaux and to Delcassé in 1895. After considerable additional confusion and a reshuffling of cabinet posts, Marchand gained approval for his project and departed from the French Congo overland, with a knock-down iron steamer to propel him along his way — when it was not being conveyed in numbered pieces by African porters. This was in 1896.

In the same year the British government took action in the Sudan, both to avenge the death of Gordon and to reassert its authority there. However, realization of the latter objective was not clearly prescribed at the outset. The most recent authority on the subject insists that military conquest was initially in neither the public nor the official mind.[45] Lord Kitchener, head of the expeditionary force, is quoted as having said that any operations south of Khartoum, the bottom of the English "sphere," should be kept to a minimum. Whatever the outcome, the preliminary intentions were not to impose firm British rule in the southern Sudan. Nevertheless, after the Battle of Ombdurman in September 1898, when Kitchener "cleaned" the British flag with the blood of twenty thousand dervishes, the public, aroused by journalistic accounts, looked upon the Sudan with a possessive collective eye.

The Anglo-French political intersection and confrontation occurred when Kitchener turned his attention and part of his troops southward to

[44] Christopher Andrew, *Théophile Delcassé and the Making of the Entente Cordiale: A Reappraisal of French Foreign Policy, 1898–1905* (London: Macmillan, 1908), pp. 21–25.
[45] Sanderson, "The Origins of the Anglo-French Confrontation," pp. 295–296.

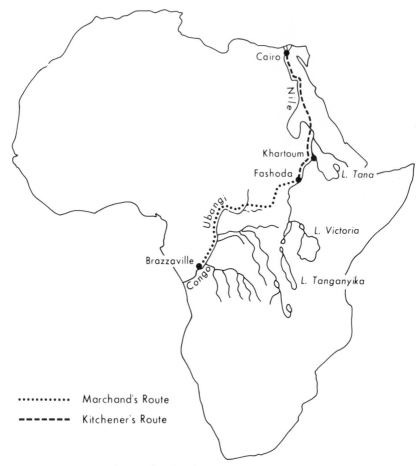

.... Marchand's Route

------- Kitchener's Route

Anglo-French political intersection at Fashoda, 1898.

greet the French in Fashoda, over which the tricolor now flew. Suddenly and briefly, the metaphysics of European power were located on a meander of the River Nile. Britain's status as a great power was questioned, if not threatened. France, that is, the government and *comités coloniaux*, was hoping through its national presence at Fashoda to dislodge Britain militarily from Egypt. The form of the crisis was, therefore, diplomatic, as was — fortunately for the peace of Europe — its solution.[46]

The lack of European response to the situation left France starkly

[46] *Ibid.*

confronting Great Britain, and the British were in no national mood for any type of accommodation. From the French perspective, the alternatives were dreadfully clear: retreat or fight. The prospects of a naval war against England, which then had a fleet twice the size of France's, appeared very dismal to Delcassé.[47] Therefore, a reluctant Marchand withdrew at the request of a worried Delcassé. The tricolor never again was seen on the Nile.

Fashoda was the climax of Anglo-French colonial rivalry around the world. It also was the dramatic conclusion of the diplomatic process or confused activity by which the European nations had acquired political dominion over Subsaharan Africa. From the core, the remaining action now moved centrifugally to the extremities of the continent. As at the beginning, so at the end, British involvement in South Africa and French involvement in North Africa dominated.

The African Antipodes, North and South

The South African problem had grown to enormity as the difficulties of white settlement had extended. It was all the more aggravated by the discovery of diamonds in 1867 and of gold in 1886, which by the peculiar alchemy of imperialism were to be turned into gunpowder. The basic issue was one not only of control of this wealth but also of the political implications such wealth had for the balance of power in South Africa. The diamond-yielding territory of Griqualand West was, after some local manipulation and Boer resistance, brought under British control, but the gold lay in the hills of the Witwatersrand and thus within the borders of the primarily pastoral South African Republic. The gold became the focal point of a century of political discontent.

Around that focal point, and therefore necessitating some attention, whirled another significant character in the scramble for Africa. This was Cecil Rhodes. Wealthy from his diamond mines and ambitious for his country as well as for himself, Rhodes dreamed of a large-scale South African federation joining Briton and Boer, possibly even Bantu. He also dreamed of a grand empire running north to Cairo. The South African Republic of the Transvaal destroyed these reveries. Its president, Paul Kruger, longed for a Boer-dominated sphere, exclusive of the British and their imperial pretensions. For Rhodes, then, the isolation if not the

[47] Andrew, *Delcassé*, pp. 102–103.

reduction of the Transvaal state was essential. As premier of the Cape Colony, he hoped to fuse Briton and Boer politically; as president of the British South African Company, founded with his wealth and royally chartered, he hoped to outmaneuver Kruger territorially. By ruse, war, and more conventional political means, the company had extended itself north of the Transvaal and had acquired an impressive amount of territory, grandly denominated "Rhodesia" in 1895.

A more direct confrontation between Rhodes and Kruger occurred through the Jameson Raid of 1895, itself precipitated by the side effects of the gold rush. Kruger and his associates neither welcomed the influx of foreigners nor relished the "modernizing" process they imported. Johannesburg rose from the land as had many a western American boomtown, a monument to human acquisitiveness. The "uitlanders" — an Afrikaner term for the foreigners working in the mines and quickly populating Johannesburg — suffered both politically and economically at the hands of the Boer government. First, they were without franchise and the prospects of receiving it grew dimmer as the government continued to extend the residency requirements. Secondly, they had to purchase their dynamite for mining purposes at high prices maintained through a governmental monopoly. To this internal irritation was added an external cause for disturbance. Kruger ordered a railroad to be built eastward to the sea, which would weaken the one economic bond between South Africa and the Transvaal, the existing railroad that ran through the Cape Colony. Needless to say, the combination of these factors only aggravated Rhodes further.

The explosive situation culminated in the ill-fortuned Jameson Raid, an attempt to create an uprising in the Transvaal through military intrusion. Rather than being seriously disturbed by the raid, the Kruger government responded with dispatch and to good effect. The raid was a fiasco, a source of embarrassment to the British government, and the reason for Rhodes's downfall in Cape politics. Most important of all, the raid further widened the rift between Briton and Boer. From this time on diplomatic negotiations were unsatisfactory, because more provocative than conciliatory. The outcome, as is well known, was hostilities. The Boer War of 1899–1902 was the most significant of the colonial wars. It stirred up strong feelings of political acrimony in Great Britain and gave to the word *imperialism* its immoral connotation.[48] Furthermore, it caused Great Brit-

[48] See Alfred Koebner, "The Concept of Economic Imperialism," *Economic History Review*, 2nd ser.; 2:1–29 (1949).

ain some humiliation in Europe and seriously embittered Anglo-German relations because of the German sympathy for the Boers and the kaiser's ill-timed and ill-considered statements. But the war ended in a considerable extension of the British empire, the last acquisition of such proportions.

Although not set on a battlefield, French imperialist maneuvers in the north eventually aroused warlike concern, despite the fact that they were initially predicated upon Anglo-French cooperation. The issue was Morocco, a country stumbling into the twentieth century on the debris of a state, "an incoherent jumble of constantly shifting peoples, bound only by a nominal spiritual submission to one man."[49] The advent of imperialist interest in Morocco was not then and is not now surprising considering its general condition of political chaos and financial insolvency. Morocco, which lies to the west of Algeria, certainly tempted the argument of territorial propinquity — and the French did use it when they spoke of a well-rounded North African empire. Yet the initiative was neither economic nor geographical, but rather political, and directly linked to Egypt. The outcome at Fashoda had convinced certain members of the *parti colonial* to turn from futile thoughts about Egypt to fruitful thoughts about Morocco.[50] In broad terms, the Entente Cordiale reached between England and France in 1904 solved this major colonial problem by allowing the French a free hand in Morocco in return for their acceptance of the British position in Egypt. Delcassé, who was responsible for the realization of this colonial agreement, had been brought to that position by the persuasive arguments of the *parti colonial*; now he hoped to assure the *pénétration pacifique* of this colonial territory-to-be.

French efforts to reorganize Morocco economically were not very far advanced when Germany remonstrated with the dramatic appearance of Wilhelm II at Tangier. Although the kaiser had no heart for the matter — and would in the future privately protest against German involvement in Morocco — his presence and a timely speech at Tangier convinced the sultan to balk at Delcassé's reform plan; continuing German diplomacy was iron-fisted enough to knock Delcassé out of the foreign ministry. The result was a multilateral diplomatic debate instead of a unilateral "peaceful penetration." The first Moroccan Crisis was settled at the small Spanish town of Algeciras where repre-

[49] Stephen H. Roberts, *The History of French Colonial Policy, 1870–1925* (Hamden, Conn.: Archon Press, 1963; first published, 1929), p. 547.
[50] Andrew, *Delcassé*, pp. 103–104.

104 ANNEXATION AND ACCUMULATION

sentatives of interested European nations, plus the United States, met to discuss two particular points, but in effect the future disposition of European power: an international bank and an international police force. The latter issue was the nubby one with the Germans strongly expressing their uncompromising disapproval of the French-proposed plan. The final arrangement whereby France and Spain were to man the force which would be under a Swiss captaincy was proof of Germany's diplomatic isolation and of Britain's support for France. Politically, Germany gained nothing at Algeciras but the rebuke of Europe; France was now in a position to extend its sphere of influence in Morocco.

The second Moroccan Crisis of 1911 reflected France's increasing political involvement in that country. Internal disorders, already bothersome, were severely aggravated by a civil war waged over control of the sultanate. As the situation descended to desperate depths, the French responded to the request of the then besieged sultan by sending troops to Fez in 1911. The German government, now concerned lest this military occupation should become permanent, sent the gunboat *Panther* to Agadir as a warning. Moreover, the German foreign minister, with the presumption characteristic of this imperialistic era, demanded "compensation" in the form of the French Congo. The Franco-German diplomatic encounter was extended when the British vigorously entered the debate through a speech by Lloyd George in which he stated that Great Britain would not be ignored where its interests were clearly involved. The tone was ominous, even though the purpose of the speech was to force a resolution of the Franco-German conflict. For a moment, "the nations faced each other in a 'pre-war' spirit," indicative of increasing political tension — although that tension at the moment was between Great Britain and Germany.[51]

Yet territorial compromise was still possible at the diplomatic table. The second crisis dissipated when Germany recognized French interests in Morocco in return for a guarantee of an "open door" economic policy and a compensatory piece of the French Congo which thereafter was affixed to the German Cameroons. Finally, enjoying a quid pro quo with Italy over Tripoli, which Italy annexed following a successful war against Turkey in 1911, France proceeded unobstructedly to the creation of a protectorate over Morocco in 1912.

With French political residency established alongside and behind the

[51] Taylor, *Struggle for Supremacy*, p. 473.

Cherifian government in Morocco, the coastal dependencies of the Ottoman empire were all once again politically disjointed from the continent
of which they were geographically a part. The entirety of North Africa was
now forcefully integrated into a new Mediterranean imperial order directed from the dominant continent directly to the north. Thus the
scramble for Africa concluded. Similar European activity farther to the
east had already subsided.

East of Suez Again

The vast measures of sea and land to the east of Suez remained within the
confines of European imperialist politics, but provided less historical
drama than Africa did in this period. Imperialism in the Far East was
somewhat less frenetic and somewhat more purposeful: the inter-
European rivalry was not as acute, although the presence of Japan was
militarily disturbing, even soon defeating for Russia; the trade relationships, on the other hand, were more obvious and persistent. However,
the general pattern of political activity was not sharply differentiated from
that of Africa. There was a veritable "scramble" along the China coast and
among the hitherto politically isolated islands of the Pacific.

Characterized by a sudden intensity comparable to that seen in Africa,
Far Eastern politics was an unusually complicated tangle of commercial
concerns, national fears, and naval strategy. If there is a historical distinction, it is to be found in the flag, which followed trade more noticeably in this region than anywhere else. American sugar interests in
Hawaii provide the most obvious example, but there are others. In sum,
earlier commercial activity acquired national dimensions and political
purposes in the last years of the century.

The convergence of Europe was still limited to the China coast, but
imperialist activity had become so competitive — with Germany, Russia,
the United States, and Japan joining France and England — that territorial division finally defied the principles of political arithmetic. Nevertheless, this was not how the situation looked in 1895. Then, British statesmen believed that the partition of China was about to begin.

China, although never treated metaphorically as a sick man, was in a
state of political illness nearly as acute as that of the Ottoman empire. Its
century-long political disorder was further intensified by its resounding
military defeat in the Sino-Japanese War of 1894–95. Forced to pay a

heavy indemnity, China turned to the West for loans and received, along with the money, demands for concessions and other privileges. Western apprehension was heightened by the Japanese factor, particularly disturbing because of the intended annexation of Liaotung Peninsula, an outcome of the peace terms. Momentarily joined together in a coalition of protest, France, Germany, and Russia warned Japan against annexation, a warning which the Japanese heeded.

This local Asiatic situation was aggravated by the extension of European-based issues. Germany, in the person of the kaiser, desired a more obvious and significant presence in the Far East. In mawkish rhetorical fashion he cast Europe in the part of crusader and gave visual shape to that proposed role in a well-known allegorical painting of Europe being led by the Archangel Michael. On a more realistic political level, Germany wished to hamper the newly formed Franco-Russian Alliance by directing Russian attention to the Far East, and at the same time it wanted to establish a suitable commercial and naval base there with Russian support.[52] As before, France was trying to assert its own national interests, now by way of a proposed railroad from Tonkin to Yunnan province.

Through 1895, Britain's trade position in China showed no overt signs of weakening, and its official policy was to continue the maintenance of free trade, the practice of the "open door." From 1895 until the end of 1898, British policy was defensive, marked by a series of diplomatic attempts to avert the establishment of spheres of influence which would be disadvantageous to Britain's commercial preponderance. "Spheres of influence we have never admitted," remarked Balfour in a nicely balanced phrase, "spheres of interest we have never denied."[53]

The "scramble for leases" and the "scramble for concessions" now began, a confused combination of competing European demands for port facilities and private commercial concessions — generally railroads, shipping and mining rights. These but thinly disguised a deeper European national concern: avoidance of exclusion from a China about to be politically disassembled. Thus a prelude to partition occurred, but the effective diplomatic response of the Manchu government and the complexity of imperialist rivalries inhibited ultimate territorial division.

The causes of intensifying European rivalry were several, but the im-

---

[52] Langer, *Diplomacy of Imperialism*, p. 448.
[53] Statement of April 29, 1898, Parliamentary Debate, quoted by L. K. Young, *British Policy in China, 1895–1902* (Oxford: Clarendon Press, 1970), p. 92.

mediate precipitant was the use of a new device: territorial leasing. Introduced by Germany, responding indignantly and advantageously to the
murder of several missionaries, the lease took form in the German acquisition of Kiaochow Bay in late 1897. It was followed by the Russian acquisition of Port Arthur and, in turn, by the French leasing of Hangchow Bay.
Concurrently, during the spring and summer of 1898, the "scramble for
concessions" took place.

Once again the railroad became the spearhead of territorial invasion,
proving that Rhodes was right when he stated that rails go farther than
bullets and cost less. From the European perspective, rail construction
was an important aspect of political penetration, a means of defining a
sphere of influence; from the Chinese perspective, the railroads might
strengthen national defenses, which had proved to be lamentably weak
during the recent war. The concessions granted by the Chinese, however, followed no finely wrought scheme of foreign claims; on the contrary, the concessions were mixed in national allocation in such a manner
that they caused a conflict of interests and ultimately helped to "frustrate
the whole process."[54]

The ongoing scramble threatened Britain's privileged position at Hong
Kong, the previously established system of treaty ports, and, of course,
the entire concept of the "open door." British diplomacy now actively
engaged the competing powers, both to check the scramble and to assure
that Great Britain profited from it. Britain leased territory on Shantung
Peninsula and pushed demands for concessions. But its willingness to
compromise and the subsequent willingness of the other powers to
negotiate led to the abatement of the scramble. Through a series of ac-
cords with Germany, France, and Russia, Great Britain managed to retain its preeminent position in the region along the Yangtze River. This is
a further indication that the practice of the sphere of influence now predominated in European relations with China.

By this method the external commercialization of China was quickly
advanced, and the "open door" was thereby unhinged. That well-known
commercial device received its fullest expression in a note circulated by
the American secretary of state John Hay on September 6, 1899, after the
scramble had ended. Hay requested the powers in China now holding
spheres of interests and leases not to "interfere with any treaty port or
vested interest. . . ." His statement not only was an assertion of Ameri-

[54] *Ibid.*, p. 79.

can commercial interests, but it also demonstrated how attenuated Chinese sovereignty had become in the face of European commercial and political intrusion.

The final Chinese response to the European scramble came not from the government but from an ill-defined, if clearly directed, group of malcontents called the Boxers. Both fundamentally patriotic and religious, the Boxers protested against the foreigner and against Christianity. The outbreak of the Boxer Rebellion (1900) was caused by a combination of deteriorating domestic conditions, such as unemployment and a retrenchment of the militia, and by irritation over the peremptory demands of the Europeans. The most recent and obvious of the latter was an Italian naval display in 1899 which was intended to produce a sphere of influence but which only aroused the anger of the coastal populations against the foreigner.[55]

Like the Taiping Rebellion before it, the Boxer Rebellion disturbed the Europeans as well as the domestic situation in China. Again, the European response was one of solidarity through a military front. All the interested powers cooperated, gaining results not dissimilar to those achieved in the past. The Boxer Rebellion was crushed, and the Chinese government was weighed down by still another indemnity, which was to be secured by further European control of Chinese maritime customs and duties. "The function of the Manchu Government was now little more than a debt-collecting agency for the Powers."[56] In this manner China entered the twentieth century, almost a subject nation.

The competitive China trade was in considerable measure the cause of further French activity in Indochina, as the search for the means of fluvial access to South China continued.[57] After exploration had proven that trade with China by way of the Mekong River was futile, French interest shifted to the Red River which, thanks to the location of Hanoi and its port of Haiphong, provided ready access to the imagined lucrative markets of South China, notably that of the province of Yunnan. Politically, Tonkin was the focus of attention, the territory through which much of the Red River flowed and in which the two cities just mentioned were situated. Actually, the French government arrived in that region indi-

[55] Victor Purcell, *The Boxer Uprising: A Background Study* (Cambridge: At the University Press, 1963), p. 179.

[56] Charles Tan, *The Boxer Catastrophe*, quoted in *ibid.*, p. 261.

[57] See Georges Taboulet, "Le voyage d'exploration du Mekong (1866–1868)," *Revue française d'histoire d'outre-mer*, 57:63 (1970).

rectly, as a result of political and commercial confusion. A French merchant, Jacques Dupuis, who would have qualified as an "old China hand," had been engaged in Chinese commerce since 1855 and was now making shipments between Yunnan and Hanoi via the Red River. His unauthorized traffic in salt provoked the Annamite government which held sovereignty over Tonkin; in turn, the French governor-general in Cochin China dispatched a mission of investigation headed by Francis Garnier. He attempted to open the Red River to his nation's trade but ended up — and not unwillingly — seizing the delta and occupying Hanoi in response to the recalcitrance of the Annamite government, though at the loss of his life. This particular action did not yield France territory only because its government was disinterested, yet it did establish by treaty in 1874 a vague protectorate over Tonkin and did open the ports of the Red River to French trade.

The ill-defined issue of "protection" was reconsidered by the French in the 1880s when the anticolonialism displayed by the government a decade before was replaced by the colonial interests of Jules Ferry's second ministry from 1883 to 1885. The situation in Tonkin had meanwhile deteriorated. The Annamite emperor had invoked an old Chinese claim to suzerainty in hopes of gaining that nation's support. The activities of the Black Flags, a militant offshoot of the Taipings, now joined by irregular Chinese forces, threatened to disrupt severely the French trade position, for which reason a mission under Lieutenant Henri Rivière was sent northward to intercede in the spring of 1883. Like Garnier before him, Rivière took Hanoi, and, again like Garnier, his life was taken shortly thereafter. To avenge these two deaths, to assure that the "protectorate" meant order, Ferry authorized a force of four thousand men from Cochin China to occupy Tonkin and to establish definitely the protectorate previously hinted at. However, the Chinese government reacted by supporting the Black Flags with regular troops so that the river war now took on broader dimensions. By autumn negotiations with both belligerent parties had led to two separate treaties which apparently guaranteed France control of Annam and peace without Chinese interference. The Chinese reluctance to withdraw their troops quickly, however, led to another confrontation at Lang-son in the following year.

This newest incident annoyed the heretofore acquiescent, even enthusiastic French parliamentarians who now balked at Ferry's demand for more funds to settle the military dispute. An incredible display of public opinion, reaching the heights of emotionalism and the depths of mob action, was directed against Ferry who was derisively called "le Tonkinois." His ministry fell, but he was able to pursue diplomatic negotiations to the point of establishing definite peace. Then, in June 1885, China signed a new treaty with France in which it gave up claims to suzerainty over Annam and assured compliance with the arrangements earlier made between France and Annam. This final agreement did not stifle domestic discontent; a general attitude of disfavor toward French involvement in Southeast Asia persisted for many years.[58] But by 1893, as a result of a treaty of protectorate over Laos and of the widening of the narrow "stick" center of Annam, France controlled a vast region which has been labeled on colonial maps as Indochina. Scorned in Ferry's day, it was to be described as the French equivalent of British India in the later annals of empire.

In comparison with the forays of French policy in Indochina and the intensity of European activity in China, the islands of the South Pacific were disturbed but gently, and only very late in the imperialist afternoon. Yet their claim on European attention went back to the late eighteenth century when voyages of discovery and commerce made of this watery portion of the globe a congeries of ports of call and small-scale trading centers, marked with the crosses of missionary stations.

In general the political and economic attitudes of the European states toward the South Pacific were one in the same, which is to say that all parties in the metropolises, save the evangelists, were indifferent to the area. There were, of course, exceptional occasions, primarily provided by the French. In 1842 there was an example of missionary imperialism in Tahiti which became France's exotic addition to empire. A year later the soil of New Caledonia was trod upon and, under Napoleon III, was converted into a protectorate and vast tropical penal colony — to which many of the Communards of 1871 were later dispatched.

British interest in the region was much more colonial than imperial, with settlers in Australia and New Zealand frequently asserting themselves to bring the "imperial factor" into play against the presence of the French and, later, the Germans. British interest, too, was generated by the antislavery movement which saw in the forced migration of laborers from the region another instance of the vile traffic in humans. An

[58] See Eric Schmieder, "La chambre de 1885–1889 et les affaires du Tonkin," *Revue française d'histoire d'outre-mer*, 53:153–244 (1966).

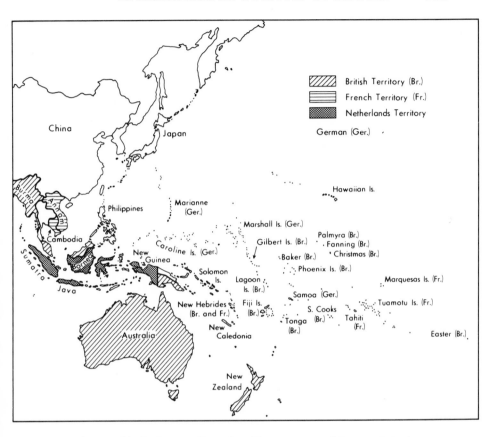

The scramble for Oceania. (Reproduced by permission of Hammond, Inc.)

erratic practice begun in the sandalwood trade, such deportation reached large proportions in the 1860s when workers were shipped to cotton and rice plantations in Peru. On the whole, however, British officials still found the Pacific Islands a "tiresome nuisance."[59]

By the last quarter of the century this political casualness began to give way to serious consideration. The advent of the steam age had brought the southern side of the Pacific closer to home, whether that be Liverpool or Hamburg; and the subsequent need for coaling stations raised the issue of possible naval bases in thought expressed in Washington as well as in the capitals of Europe. The great Hamburg shipping firm of J. C. Godef-

[59] W. P. Morrell, *Britain in the Pacific Islands* (Oxford: Clarendon Press, 1960), p. vii.

froy and Son had become interested in the coconut oil trade in Samoa in the 1860s, and even more interested when one of its agents happened to discover the copra — dried coconut — process. The American navy negotiated in 1872 for a base in Pago Pago Harbor, Samoa, while the French had even earlier seen the strategic value of New Caledonia. Intensifying trade, with its internecine political complications, and expanding naval power, with its need for coaling stations, brought new powers into the South Pacific. The ensuing "scramble for Oceania" was conditioned by the scramble for Africa; for example, Great Britain's involvement in Egypt allowed it less leverage for the settlement of problems arising in the Pacific, particularly when it had to deal with Germany, whose diplomatic weight was worrisome to the English because it might have been shifted to the French side in the Egyptian scale. Yet there was no well-concerted British policy for the Pacific area; rather there was a series of reluctant responses to various local conditions which were generally tempered, if not solved, by negotiation with the new arrivals.

However far extended in territorial range, the problems primarily clustered around the island groups that sweep out eastward from the northern waters of Australia. Of the lot, the Fiji Islands were the most easily regulated because their situation was the least complicated internationally. Previous relations between local governments and the resident British had generally been unsettled. Nevertheless, it was the threat of impending anarchy caused by militant competition among local rulers that first involved the home government, when the resident British consul inquired whether the government would consider annexation as a solution to the crisis. In response it commissioned two men in June 1873 to investigate the situation and suggest appropriate modes of action. They favored annexation, as did Sir Hercules Robinson, appointed some months later by the incoming Disraeli government to review the matter also. Sir Hercules, governor of New South Wales, was no disinterested observer; he moved ahead quickly to fulfill his commission of investigation and his desire for annexation; his work was concluded on September 30, 1874, when the Fijis, by deed of cession, came under the British crown.

Rapid in execution and not long premeditated, the annexation of these islands pleased the Australians and seriously disturbed none of the European nations treading water in the vicinity. The result was regionally unique at this moment when nationalistic rivalry affected all other acquisitions.

Competition leading to compromise summarizes other such occurrences in the New Hebrides, New Guinea, and the Samoa Islands. Each instance caused great anxiety among the Australians, who feared the geographical proximity of potentially unfriendly powers and the possibility of foreign involvement in local commerce. This general sentiment was particularly strong in the case of the New Hebrides, where worry about the possibility of these islands being converted into a forced residence for recidivist French convicts was intense. These compelling colonial concerns were seldom matched by the British imperial response which was necessarily multidirectional in the hectic 1880s when scrambling seemed to be occurring nearly everywhere.

In brief review, the many events in the Pacific produced the following historical pattern, here arranged according to increasing complexity, not chronological order. On the New Hebrides commercial rivalry was accelerated with the appearance of a New Caledonian–based French company bent upon buying up land and sponsored, interestingly enough, by an English-born resident who saw the New Hebrides as a valuable labor supply for French mining interests on New Caledonia. The success of the French company was internationally disturbing, particularly to Australians who were not prepared to enjoy the French as neighbors. Negotiations between England and France ensued and ended in 1887 with the establishment of a joint naval commission charged with the regulation of local problems involving each other's nationals. In effect, and in fact after 1906, they were founding a political condominium over the islands.

Northwestward, on the large island of New Guinea, the rivalry was of a different national order and of different proportions. While the western half of the island had languished politically in the hands of the Dutch since the early eighteenth century, British interest in the south coast of the still "unclaimed" eastern part was keenly motivated by trade and advantageous navigational routes. In 1883 preliminary commercial probes by Germany were more definitely defined in the formation of a government-sponsored New Guinea Company. Again, Australian fears were accordingly magnified, and the British government aroused. Negotiations between Britain and Germany led to the formation of spheres of influence; in April 1886 a line of demarcation was finally drawn, running from New Guinea, through the Solomon Islands, the northwestern tip of the Gilbert Islands, and on to the Marshall Islands. Germany retained the northern sphere, Great Britain the southern.

Perhaps the most serious complications arose in Samoa where Godef-froy's copra interests were principally situated and where the German colonial party focused its attention at the end of the 1870s.[60] Great Britain and the United States were also involved politically and economically, thereby triangulating the local imperialism. Questions of sovereignty, of acquisition of harbor rights, and of commercial concessions were compounded by the financial collapse of the House of Godeffroy in 1879 and by the even more apparent involvement of the German government, impelled by Bismarck's newly accepted imperialist policy.

The outcome was unintentionally arranged with chronological symmetry but suffered from political imbalance: three decisions were effected at ten-year intervals. First, in 1879 Britain, Germany, and the United States came to a joint agreement over mutual consular control of municipal politics in Apia, the center of concentration of their nationals on the islands. Second, in 1889 a conference was held at Berlin which led to further control, both through support of a mutually agreed upon king and through the appointment of a European judicial official who would serve in several advisory and administrative capacities in the Samoan government. Third, in 1899 the arrangement of 1889 gave way to outright annexation. Although the final adjustment favored Germany, the Samoa Islands were divided between Germany and the United States. Great Britain was accommodating — for 1899 was hardly a propitious year, what with war unleashed in South Africa — and received compensation for its interests through territorial adjustments in the Tonga and Solomon islands and on the west coast of Africa.

While these were the major political decisions reached as imperialism swept across the waters of the Pacific, others involving Japan, the United States, Germany, Great Britain, France, and, obviously, Spain also were accomplished. The sum of these parts is a whole history of oceanic imperialism in which, for the first time, the expanding nations of several continents met in what can properly be called a *Weltpolitik*.

The twentieth century opened in the Pacific with a new disposition of political and naval power. Both the Spanish-American War and the Russo-Japanese War demonstrated the limits of European imperial

[60] *Ibid.*, p. 225.

capabilities and clearly proved that the age of European hegemony was nearing its close. Granted the world still remained Eurocentric until 1918, European power had already crested — and astute European statesmen at the time were already aware of this painful fact.

Imperialism and the Outbreak of World War I

A subject of anxiety in the first years of the twentieth century, as it had often been a subject of indifference in the middle years of the nineteenth, imperialism was the political agency by which the global age was forced into crude existence. The sequence of international events crowded into the years between the scramble and the outbreak of war in 1914 tempt the conclusion that imperialism was a major cause of the war.

Certainly the awesome title historically affixed to that war, "The World War," suggests that the lines of engagement paralleled, if they were not coextensive with, the lines of imperialistic rivalry. Moreover, the considerable literature that appeared after the war answered the question of responsibility affirmatively. Indeed, in 1914, only three months before the war broke out, the English Fabian Henry N. Brailsford published *The War of Steel and Gold*, in which he established an argument that was later to be repeated frequently. "The potent pressure of economic expansion is the motive force in an international struggle," he asserted, but "the startingpoint in such a rivalry is soon forgotten." Discussion and demands are cast in terms of national exclusion, of encirclement, and then rivalry "becomes a general engagement, and all the channels of human folly pour into it their reserves." However, the balance of power is always motivated by economic interests. Lenin, who followed Brailsford by but a year, already had the war to observe. It was, he insisted, "a war for the division of the world, for the partition and repartition of colonies, 'spheres of influence,' of finance capital, etc."[61]

Less theoretical and economically causal than these interpretations were the historical monographs that reviewed the causes of the war and placed great emphasis on imperialistic political activity. The crises in Morocco, British naval anxiety, the belief of many Germans that Ger-

---

[61] Henry N. Brailsford, *The War of Steel and Gold: A Study of the Armed Peace* (London: G. Bell, 1914), pp. 42 and 46; V. I. Lenin, *Imperialism, the Highest Stage of Capitalism* (New York: International Publishers, 1939; first published, 1917), p. 9.

many need forcefully break out of continental bondage, the constant diplomatic friction over the decaying Ottoman empire — determinants such
as these were paraded in solemn array after the war.[62]

Yet a stronger argument can be made that imperialism was more a
reflection than a severe conditioner of the European state of mind and the
politics it engendered. Anxieties raised in Europe made their way around
the world. Moreover, because of their geographical origins, these anxieties were most often resolved peacefully when manifested overseas.
Fashoda is the classic example, but Morocco, the islands of the Pacific,
and the situation in late nineteenth-century China can also be regarded in
similar manner. Of greater interest is the fact that the two major overseas
rivals throughout the nineteenth century had attained a workable understanding just before the war: France and England arrived at the Entente
Cordiale in 1904.

The alignment on the Continent was preceded and prepared by the
settlement of problems abroad. Fashoda was the pivotal event but less
dramatic encounters and solutions had come before it. In 1890 both nations effected a belated regulation of the West African scramble by describing an arbitrary line of division running from Lake Chad to the Niger
River. While not so clean in realization as in design, the arrangement was
an attempt to avert direct confrontation and possible conflict. In a similar
way an accord was reached over Siam in 1896 whereby the new French
possession of Laos — also the former satellite territory of Siam — was
recognized by the British with the French accepting the political buffer
that Britain had made of Siam.

Fashoda therefore may be considered both the climax of Anglo-French
rivalry and a near deviation from a pattern of negotiated compromise
established at the beginning of the decade in which that encounter occurred. Not overseas involvement, but continental isolation was the
primary cause for these arrangements. Both France and England had
little desire to stand alone before a troublesome Germany. As the British
press had commented at the time of the Anglo-French accord over Siam,
cordiality with France was desired above all else on the Continent.[63]

But British diplomacy did not stop there. After the Entente Cordiale
England moved to stay its competition with Russia in the Near East with

[62] See, for instance, Sidney B. Fay, *The Origins of the World War*, 2 vols. (New York:
Macmillan, 1928).
[63] See Langer, *Diplomacy of Imperialism*, p. 251.

a 1907 entente covering Persia, Afghanistan, and Tibet, an agreement cast in the newest mold, that of spheres of influence. Tibet was marked out as a neutral buffer; Afghanistan was simply described as "outside the sphere of Russian influence"; and Persia, like China, was divided by the two nations into commercial spheres.[64]

Great Britain extended its negotiations to Germany as well. The arrangements in East Africa and China have already been noted, and to them was added an agreement over relations in the Near East, where the Berlin-to-Baghdad Railroad was viewed as a thrust of steel in India's direction. More mysterious and most ineffective was a secret Anglo-German treaty in 1898 which stipulated the possible division of Portuguese Africa should the finances of the Portuguese state collapse. Nothing resulted immediately, other than a new treaty between Britain and Portugal refurbishing the ancient treaty of 1661 and, consequently, irritating the Germans who had diplomatic intimation of it. Again in 1912–13, negotiations between Great Britain and Germany were undertaken, and the secret treaty of 1898 reworked. Yet the new treaty remained unsigned by the German chancellor Bethmann-Hollweg until the very day that the German ultimatum to Belgium was prepared. Ironically and unbeknown to most of the imperialist world, negotiations over colonial settlement persisted nearly to the outbreak of World War I.[65]

While overseas negotiations thus continued to function, continental diplomacy collapsed in the summer heat of 1914. The ensuing war was caused as much by recklessness as by calculation, by highly localized problems as much as by grand continental schemes. It was all a sad commentary on contemporary diplomacy and the individuals who manipulated it.

Perhaps imperialist affairs were not handled with any more adroitness; the point is they were less significant in the context of European politics. In no obvious way was imperialism a cause of the war. Yet it did, of course, condition the nature of that war. From the western front to the deserts of Arabia, across the lakes of East Africa, and among the islands of the Pacific, the war extended — not in the opposite direction. The process seemed to be directed by some law of political centrifuge, as had been so much of the expansion that had occurred before it.

[64] For a brief resume, see Moon, *Imperialism*, pp. 278–281.
[65] See *ibid.*, pp. 118–120, and Jacques Willequet, "Anglo-German Rivalry in Belgian and Portuguese Africa," in *Britain and Germany in Africa*, pp. 265–270.

PART II

Imperialism: Mission and Need

I see no evils in the world — except, of course, natural evils — that cannot be remedied by freedom, self-government, and English institutions.

Broadbent in George Bernard Shaw,
John Bull's Other Island

Imperialist thought, while not exceptionally rich, was bountiful, pouring from many minds of different intellectual turns. Although constantly re-iterated, its major themes were limited. They were later well joined in Lord Lugard's phrase, the "dual mandate." "Europe is in Africa for the mutual benefit of her own industrial classes, and of the native races in their progress to a higher plane," he wrote. "The benefit can be made reciprocal, and . . . [it] is the aim and desire of civilised administration to fulfil this dual mandate."[1] It was the presumed economic benefits and the assumed cultural duties that the imperialists verbally dwelt upon — as did their critics. The political justifications of empire, however, were never so extended over pages of argument; they were generally considered to be self-evident.

Historically, there is nothing unusual in this combination of economic advantage and cultural obligation, simply because it befitted the age. As a result of industrialization, Europeans were materialistically conscious as none of their ancestors had been; the methodical inventiveness upon which the industrial process was later predicated led to a belief in Euro-pean cultural superiority and, therefore, to a self-assumed responsibility for the betterment of the "lesser breeds."

Mark Twain once commented that the "van leader of civilization" is "always whiskey," which is then followed by the missionary, the emi-

---

[1] Lord Frederick D. Lugard, *The Dual Mandate in British Tropical Africa* (3rd ed.; London: William Blackwood, 1926; first published, 1922), p. 617.

grant, and a band of self-seekers.[2] Advocates of empire would not have disagreed with the idea that both the material and the spiritual were packaged for export, but they would no doubt have desired to alter Twain's order of arrivals. Furthermore, their evaluation of this expansion was not cast in Twain's cynicism. Imperialists generally concurred that their expanding civilization was dynamic and good because it was rational: logical in its thinking, technological in its production.

Yet the arguments that supported as well as denounced imperialism were not always arranged and presented in that would-be orderly western way. Emotion and invective gave a particular bite to the debate over imperialism. Again, this is easily appreciated. Proponents were forced to exaggerate in order to stimulate public political interest; they were also driven to poetic license by their own larger aspirations. Opponents heard a hypocritical and dreadfully bombastic tone emanating from the grand phrases. The notion of a dual mandate might be exemplary; it might also be crassly exploitive. Both conclusions were drawn.

[2] Mark Twain quoted by Paul Sharp, "Three Frontiers: Some Comparative Studies of Canadian, American and Australian Settlement," *Pacific Historical Review*, 24:372–373 (1955).

CHAPTER 4

Economic Ideas and Interests

Behind empire, it has been asserted, is seen the glimmer of gold. Whatever the justifications adduced to persuade a God-fearing or flag-waving public to support governmental action abroad, the men of the City of London — and their equivalent on the Continent — have been accused of moving all, and all for their own measurable purposes. "Imperialism," wrote its most significant critic, J. A. Hobson, "implies the use of the machinery of government by private interests, mainly capitalists, to secure for them economic gains outside their country."[1]

Since so stated, that argument has been particularly compelling in analyses of nineteenth-century expansion. Europe in this age was "rationalizing," ordering its industrial and financial institutions and arranging its economic ways in a manner of refinement matched only by the military. Foreign trade and foreign capital investment increased incredibly, appearing in one form or another in the souks of Tunis, the railroads spanning Utah, and the ledgers of the Imperial Bank of Persia. The surge in such exportation roughly corresponded to the increase in territory acquired abroad, particularly toward the end of the century. With little effort the correspondence can be converted into a condition of causality, and so it frequently has.[2] But the economics of empire defy such simplistic interpretation.

[1] J. A. Hobson, *Imperialism: A Study* (London: Allen & Unwin, 1954; first published, 1902), p. 94.

[2] "The two essential characteristics of this period, 1878–1914, are the industrial surge and colonial expansion, the first determining the second." Maurice Baumont, *L'essor industriel et l'impérialisme colonial, 1878–1914* (3rd ed.; Paris: Presses Universitaires de France, 1965), p. 2.

Like the threads of gold that bound European finances in the nineteenth century, the lines of economic dependency and exploitation between colonial region and colonizing country were a complex maze, still unsorted by historians. The theorists at home often intended one thing while colonial policy realized another; the merchant on the spot frequently was concerned with matters which were of no importance to the entrepreneur at home; and the industrialist, cautiously regarding world markets, quite regularly saw colonies as only so many acres of sand. It is true, and ultimately more important, that regional trade patterns in which the colonial factor may have originally been the most dominant — for example, in India, Southeast Asia, and China — were giving way by the end of the century to more complicated global patterns of trade in which the colonial factor as such was not so discernible.[3]

The relationship of the expansion of European trade and investment to territorial expansion is not a direct ratio; it is so fractionalized that general correlations are difficult to find. Indeed, with the notable exception of India, which was considered a major source of British economic strength, none of the colonial regions acquired in the nineteenth century rivaled the English trade or investment in the white-settled dominions and the United States. French trade, based primarily on luxury goods, found few fitting markets in the portion of tropical Africa under French control; instead it moved westward to England, just as French capital was to move further in that direction to new American railroads — and later beyond the frontier of Russia. In short, nineteenth-century trade did not necessarily follow the flag, and the flag often flew over marketplaces not soon frequented by local distributors of European goods or extended by the presence of European capital.

Yet the prescribed causal relationship of late nineteenth-century territorial expansion with foreign trade and investment is, despite innumerable qualifications and refutations, still the most popularly appealing. In fact, the word *imperialism* has acquired the clear connotation of economic exploitation. As a term it entered the vocabulary of social scientists only at the turn of the twentieth century, and chiefly by the pen of Hobson who sought the "economic taproot" of it all.[4] Hobson's essay was preceded by the thought and writing of many others who, for different

[3] S. B. Saul, *Studies in British Overseas Trade, 1870–1914* (Liverpool: Liverpool University Press, 1960), pp. 44 and 60.

[4] Richard Koebner, "The Concept of Economic Imperialism," *Economic History Review*, 2:1–29 (1949).

reasons and under different circumstances, also saw in colonization economic benefit.

Theories of Economic Imperialism

Before the latter part of the nineteenth century, the major body of economic opinion on colonies was, not surprisingly, English. As the "old colonial system" fell into decay and disrepute in the first years of the century, a reevaluation of the purposes and profits of empire ensued. Such men as Smith, Ricardo, Bentham, and James Mill shortly before or during this time offered treatises in which they maintained that colonial monopoly was gravely disadvantageous, that colonies were financially draining as well as worthless, but that an unregulated flow of investments and goods worked wondrously in accordance with the laws of nature and of common sense.[5] These thoughts and arguments, endorsed later in ponderous pronouncements by statesmen before the houses of Parliament, were neatly bundled together into a grand historical assumption that a "Little England" era of anti-imperialism existed, an era which roughly spanned from the publication of Smith's Wealth of Nations in 1776 to the abolition of the Navigation Acts and the Corn Laws in the 1840s.[6]

Reconsideration of both the thought and the activities of this period has led to a total historical reassessment and also to the realization that a historical myth had been fabricated over the years.[7] No scholar would disagree with the assertion that outspoken comments against colonies and empire abounded at this time, but beside them, and often housed in the same mind, dwelt a number of arguments for the retention, if not the expansion of colonies. Jeremy Bentham, for instance, wrote a provocative pamphlet entitled Liberate Your Colonies, which he intended to dispatch to the French revolutionaries in 1793; yet he reached quite different conclusions in the first years of the nineteenth century, when he wrote, "Taking futurity into the scale, the well-being of mankind appears to have been promoted upon the whole by the establishment of colonies."[8] Such a shift was the result not of Bentham's intellectual rambling but rather of

[5] On this subject, see Donald Winch, Classical Political Economy and Colonies (Cambridge, Mass.: Harvard University Press, 1965).

[6] See the significant article by Robert Schuyler, "The Climax of Anti-Imperialism in England," Political Science Quarterly, 36:537–560 (1921).

[7] John S. Galbraith, "Myths of the 'Little England' Era," American Historical Review, 67:34–48 (1961).

[8] Economic Writings, III, 91, quoted in Winch, Classical Political Economy, p. 32.

new considerations and the persuasiveness of other opinions.[9] In this respect he was not alone. Indeed, one critic, speaking broadly of the colonial thought of Bentham's era, has insisted that out of the opposition to the old mercantile system of colonization emerged a new doctrine of imperialism which complemented the "imperialism of free trade."[10]

What is thus being suggested is the compatibility, if not the logic, of free-trade doctrine and practice and the retention of colonial empire. The argument depends on the assumption that an expansionist Britain looked throughout the century for areas toward which to export. Where economic domination (informal empire) was possible, political control (formal empire) was avoided. But, in accordance with the events of the period, the theory suggests that both approaches worked simultaneously at the end of, and, indeed, throughout much of the century. The constant interplay of the two, with both derived from the same economic source, accounts for the otherwise inconsistent colonial behavior of Great Britain in the 1800s. The theory, as originally expounded, therefore sounds like an elaborate exegesis of Lord Shelburne's famous comment, made at the time of peace negotiations with the American colonies, that England preferred trade without domination where possible but accepted trade with domination when necessary.[11]

Recent reviews of the thought of the "Little England" era indicate that there did exist an incipient ideology supportive of imperialism. That ideology was grounded in a reinterpretation of classical economic thought — the liberal laissez-faire approach to economics — and particularly revolved around the problems considered in the famous law of Jean-Baptiste Say, a pure free trader and anticolonialist.

Say's law was one of economic equilibrium in which all value produced was value destined to be consumed; in other words, supply created and hence regulated demand. As redefined by James Mill, who strongly endorsed it, the theory reads: "Every arm could be employed and every article of the annual produce could be sold, if the country were surrounded by Friar Bacon's Wall of Brass, a thousand feet high."[12] Conditions in early nineteenth-century England were not hidden behind such a

[9]*Ibid.*, pp. 25–26.
[10] Bernard Semmel, *The Imperialism of Free Trade: Classical Political Economy, the Empire of Free Trade and Imperialism, 1750–1850* (Cambridge: At the University Press, 1970).
[11] The seminal piece on free-trade imperialism, from which the argument above derives, is Ronald Robinson and John Gallagher, "The Imperialism of Free Trade," *Economic History Review*, 6:1–15 (1953).
[12]*Commerce Defended*, pp. 106–107, quoted in Winch, *Classical Political Economy*, p. 86.

wall, what with the post-Napoleonic economic depression causing considerable concern. This domestic situation, aggravated by unemployment and a fall in the rate of profits, gave rise to a new set of arguments for colonization.

Throughout the history of modern European imperialism, there existed the perplexing demographic question which Marx would translate into the provocative phrase, "the surplus army of the unemployed." The Malthusian mood, which made of economics the "dismal science," hung over the thinking of many English economists and caused them to ask how, other than through the ineffective system of the poor laws, the condition of the working classes might be alleviated. Several influential thinkers — among them Edward Gibbon Wakefield, Robert Torrens, and a then maligned but recently rehabilitated R. J. Wilmot-Horton — expressed their views on this matter by advocating what has been called "systematic colonization."

All agreed that through colonization the glut of laborers would be reduced, even removed. Beyond this there were disagreements and qualifications. Wilmot-Horton, who bears the honor of having been the first to enunciate such a plan fully and uphold it vigorously, proposed that the state aid pauper families by directing them to the lands then opening up in Canada. This action would be financed by mortgaging the parish poor rates. Wakefield's scheme geographically was centered on southern Australia and differed in two respects from Wilmot-Horton's. First, the migrants themselves would indirectly pay for their passage (as is explained below). Secondly, the migration would be of the young rather than of paupers so that both a laboring and a child-begetting portion of the population would be removed from domestic concern.[13]

Because Wakefield's proposal gained the support of a number of influential people, including Mill and Bentham; because he was able to discredit Wilmot-Horton; because his plan was tried in modified form in southern Australia; and, finally, because his general interpretations of colonization have been considered to have had an indirect effect on the thinking of Hobson and Lenin, the "systematic colonization scheme" merits some consideration.

Wakefield's thought concentrated primarily on the basic land-capital problem he defined as the "field of production" or the "field of employ-

[13] See R. N. Ghosh, "The Colonization Controversy: R. J. Wilmot-Horton and the Classical Economists," *Economica*, 31:385–400 (1964); and Winch, *Classical Political Economy*, chapters 5 and 7 on Wakefield.

ment." While the concept originally had spatial connotations, it was not always so restricted. "It is not the land that we want," he insisted, "but the use of it." This could be obtained by exchange. "Every fresh importation of food by means of exporting more manufactured goods, is an enlargement of the field of production; it is like an acreable increase of our land."[14] But because other nations might turn to industrial production themselves or might place tariffs on products imported from Great Britain, the field of production outward toward independent states could be severely circumscribed. No such restriction could be imagined with respect to the colonies.

Wakefield's assessment thus centered on the colonial issue, which he had first seriously considered while in jail on a charge of abduction; out of forced consideration appeared his most famous work, *Letter from Sydney*. He contended that not the quantity of land but the nature of the distribution of the population over it was the important aspect of colonialism. He remarked that new colonists acquire land for themselves, thus dispersing from previously established centers and taking with them their labor which, on the new land, would be used for self-sustenance, not for the creation of new wealth. He therefore proposed what Bentham ponderously denominated the "Vicinity-Maximizing-or-Dispersion-Preventing Principle." Forced population concentration, achieved by a sufficiently high price placed on "free land," would require the new emigrant to work for three years in an already established center. In this way the existing lack of division of labor, necessary for profitable productivity, would be satisfactorily filled.

Wakefield's general conclusion was one which suggested both domestic and colonial benefit from such an arrangement. "Thus, employment for capital and labor would be increased in two places and two ways at the same time; abroad, in the colonies, by the removal of capital and peoples to fresh fields of production; at home, by the extension of markets, or the importation of food and raw materials."[15]

What Wakefield was demonstrating is what Torrens, in agreement with him, saw as a meaningful solution to the redundancy of both labor and capital. In the world economy of which Great Britain was a part, Torrens imagined a situation in which the capital employed in home industries increased disproportionately to that employed in the countries from

[14] Edward Gibbon Wakefield, *A View of the Art of Colonization in Letters between a Statesman and a Colonist* (Oxford: Clarendon Press, 1914; first published, 1849), p. 89.
[15] *Ibid.*, p. 92.

which raw materials were derived, thus causing a surfeit of capital in England for which domestic employment could not be found. The colonies would remove this condition, opening to "British capital and labor, an expanding field of beneficial employment." Later Torrens went further, abandoned the principles of free trade, embraced those of commercial reciprocity, and spoke, well before Joseph Chamberlain, of a colonial zollverein.[16]

The debate, briefly discussed here but including many more personalities, was germinal of subsequent imperialist theory. Much of the thought of Wakefield and Torrens anticipated Marx and Lenin's ideas on the need for exportation of capital.[17] The emigration problem and, coupled with it, the concept of a "field of employment" would later be recalled, as the century ended, in theories of diminishing "waste lands" and the need for *Lebensraum*. The notion of opening new worlds, such as southern Australia, to the productive use of Europeans is not far removed from propositions, such as Lord Lugard's, about the European mandate to make the resources of the world available to all — or, as others insisted, to employ the lands inadequately exploited by indigenous populations. In brief, the economic arguments that dominate the debate over imperialism during the nineteenth century were articulated early and in an England at the time supposedly anti-imperialist.

All this suggests a further factor of considerable importance. Much of the economic argument, both for and against imperialism, was based on incipient, not advanced industrialism. It was predicated upon an "underconsumptionist" interpretation of the results of the productive process and, later, upon a sanguine view of the previous success of free trade. The theories of redundancy and of economic stagnation which Wakefield and Torrens so well expressed were to recur over and over again. Thus the opinions voiced after 1880 about the need for colonial "outlets" had the resonance of words uttered a good half-century before.

During the 1870s Britain's well-aired economic concern with colonies and empire crossed the Channel to France. However, British interest at this particular time was turning toward the issue of imperial political consolidation, and that issue slowly evolved into the Imperial Federation movement of the next decade. French concern was, as it were, a step

---

[16]*Colonization of South Australia*, pp. 269–270, quoted in Lionel Robbins, *Robert Torrens and the Evolution of Classical Economics* (London: Macmillan, 1958), p. 181. On the zollverein idea, see *ibid.*, p. 187.

[17] Semmel, *Imperialism*, p. 214.

behind the British; there was not yet sufficient effort directed toward empire, let alone its consolidation. Indeed, the economic arguments expounded in France after 1870 were often belated statements of earlier English thought.

Although the matter of colonization — that is, emigration — was not ignored, French imperatives were in no sense demographic; rather, protectionism, an essential part of French economic history, was now cast in imperial terms as the need for markets.

If there was a systematic expositor of economic colonialism it was the economist and publicist Paul Leroy-Beaulieu, who at an early age wrote a work which may well be considered the seminal French imperialist study. *De la colonisation chez les peuples modernes* first appeared in 1874 but only gained a wide reading audience and hence influence with the second edition in 1882. The book offered a long review of previous European colonization and a briefer evaluation of the advantages of colonization for the modern state and economy. In his analysis, Leroy-Beaulieu both borrowed from and disagreed with Wakefield, Torrens, and others. He saw no domestic benefits to be derived from emigration, but he did concur with the English theorists' general assumptions about the value of colonies as places for investment and markets. Almost as if in direct French translation, he stated that overproduction of goods could lead to overcapitalization and consequent reduction in profits. To avert this unfortunate trend, the investment of capital in new regions should be encouraged, as indeed it had been in England where the multiple benefits were apparent. Colonies thus not only absorbed but also generated greater national wealth, a cause for congratulation.[18]

The same conclusion, he argued, ought to be drawn about the market value of colonies. Again, like Torrens, he emphasized the advantages colonies had over general foreign trade. Neither tariff walls nor war could disrupt or destroy colonial trade, and, more positively, the tastes and habits of the colony would be both more stable and more consistent with those of the founding country. The sum was that "trade between the metropolitan country and the colonies approaches the regularity and permanence enjoyed by domestic trade."[19]

Yet Leroy-Beaulieu was fully aware that the colony of settlement (*col-*

[18] The best analysis of Leroy-Beaulieu is that of Agnes Murphy, *The Ideology of French Imperialism, 1871–1881* (Washington, D.C.: Catholic University Press, 1948), chapter 3.

[19] Paul Leroy-Beaulieu, *De la colonisation chez les peuples modernes* (3rd ed.; Paris: Guillaumin, 1886; first published, 1872), pp. 564–565.

onie de peuplement) was the one least available to modern France. Either trade colonies (*colonies d'exploitation*) or colonies with a French cadre and a potential indigenous market (*colonies mixtes*), such as Algeria, were the most likely. It was to Africa and to Asia that he invited the French to direct their attention so that the markets he envisioned would be created. Of course the ultimate purpose of colonies was Eurocentric: they were to expand metropolitan commerce, stimulate metropolitan industry, and "furnish to the inhabitants of the mother country, to its industrialists, workers and consumers, an increase in profits, wages or benefits."[20]

By the time the second edition of Leroy-Beaulieu's work was published in 1882, a large number of economically oriented statements on empire were appearing in pamphlets, books, parliamentary debates, many of which gravitated around the newly enunciated economic imperialist arguments of Jules Ferry. Ferry, like Leroy-Beaulieu, saw colonial enterprise as based on the exportation of capital and goods. Also like Leroy-Beaulieu, he affixed as a motto to his thought John Stuart Mill's assertion that "colonization in the present state of the world, is the best affair of business in which the capital of an old and wealthy country can engage."[21] The present state of the world, as Ferry interpreted it, was one of grave industrial competition, of the drying up of outlets. He ardently endorsed the protectionist position, because he imagined the United States and Germany to be threatening commercial rivals, and consequently he feared for the welfare of France since it had not yet secured sufficient markets through colonial enterprise. It has been maintained that most of Ferry's assertions were ex post facto, justifications for action already taken but not eagerly accepted by the electorate at home.[22] In truth many of his statements were made after territorial acquisition, as for instance his most elaborate defense in the preface to *Tonkin et la mère-patrie*, which appeared in 1890, several years after his fall from office over the Tonkin incident.

A more serious criticism of Ferry, and one detected by a contemporary who supported his colonial policy, was his failure to appreciate that the markets he desired in the colonies could not be obtained immediately. The France of Ferry suffered not from excessive production and certainly

---

[20] *Ibid.*, p. 542.

[21] From Mill's *Principles of Political Economy*. Leroy-Beaulieu made these words "the theme of his whole book." Murphy, *Ideology*, p. 120. See Ferry's statement in his *Discours et opinions de Jules Ferry* (Paris: A. Colin, 1895–1898), IV, 525.

[22] Thomas F. Power, *Jules Ferry and the Renaissance of French Imperialism* (New York: King's Crown Press, 1944), pp. 196–197.

not from a surfeit of cheap commodities which could be absorbed in non-European markets. The comparable "tastes" of which Leroy-Beaulieu had spoken were not to be found anywhere in the colonial empire, except, perhaps, among the then small settler population in Algeria. Recognizing, indeed emphasizing, this difficulty, the most indefatigable of French imperialist advocates, Joseph Chailley-Bert, insisted that the colonies had not arrived at the age of commerce; they were in the "age of agriculture."[23]

To the question of whether Ferry was correct in stating that the colonies would be new outlets, Chailley-Bert responded that he was right in principle, but wrong in timing. The indigenous populations were not French consumers because they were unable to pay for French products, not because they were unwilling to have them. Commerce would have to wait until agriculture was sufficiently developed. Offering a sketchy stage theory of development, similar to that of Adam Smith, Chailley-Bert argued that the duration of economic periods might be reduced, but the order of advancement — from agriculture, to commerce, and then to industry — could not be disturbed. The process of development which he hinted at would later be called the *mise en valeur* of the colonies, the development that would allow them to assume a complementary economic relationship to metropolitan France.

The main lines of French economic thought were established and popularized by the three men just discussed. Frequently repeated and seldom deviated from, this thought formed the basis for a protectionist theory of imperialism which critics have described as neo-mercantilist. In so thinking and proposing, the French were not alone. However, France did avoid the severe problems that seemingly threatened the more advanced and commercially extended industrial states.

For such states the imperialist issue reached beyond the marketplace to the commonweal itself. This broad issue was primarily aired in the industrially polluted atmosphere of Germany and Great Britain. Whatever the differences in expression, critics in both countries were aroused by the growing "social question," one for which imperialism seemed to have a ready and tempting answer. The still precarious condition of the factory worker and the political implications of that condition were worsened by

[23] On Chailley-Bert, see principally his *Où en est la politique coloniale de la France: L'âge de l'agriculture* (Paris: A. Colin, 1896).

the economic instability of Germany and Britain in the last decades of the century. Unemployment and pending social discontent could be channeled outward, to the still growing world of empire. Cecil Rhodes, in a frequently cited statement, provided the gist: "The Empire, as I have always said, is a bread and butter question. If you want to avoid civil war, you must become imperialists."[24] His contention was as appreciated by supporters of empire in Germany as it was by their counterparts in England.

The initial military success of the new German nation, by which it had in fact been united, led to no comparably joined social community. As has already been mentioned, growing difficulties in the parliamentary politics and the industrial economics of the 1880s were disturbing to Bismarck and the state he served. From this historical perspective, German imperialism can be seen as having been provoked and formed by internal conditions, not by the general international situation.[25] And just such a perspective was appreciated not only by Bismarck but also by the majority of German theorists of modern imperialism.

The basis for German economic imperialist theory can be traced back to the publication of Friedrich Fabri's popular essay *Bedarf Deutschland der Kolonien?* in 1879, which was a warning that without colonies Germany's problems of population and market would explode into major social issues. However, the essential core of such thought was not established until later. It was out of the academic debate of the *Kathedersozialisten*, "socialists of the chair," as these scholar-advocates were derisively labeled, that a significant imperialist ideology emerged.[26]

Generating what was a form of social imperialism, they fused concerns about general social welfare with those of overseas expansion and recognized the resolution of Germany's major national problems to lie in that fusion. The *Kathedersozialisten* exercised enormous influence, as they held every major university chair of economics and were listened to with favor in the corridors of governmental power.[27]

Their chief spokesman was Gustave Schmoller, a professor at Tübingen

[24] Quoted by V. I. Lenin, *Imperialism, the Highest Stage of Capitalism* (New York: International Publishers, 1939; first published, 1917), p. 79.

[25] Hans-Ulrich Wehler, "Bismarck's Imperialism, 1862–1890," *Past and Present*, 48:124 (1970).

[26] Abraham Ascher, "Professors as Propagandists: The Politics of the Kathedersozialisten," *Journal of Central European Affairs*, 23:286 (1963).

[27] *Ibid.*, pp. 283 and 300–301.

and then at Halle and Berlin. Best known for his general study of mercantilism, Schmoller was both an active editor and writer who seized upon the theme of imperialism in 1899.

Like the majority of German economists from the days of Friedrich List on, Schmoller denied the wisdom of English laissez-faire economics. He perceived such a policy as socially pernicious, in no way relieving the real problems derived from competitive capitalist industrialism, particularly the development of class fissures. A form of national economy, of protectionism under the guidance of the bureaucratic administration of the state, would mitigate the social tension and prevent the further decline of a large segment of the population into the lower-class strata. Schmoller was no egalitarian and no democrat; his state was to assume a benevolent authoritarianism over the population, resolving national differences rather than accommodating to them. The immediate problem he saw begging for solution in the 1890s was that of overpopulation. In a mode of thought not dissimilar to that of Wakefield, Torrens, and even Leroy-Beaulieu, he contended that the possession of colonies would avert the loss to the nation of capital and of people caused by overseas emigration. Without colonies, he further argued, the outcome would be "a lowering of wages . . . a proletarianization of the masses."[28]

Schmoller's thinking, like that of the *Kathedersozialisten* in general, had Marxist undertones, though not Marxist purposes. Concern with the social problems of overcapitalization and overproduction reached the point of fear of possible class struggle and of the ultimate destruction of the national fabric. By releasing internal tension through the external channels of colonies, Germany would both be assured of domestic peace and acquire national grandeur. This form of social imperialism was to be situated in much of European thought from the 1890s until the demise of Hitler's Third Reich.[29]

The discussions over imperialism that intensified in Great Britain and in Germany at the turn of the twentieth century were similar in that they both linked economic interests with social welfare. But Britain's had its own peculiarity formed by the national tradition of free trade. As a result of the ill effects of serious foreign commercial competition and the new colonial demands for preferential tariff treatment, the principle to which liberals had long been happily wedded and which even the working

[28] Quoted in *ibid.*, p. 291.
[29] Wehler, "Bismarck's Imperialism," pp. 154–155.

classes did not see as obsolete was questioned, though not quickly discarded. "The establishment of Free Imports," stated a Fabian Society tract written by George Bernard Shaw with his ironic wit, "seemed as stable and final as the disestablishment of the Irish Church, of Purchase in the Army, of dueling, and of property qualification for the franchise."[30] Free trade, however anachronistic it appeared to some, continued as state policy until after World War I, even though it was now seriously debated.

With the spread of protective tariff measures across the Continent in the 1870s and 1880s, a policy of "fair trade" was advocated in Britain, one whereby either English goods would be allowed equality of market conditions abroad or corresponding duties would be imposed on goods imported from the discriminating nation.[31] Although "fair trade" did not imply complete abandonment of free trade, it was a theoretical step toward protectionism; nevertheless, it was never adopted as governmental policy. Yet, by the last years of the century, protectionism was being widely aired, and by no one with more vigor than Joseph Chamberlain. With him tariff reform was closely related to colonial development.

Chamberlain, who had been mayor of Birmingham and an early proponent of municipal socialism, exercised his greatest influence as colonial secretary between 1895 and 1903, when he formed his concept of a "constructive imperialism" in which colonial development, domestic prosperity, and social welfare were directly linked.[32] He first argued, as early as 1888, that the empire was vital to England's economic well-being, for, if that empire were reduced in size to the United Kingdom, "half at least of our population would be starved."[33] Later he extended his economic theory to include the idea that the regions of the empire still commercially undeveloped should be regarded as if they were estates to be readied as markets. To this end he even recommended national state aid to the colonies — a modest forerunner of later development plans — but the suggestion gained little support.[34] Most impressive and embracing of all

[30] Tract 116, quoted by A. M. McBriar, *Fabian Socialism and English Politics, 1884–1918* (Cambridge: At the University Press, 1962), p. 131.

[31] Donald C. M. Platt, *Finance, Trade and Politics in British Foreign Policy, 1815–1915* (Oxford: Clarendon Press, 1968), pp. 82–84; and Sydney H. Zebel, "Fair Trade: An English Reaction to the Breakdown of the Cobden Treaty System," *Journal of Modern History*, 12:161–185 (1940).

[32] J. B. Saul, "The Economic Significance of 'Constructive Imperialism,'" *Journal of Economic History*, 17:173–192 (1957).

[33] Speech of May 14, 1888, quoted by William L. Langer, *The Diplomacy of Imperialism* (New York: Alfred A. Knopf, 1935), I, 77.

[34] Saul, "Economic Significance of 'Constructive Imperialism,'" pp. 188–189.

his propositions was a zollverein which he believed would "establish at once practically free trade throughout the British Empire, but would leave the separate contracting parties free to make their own arrangements with regard to duties on foreign goods."[35]

None of these schemes met with any obvious success, and Chamberlain's political approach was accordingly modified. Indeed, the zollverein, which then appeared to be the only immediate solution to imperial reorganization, was rejected by the colonial ministers at the Imperial Conference of 1897. What these leaders desired was no grand economic union but simply preferential tariffs which would allow their products easy access to British markets. Such an arrangement was not readily appreciated as being advantageous to Great Britain, but through Chamberlain imperial preference was to become a national issue. Speaking against the dangers of continued free trade, he warned an audience in industrial Birmingham that the tariffs, bounties, and subsidies prevailing in continental Europe were "designed to shut out this country, as far as possible, from all profitable trade with those foreign States and, at the same time, to enable those foreign States to undersell in British markets." He continued in ominous terms: "If we do not take every chance in our power to keep British trade in British hands, I am certain that we shall deserve the disasters which will infallibly come upon us."[36] The "chance" was, of course, to tie the empire together by economic bonds.

In 1903 Chamberlain, as a member of the cabinet, openly espoused the cause of imperial preference by demanding the implementation of such a policy. He thus made the matter a political issue of national interest. A general protest quickly gathered around the effects of imperial preference on food prices, because colonial imports were primarily agrarian. "Free food" became the slogan of the opposition, but concern over the possible rise in prices of the raw materials upon which British industry depended was also keen. Principal opposition to the preference plan centered on its social inequity; it amounted to a tax on the poor, not on the rich. As the president of the Trades Union Congress remarked in 1903, "If the people of this country have to be taxed heavier than they are at the present time

[35] Quoted in Sydney H. Zebel, "Joseph Chamberlain and the Genesis of Tariff Reform," *Journal of British Studies*, 6:140 (1967).

[36] Speech of May 16, 1902, quoted in George Bennett, ed., *The Concept of Empire from Burke to Atlee, 1774–1947* (London: A. C. Black, 1953), p. 328. On Chamberlain and imperial preference, see Peter Fraser, *Joseph Chamberlain: Radicalism and Empire, 1868–1914* (South Brunswick: A. S. Barnes, 1966), chapter 10.

for our offspring in Canada and the Australian colonies, we require to know more of what we are likely to get in return."[37]

Political alliances also fell apart. The Liberal Unionist party, then in power, split over the issue, and a similar destructive division occurred within the newly instituted intellectual discussion group called the "Coefficients," which was formed by the Webbs and listed in its membership such men as H. G. Wells, Bertrand Russell, and Sir Edward Grey. Only the Fabian Society held firm by saying much and committing itself to little, another of the intellectual legerdemains performed by Shaw. In its pamphlet *Fabianism and the Fiscal Question*, both free traders and protectionists were equally treated to biting scorn, with the resulting ambiguities preventing a split within the society.[38]

Chamberlain's tariff reform failed, but its historical importance was not thereby diminished. A "bread-and-butter" matter in the eyes of its advocates and a "squalid argument" in the eyes of its opponents, it was addressed to social issues arising from economic problems, as well as to the economic problems themselves. All critics agree that Chamberlain's earlier interest in municipal socialism continued to affect his thought. He was genuinely concerned with the condition of the working classes, and he clearly saw empire as the means of improving it. As he stated most emphatically on October 6, 1903, in Glasgow: "Your colonial trade as it stands at present with the prospective advantage of preference against the foreigner means employment and fair wages for three-quarters of a million of workmen, and subsistence for nearly four millions of our population."[39]

In the Chamberlain era, then, the British public was harangued with economic arguments for empire as strident as those made in Germany and France, but with little more effect. Counterarguments from the anti-imperialists followed a similar pattern of development about the same time, although their great impact was not felt until after World War I.

Theories and Arguments against Economic Imperialism

Put starkly, the economic arguments presented by the anti-imperialists were generally the same as those offered by the pro-imperialists but with

[37] W. B. Hornidge, Presidential Address to the Trades Union Congress, September 8, 1903, quoted in Bennett *Concept of Empire*, p. 337.
[38] See McBriar, *Fabian Socialism*, p. 133.
[39] Quoted in Semmel, *Imperialism and Social Reform*, p. 84.

inverse moral and social implications. Expansion was seen as either voluntarily or deterministically predatory — and with little or no redeeming benefit to mankind. The most obvious origin of this thought was Marxist, for in Marx's world view expansion was an integral part of capitalism, as inevitable as it was exploitive. In the *Communist Manifesto* he had asserted that "the need of a constantly expanding market for its products chases the bourgeoisie over the whole surface of the globe," an interpretation entertained by all radical critics, regardless of whether they were of Marxist persuasion.

Toward the end of the century many expressions of concern over and discontent with the apparently deleterious effects of industrial capitalistic competition were offered and were logically bound up with the "New Imperialism" which had already been given a firm economic base by such men as Jules Ferry. Although the socialists were to be imperialism's primary critics, the first significant work on the economic disadvantages of imperialism emanated from the mind of an English liberal journalist and university professor whose views were part of a "new radicalism" directed toward social reform.

J. A. Hobson's *Imperialism: A Study* was published after the Boer War and reflects in some measure his experience as a correspondent during that war. However, Hobson's ideas on imperialism extend further back in time and depend more greatly on other influences. Above all, his economic interpretation of imperialism was but a portion of a broader interpretation of imperialism which, in turn, was subordinated to what was his major interest, the "social question." Influenced by Bosanquet, Herbert Spencer, and John Ruskin, he was opposed to the individualism and the "Invisible Hand" idea of the Manchester School; as an alternative he offered an organic theory of social relationships in which the well-being of society, not of its individual members, was the basic issue. From Ruskin in particular, Hobson had learned to look beyond monetary values, "to reach the body of human benefits and satisfactions which give them meaning." It was with this broad social bias in mind that Hobson analyzed imperialism.[40]

Hobson's first strong statement on the economics of imperialism was

[40] The best analysis is that of Bernard Porter, *Critics of Empire: British Radical Attitudes to Colonialism in Africa, 1895–1914* (London: Macmillan, 1968), notably pp. 168–179. The quotation from Ruskin is a familiar, frequently cited one. See *ibid.*, p. 171; and the introduction of Philip Siegelman to *Imperialism: A Study* (Ann Arbor: University of Michigan Press, 1965), p. ix.

occasioned by the "scramble for concessions" in China in 1897. To the then heated question of whether Britain should follow Germany's lead in leasing territory, Hobson provided an answer that went beyond the issue of free-trade imperialism and protectionism to the basic operations of the economy as he understood them. He explained everything by a theory of underconsumption, a theory from which he did not seriously deviate at any time and which, therefore, became the basis for his economic interpretation of imperialism. The underconsumptionist theory in a way harkened back to Say's law that all production would be consumed, for Hobson argued that if there was no maldistribution of wealth, goods would find satisfactory outlets in a domestic market. Production exceeded consumption, hence external outlets were needed simply because the well-off were unable or unwilling to consume it all. "Our surplus products, which the working classes cannot buy and the wealthier classes do not wish to buy, must find customers among foreign nations . . ."[41]

The results of his experience in and examination of the Boer War led Hobson to add a new dimension to his theory, that of conspiracy. Denouncing the war, he interpreted it as a plot by financial capitalists to seize control of the Rand gold mines. More particularly he singled out Jewish interests which he identified in a manner that was anti-Semitic.[42] From this two-strand analysis, he wove *Imperialism: A Study* which, since its publication, has been honored as the number one study of imperialist ideology.

The crucial chapters of the work are four and six, respectively entitled "The Parasites" and "The Economic Taproot of Imperialism," but even a glance at its contents will suggest that few aspects of imperialism, noneconomic as well as economic, escaped Hobson's attention. His economic appreciations include a recapitulation of the arguments and issues discussed since mid-century as well as his underconsumptionist theory, which critics agree is his most original contribution to the general subject.

Denying the value of industrial trade in the tropical regions under European domination, discounting the argument of overpopulation and the need for colonial emigration, and insisting that protectionism through colonial possessions cost nearly as much as is gained by the colonial trade

---

[41] Hobson, "Free Trade and Foreign Policy," *Contemporary Review*, August 1898, p. 178, cited in Porter, *Critics*, p. 198. Porter is the first to draw attention to the role of this significant article in Hobson's thinking.

[42] On this "conspiracy theory," see *ibid.*, pp. 200–206.

thereby acquired, Hobson asked the obvious question, To whom was the activity of profit and benefit? The answer was the capitalist. "Aggressive Imperialism, which costs the taxpayer so dear, which is of so little value to the manufacturer and the trader, which is frought with such incalculable peril to the citizen, is a source of great gain to the investor who cannot find at home the profitable use he seeks for his capital, and insists that his Government should help him to profitable and secure investments abroad."[43]

The wealth acquired by these people is, as was mentioned earlier, the result of maldistribution. According to Hobson, underconsumption is caused by oversaving. If income were distributed according to needs, "it is evident that consumption would rise with every rise of productive power." Since this does not happen in reality, certain people have a surplus of capital, beyond their needs to consume; this brings about a condition of oversavings which in turn suggests the need for investment abroad. "Thus we reach the conclusion that Imperialism is the endeavor of the great controllers of industry to broaden the channel for the flow of their surplus wealth by seeking foreign markets and foreign investments to take off the goods and capital they cannot sell or use at home."[44]

Here, then, were the finance capitalists, the unwanted offspring of oversaving, who turned politics, hence imperialism, to their own interest. In his famous and appropriately industrial metaphor, Hobson described finance as the governor of the expansionist engine; it controlled it while other groups — adventurers, militarists, missionaries — drove it on.[45] Hobson succumbed to no historical determinism, however. His underconsumptionist theory was saved from inevitability by his conspiratorial theory. The financiers could be checked. He therefore argued for a genuine democracy which would not tolerate such disparities of wealth.[46]

Hobson's remained the most effective statement against imperialism before World War I, even though the trend toward analytical criticism was not English, but German. In both Germany and Austria, socialists began to face the theoretical implications of imperialism for a capitalist system to which they were doctrinally opposed. Their intellectual activity was chiefly post-Hobsonian, yet it followed no simple direction; certainly it demonstrated no simple adherence to or amplification of Hobson's

[43] Hobson, Imperialism, p. 55.
[44] Ibid., pp. 83 and 85.
[45] Ibid., p. 59.
[46] See Porter, Critics, chapter 7.

thoughts. In fact, the social democrats on the Continent, not just in Germany, were unified only by their all having read Marx; their explications of his theory, as their supplements to it, followed two distinct lines. The revisionists, of whom the German Eduard Bernstein is the best known, were social evolutionists not wedded to notions of impending revolution, but accepting the principle of socialism achieved through political reform. The orthodox Marxists were firm in revolutionary dogma, finding any accommodation to capitalism a form of untenable compromise. These two schools of interpretation provided, as should be expected, different evaluations of the new phenomenon of imperialism.

There was no doctrinal disagreement with the assertion that imperialism was a politico-economic function of capitalism. Concerning the intimacy and significance of this relationship, however, there was a variety of subtle differences of interpretation, which can be generally subsumed in two sets: the issue of whether socialism should condemn all imperialism and thereby avoid any consideration of a humane colonial policy; the issue of whether imperialism was simply a policy of capitalism or part of an inevitable historical process.

The notion of converting what was regarded as a rapacious imperialism into an "efficient," or constructive one was far from unknown left of center. The Fabian Society in England had, through the efforts of George Bernard Shaw, issued the tract *Fabianism and the Empire*, which urged greater state control of the empire, with public replacing private enterprise in several domains, such as the South African mining industry.[47] In like manner, some continental socialists of the revisionist school stressed the need of formulating an intelligent colonial policy in the event — not unlikely — of their accession to political power and therefore of their assumption of previously determined international responsibilities. This particular line of socialist thought, set along the scale of the nineteenth-century doctrine of progress, measured the time until the benefits of the industrial system would spread generously over the world and through all classes. The obvious objection, therefore, was not to European involvement in other parts of the world, but to the exploitation that it then implied.

However, such expressions of humanistic concern were not motivated by pure sentiment alone. Like the English liberal imperialists who saw in

[47] See McBriar, *Fabian Socialism*, pp. 119–130; and Semmel, *Imperialism and Social Reform*, pp. 57–62; and chapter 5 below.

expansion the advantage of employment for the working class, some of the revisionists related overseas activities to working class interests. Jean Jaurès, for instance, spoke in this vein to the Socialist Congress of Bordeaux in 1903, when he stated that French foreign policy should be designed so that "a part of the foreign markets, in China or elsewhere, shall be assured to the peaceful penetration of industry, which is the necessary condition of good wages for the proletarian class." Regarding the other, the "input," end of the industrial system, Henri Van Kol addressed his colleagues at the 1904 Amsterdam congress of the Second International on the increasing industrial need for the raw materials contained in the tropical regions then under colonial domination. What Van Kol desired, as did the Fabians, was the substitution of public for private colonial enterprise.[48]

To the more orthodox Marxists, such suggestions were intolerable compromise, for all colonial activity was by their definition capitalist, hence reprehensible. Nevertheless, they differed on its origins, some considering imperialism contrived capitalist policy, a few arguing that it was a historical necessity. Many of the hard-lined Marxists, like Karl Kautsky, tied colonization in with industrial capitalism, but they never used the term *finance capitalism* or came to an appreciation of the process it described, an appreciation that had given to Hobson's thought its originality. However, two Austrian economists, Otto Bauer and Rudolph Hilferding, put Hobson's thought in a newer yet orthodox frame. Their approach, nonetheless, was from a different theoretical direction, as one critic has shown. Whereas Hobson began with imperialism and arrived at finance capitalism, the Austrians began with finance capitalism and arrived at imperialism.[49]

Both Bauer and Hilferding adhered to the "theory of catastrophe"; they interpreted imperialism as a militant form of capitalist expansion, with the army and the capitalist in league, and with the course of their activity moving toward international war. Bauer was particularly concerned with the pervasiveness of nationalism and the use to which the capitalists put it. Through state policy carried on in the name of the nation, surplus

[48] On the general subject see Brynjolf J. Hovde, "Socialistic Theories of Imperialism Prior to the Great War," *Journal of Political Economy*, 36:569–591 (1928). The quotations are, respectively, from pp. 586 and 580.

[49] E. M. Winslow, *The Pattern of Imperialism: A Study in the Theories of Power* (New York: Columbia University Press, 1948), pp. 159–160. The following interpretation derives largely from *ibid.*, pp. 158–169, and Hovde, "Socialistic Theories," pp. 570–577.

goods and capital could be profitably shipped abroad, protective tariffs raised to the detriment of the worker, and international situations provoked — particularly in the Balkans — so that the new principle of divide and financially conquer would prevail.

Hilferding, in his *Finanzkapital*, published in 1910, was more concerned than Bauer with the economic aspects of imperialism and can claim credit for having integrated finance capitalism into Marxist theory, and hence imperialism into Marxism. Where he differed from his predecessors — which is to say where he was original in the socialist school — was in his assertion that industrial capitalism, in which ownership and management were combined in the same persons, had given way to financial capitalism, in which the financiers, the great banking houses, supplied the capital to the industrialists and thereby shifted foreign economic activity from the exchange of goods to the exportation of capital. "Whether colonies and new markets are now developed more or less fast will essentially depend on their capacity to serve as places for capital investment. The richer the colony is in those products which can be capitalistically produced, which have a sure sale in the world market and which are important for home industry, the greater this capacity will be."[50] This new economic activity did not allow for open exchange, but required close protection, and, as a result, the peaceful policy of industrial capitalism yielded to an aggressive policy of domination under capitalist imperialism. Hilferding thus placed considerable emphasis on the role of political power in this phase of international economics because he insisted that state policy would have to submit to the demands of the finance capitalist. In agreement with Bauer, Hilferding regarded imperialism as a development of policy, not as a result of inevitability. In further agreement with Bauer, he imagined it would end in belligerent competition, in widespread war.

Lenin was later to denounce Hilferding as he would Kautsky and others for their failure to see how parasitical imperialism was and for their complementary failure to recognize it as an integral part of the capitalist process, as the highest, or last stage of capitalism.[51]

This failure was compensated for two years before Lenin denounced it by Rosa Luxemburg, whose words were not deeply appreciated at the

[50] Quoted by David K. Fieldhouse, ed., *The Theories of Capitalist Imperialism* (London: Longmans, Green, 1967), pp. 82–83.
[51] Lenin, *Imperialism*, pp. 13 and 99.

time or even later, but who certainly centered her attention on the problem by considering capitalism exclusively in terms of colonial imperialism. *Die Akkumulation des Kapitals*, first published in 1913, was an
elaborate and intricate theory which made imperialism a definite historical stage of capitalism. In structure, Luxemburg's study is the reverse of
Leroy-Beaulieu's. The first two-thirds are devoted to a carefully wrought
criticism of preceding economic theories of capital accumulation; the last
section provides a survey of nineteenth-century history in which imperialism finally figures.

Luxemburg offers a definition of imperialism that places her and it in
the "catastrophic" mold of thought: "Imperialism is the political expression of the accumulation of capital in its competitive struggle for what
remains still open of the non-capitalist environment."[52] Accumulated
capital in Europe requires new outlets through which it can acquire
surplus value. It matters not where or how this money is employed as
long as it leads to great returns. "The important point is that capital
accumulated in the old country should find elsewhere new opportunities
to beget and realize surplus value so that accumulation can proceed."[53]
But with the intensifying capitalism among the European states and with
the conversion of precapitalist to capitalist economies in many of the
regions now touched economically by Europe, competition for the remaining untouched regions becomes intense, occasions protectionism,
aggravates international relations, and ultimately undercuts further possibilities of capital accumulation.

Unlike the commodity market in which the exchange of goods and
services can proceed peacefully, capital investment abroad is ruthless.
"Its predominant methods are colonial policy, an international loan system — a policy of spheres of interest — and war." Under these conditions,
"political power is nothing but a vehicle of the economic process."[54]

With the thought of Rosa Luxemburg the economics of imperialism
received their most intense evaluation before World War I. Yet it was
Lenin's brief study *Imperialism, the Highest Stage of Capitalism*, written
during the war, that became the standard Marxist interpretation. In all
subsequent analyses Hobson and Lenin were considered together as the
truly formative theorists of economic imperialism.

[52] Rosa Luxemburg, *The Accumulation of Capital*, trans. Agnes Schwarzchild (New Haven, Conn.: Yale University Press, 1951), p. 446.
[53] *Ibid.*, p. 427.
[54] *Ibid.*, p. 452.

Theory and Practice Disjoined

The range of argument, from the slogans of Jules Ferry to the sophisticated intellectual ruminations of Rosa Luxemburg, not only indicates the
prevalence of the concept of economic imperialism, but also demonstrates
that proponents and opponents worked the same field of thought. Today,
there is no disagreement among historians that imperialism had its
economic component. To the European mind of the nineteenth century,
empire was synonymous with wealth. Some persons certainly gained from
it; many more hoped that they would. No previous century had witnessed
such a concerted search for sources of new riches and new commodities.
Dreams of untapped African wealth were modern variations of the
Spanish quest after El Dorado; anticipations of the development of a
lucrative South China trade were consonant with profit-motivated market
trends. When Stanley described the Congo to businessmen in Manchester, he did so not in square kilometers of land, but in square yards of
cotton stuff to be exported.

However, no fixed causal connection between words, hopes, and deeds
can be easily drawn. Often commerce and colonialism were bound in no
simple relationship which was mutually inspiring or mutually reinforcing.
Whatever its excesses, the capitalist industrial system did not swamp its
overseas possessions with goods or capital, any more than it uniquely
forced territorial expansion to begin with.

For several decades now, theories of economic imperialism have been
revised, refuted, and revised again in still different form. Many
economists and non-Marxian historians have demonstrated that there was
no meaningful statistical relationship between the export of money and
finished materials and the increase of territory. The lands acquired by the
effort of the "New Imperialism," which allegedly was economically predicated, were tropical dependencies of little economic value to Europe at
the time of acquisition. That such acquisition of territory preceded the
financial phase of capitalism, so elaborately described by Hilferding and
Luxemburg, logically denies the possibility of a causal connection. And
that two of the newest imperialist nations, Germany and Italy, were generally harboring, not shipping their capital weakens any generalization
about late nineteenth-century capitalism in dire need of external sources
of investment. As for the argument produced by the imperialists themselves, that colonial empire would both protect and enhance the in-

vestments of their nationals against competing foreign capital, this, too, was proved wanting in the early twentieth century. German capital entered Moroccan extractive industries at the time French domination of that country was assured; and French and British capital was welcomed in Dutch Indonesia.[55]

Like capital, goods for export did not require colonies. As foreign markets became limited in the first years of the twentieth century, capitalist-imperialist Europe did not explode from the pressure of accumulated goods as Jules Ferry's metaphor of the steam engine demanded. Rather, the industrial nations of the world, still exchanging the greatest quantity of goods among themselves, became *"their own* best customers; as the potentialities of overseas outlets diminished, the domestic market acquired increasing importance."[56] Neither as policy nor as supposedly inevitable historical process did imperialism respond to the realities of contemporary European economic behavior in the manner classical theory required.

Furthermore, the behavior of the capitalist did not merit his being cast in the devil's role in this historical drama. The general theory, as elaborated by many anti-imperialists, bordered on the conspiratorial when it allied the high-placed capitalist with the high-placed politician. Marx, in his *Communist Manifesto*, had offered the marvelous idea and phrase that government was but the executive committee of the bourgeoisie. Early twentieth-century interpretations of capitalist imperialism, of which Hilferding's is the best known, frequently made the basic assumption that the directorates of leading banks and large corporations were closely interlocked and operated in tandem, with government regularly and generously responsive to them. "The 'personal union' between the banks and industry is completed by the 'personal union' between both and the state," Lenin asserted.[57] Here, then, was depicted a power elite driven by or acceding to one unifying purpose: the continued profitable development of national industry and investment. Pictures of the kaiser with the great shipbuilder Albert Ballin, reference to Joseph Chamberlain's industrial background in Birmingham, indications that the Earl of

[55] David Landes, "Some Thoughts on the Nature of Economic Imperialism," *Journal of Economic History*, 21:504 (1961).
[56] David Landes, *The Unbound Prometheus: Technological Change and Industrial Development in Western Europe from 1750 to the Present* (London: Cambridge University Press, 1969), p. 241.
[57] Lenin, *Imperialism*, p. 42.

Cromer, English resident in Egypt, was a member of the great English banking family of Baring are all adduced to prove the intimacy of the economic-political relationship. How could any European country make war if the Rothschilds were opposed to it? Hobson posited.[58]

Although neither Hobson nor Lenin insisted that imperialism was exclusively centered in the colonial world or exclusively inspired by the profit-motivated businessman, their analysis provided a rational explanation for what other historians have considered to be irrational, emotional behavior. "Irrational from the standpoint of the whole nation," said Hobson of imperialism, "it is rational enough from the standpoint of certain classes in the nation."[59]

The rationalism that Hobson speaks of was supposedly an expression of calculation, of double-entry bookkeeping. And it gave to "certain classes in the nation" an appreciation and understanding of their own interests — a cunning — which was apparently absent from the minds of those people located at other social stations. All this is to discount the aberrant, the action that cannot be explained in terms of "best interests" as determined by the outside, analytical observer. Hobson deplored the "psychology of jingoism," but he never deemed it to be a force that motivated the financier.

Our own age, more beset by the extent of the peculiar logic of the irrational, can understand that economic "best interests" are neither necessarily nor consistently acted upon. However, even Hobson's contemporaries were not all convinced of the operation of the calculus of cash. "Sentimental considerations have dominated those of interest," commented Norman Angell, author of the well-sold *Great Illusion*, with respect to England, the United States, and France.[60] And at times there hardly seemed to be any consideration whatsoever. Describing British investment in foreign railroad bonds, one writer mentioned that "the investor repeatedly showed a lack of discrimination which can only be explained in terms of laziness, ignorance, and prejudice."[61] Even in the

[58]*Ibid.*, p. 42; Hobson, *Imperialism*, p. 57. For such correlation just described, see Heinz Gollwitzer, *Europe in the Age of Imperialism, 1880–1914*, trans. David Adam and Stanley Baron (New York: Harcourt, Brace and World, 1969), pp. 64–76.

[59]Hobson, *Imperialism*, p. 47. Porter analyzes this particularly; see *Critics*, pp. 222–223.

[60]Norman Angell, *Patriotism under Three Flags*, p. 24, quoted by Porter, *Critics*, p. 222.

[61]A. K. Cairncross, *Home and Foreign Investment 1870–1913: Studies in Capital Accumulation* (Cambridge: At the University Press, 1953), p. 88. Herbert Feis lends support to this contention with respect to the French. See *Europe the World's Banker: An Account of European Foreign Investment and the Connection of World Finance with Diplomacy before the War* (New Haven, Conn.: Yale University Press, 1930), pp. 49–50.

vital center of that grand web of international finance, the City, thought seldom reached out as far as investment supposedly did. "Only a proposed reform could provoke the City to thought and discussion beyond the immediate course of markets."[62]

If there was a vision of empire, it was not in the eyes of businessmen. There was, of course, the occasional Cecil Rhodes who viewed profits as a means to political power, but his type was not numerous. Neither French, nor British, nor German capitalists were ready and anxious to deposit their earnings in the colonies. And the Belgians, whom Lenin viewed as the most bourgeois of the lot, found no source of pleasurable cupidity in Leopold's venture in the Congo.

Everywhere supporters of imperialism lamented the fact that their fellow nationals with the money did not have the will. French literature at the end of the century is filled with statements of complaint that are amazingly repetitious. "The economic development of our colonies," one critic woefully remarked, "demands engagement of capital, yet we must affirm that in this matter France has still a lot to do. The well-known timidity of French capital is all the more regrettable because France remains the major money market of the entire world." Another commentary ran: "What has been lacking up until now in our colonies is less men than capital. Money in France is more timid than individuals; it expatriates itself reluctantly." Or again, from still another author, "The capitalists only involve themselves timidly because African commerce carries great risks."[63]

The timidity of capital was not noticeable in all colonial endeavors, of course. However, capital's general avoidance of colonial relocation does suggest, and not just in the French instance, that the need for tropical colonies was not abundantly clear to the European capitalist. There is only one direct and constant correlation between overseas expansion and capital outlay, and it can be neatly graphed. Particularly, but not exclusively, in the British experience did capital follow white settlement. The departure of Englishmen for America in the nineteenth century was matched by investment in the United States; a similar occurrence is evident in late nineteenth- and early twentieth-century Canada and Aus-

[62] S. G. Checkland, "The Mind of the City, 1870–1914," *Oxford Economic Papers*, 9:273 (1957).

[63] Henri Lorin, *La France, puissance coloniale* (Paris: A. Challamel, 1906), p. 467; "Création d'une banque coloniale," *Quinzaine coloniale*, April 25, 1898, p. 228; Louis Vignon, *L'exploitation de notre empire coloniale* (Paris: Hachette, 1900), p. 208.

tralia. This particular affinity was the result of the need for "infrastructure" in which the British were willing to invest: new railroads to transport the settlers, new houses to shelter them. In inverse but obvious ratio, the decline in the English building trade was commensurate with the rise in the same trade in the areas to which Englishmen emigrated. Money as well as people left when the market was slack. Although the French were *casaniers* (home bodies) by tradition and in the nineteenth century because of the lack of demographic pressure, French capital also tended to follow French settlement, as in North Africa and to a lesser degree Latin America. Both a familiarity with the credit system — for nationals abroad tended to borrow from nationals at home — and a sentimental disposition, noticeably in the French case, account for this procedure.[64]

Thus, capital like trade only occasionally followed the flag, and not regularly to those areas where the national colors dipped languidly because of high humidity.

What the contemporary historian now realizes is that the classical theory of imperialism as propounded at the turn of the century was incorrect, at the very least out of chronological context. Put otherwise, the imperialist effort in the late nineteenth century was not at severe variance with earlier manifestations. New urgencies and fears of both an economic and a political sort introduced a new intensity, it is true. However, the intentions to be fulfilled by late nineteenth-century colonial possessions were not strikingly new.

When all economic theory relating to colonial expansion is distilled, only one generalization escapes evaporation: overseas empire was undertaken for commerce. From the plunder empires of the sixteenth century to the plantation colonies of the seventeenth and eighteenth centuries through the tropical empires of the nineteenth, the European economic effort overseas remained two-pronged: the search for raw materials and the establishment of new markets.

Yet to assert the obvious makes it no easier to answer the question of whether the economic purpose of empire was the primary cause of imperialism. Because of the incredible economic expansion of nineteenth-century Europe, it is reasonable to suggest that imperialism, whatever its particular manifestations, was a constant and exclusive function of an

---

[64] See Cairncross, *Home and Foreign Investment*, chapter 8; and Feis, *Europe the World's Banker*, p. 49.

outreaching industrial system. Indeed, this very argument has been the basis for the lively academic debate about the nature of "informal empire" already reviewed in earlier chapters. To stress the nature of political possession is, according to this theory, to concentrate on a secondary characteristic. With respect to British expansion, the theory reads: "[T]he many-sided expansion of British industrial society can be viewed as a whole of which both the formal and informal empires are only parts. . . . If this is accepted, it follows that formal and informal empire are essentially interconnected and to some extent interchangeable."[65]

Chronological divisions in the history of empire should not accordingly be determined by change in political activity, but by rate of growth or, even better, by extension of external markets and the governmental involvement and strategic concerns this arouses. Thus in its own broad lines this theory seems to be a fitting counterpart to the thought of Karl Marx who appreciated, if he did not respect, the far-ranging economic exploits of the bourgeoisie. To suggest that there was a "general strategy" designed to convert the non-European areas of the world "into complementary satellite economics" is to return to the tightly interdependent relationship earlier established between government and commerce, to the insistence that the political authority of the state was constantly — if sometimes indirectly — employed to guarantee private economic advantage.[66]

That such did actually occur on many an occasion in Asia and Africa, no one would deny. But when universalized both geographically and chronologically, the argument encounters difficulty. All political conduct is ultimately named a function of economic enterprise; all local activity is finally subsumed under a grander national economic policy or purpose.

In its original form the concept of "informal empire" was bound strictly to analysis of British overseas expansion. But even within this limited area of application, it has been found to be distortive. The term *imperialism of free trade* has encountered the most criticism. Those historians who dispute its historical validity have demonstrated that the official governmental attitude and practice of Great Britain during this period was consistently one of lofty disinterest in the commercial activities of its nationals abroad, that private requests for governmental assistance were only for equal, not preferential treatment, and that a governmental policy of

[65] Robinson and Gallagher, "The Imperialism of Free Trade," p. 6.
[66] *Ibid.*, p. 9.

noninterference in the affairs of other states was regularly maintained.[67] In short, neither policy nor occasion arose to provoke such imperialism. And in the instance most celebrated in recent studies, that of the Argentine financial crisis of 1890–91, the heavy losses suffered by British investors were covered only by a reiteration of Canning's old policy of noninterference.[68]

Practice of a governmental policy of free-trade imperialism, as distinct from the existence of a theory of imperialism in the free-trade era, therefore remains at best mooted and warrants further historical examination. It might help if comparisons were made with contemporary ideas about neo-colonialism. The practice of commercial domination attributed to the United States in the 1950s — and coincidental with the initial popularity of the concept of "informal empire" — has striking similarities. Indeed, a comparable theory of "informal empire," defined for the late nineteenth century as "imperial anticolonialism," holds together the broad history of American expansion, both internal and external, from the incipient days of the Republic until its more recent moments as a superpower.[69]

Certainly trade relationships developed into direct acts of imperialism; "informal empire" was transmogrified into "formal empire." Persuasion gave way to invasion: such is the spectrum of that condition described as Power. Yet the flag over the newly acquired land did not necessarily mean more than the "paramountcy" of European interests. Thus "formal empire" might not involve more than general policing, the maintenance of a local pax in which trade might flourish or taxes might be collected so that the general policing might be maintained — for just so circular did the justification for empire occasionally seem.

Again the historian is forced back to the annoying past reality of it all. Such a variety of acts, precipitated by such a number of motives, cannot be bound into a single pattern. Politics and economics were joined, but in no set or grandly symmetrical way. They were confused in actuality, if they are not in theory.

---

[67] Donald C. M. Platt, "The Imperialism of Free Trade: Some Reservations," *Economic History Review*, 21:297 (1968).

[68] *Ibid.*, pp. 298–301; and H. S. Ferns, *Britain and Argentina in the Nineteenth Century* (Oxford: Clarendon Press, 1960), pp. 487–491.

[69] The expression "imperial anticolonialism" is found in William Appleman Williams, *The Tragedy of American Diplomacy* (Cleveland: World Publishing, 1959), p. 36. On the continuity of American commercial imperialism, see *ibid.*, and Walter LaFeber, *The New Empire: An Interpretation of American Expansion, 1860–1898* (Ithaca, N.Y.: Cornell University Press, 1969; first published, 1963).

CHAPTER 5

Civilisation Oblige

When considered within the historical dimensions of the last four hundred years, the general cultural attitude of nineteenth-century European society is remarkable for its certainty, conceit, and, hence, confidence. Preceded by two centuries of critical self-evaluation and humbling cultural comparison, and followed by a century of self-doubt and seeming absurdity, the nineteenth is the sturdy European century, fashioned out of new hardware and ideas.

Hidden within this grand generalization are many qualifiers, but even when they are allowed to obtrude, they do not badly mar the total effect. Kierkegaard was far less influential in his day than Samuel Smiles, Nietzsche was not so widely read or attended with such interest as was *Popular Mechanics*, and the terrible visions of William Blake were dissipated in the artificial atmosphere of the Crystal Palace. If there was a recondite problem of some grave intellectual concern in the last decades of the century, it was the nature of electricity, but confident scientists were sure that would soon be reasonably explained. In the same period the middle-class world, now brightly illuminated by gas, displayed a spirit of exuberance.

Just as the rational mind seemed bent on reordering nature, just so the European mentality was soon adjusted, without many expressions of public disfavor, to the ongoing political domination of the world. "In the field" missionaries, both secular and religious, were prepared to bestow some, if not all of the benefits of western civilization on those peoples who dwelt beyond the pale of the pale. *Civilisation oblige* was the sentiment, if not the affixed motto.

Yet, unlike some commemorative medal, this attitude was not struck on a particular occasion. Its initial form was set in the eighteenth century. By then the western mind had accumulated a great variety of facts and opinion about other peoples and cultures. Robinson Crusoe had left his impact on European thought as visibly as he had left his footprints on the sands of the island where he had been marooned. And so had a number of real characters who in the seventeenth and eighteenth centuries treated the literate European public to accounts of near utopias, wondrous cities in faraway places, and varieties of peoples whose habits were unusual, amusing, or repulsive. The travel literature of the eighteenth century was nowhere as technical as the botanical literature emanating from the same regions, but it was rich in detail and the major source of cross-cultural judgments. The sagacious Chinese had made his appearance in printed woodcut, as had the "noble savage" and the black African, the last already condemned by many Europeans to a cultural prison of passion.

Not until the middle of the nineteenth century was there a discernible shift in western social attitudes toward that vast and interesting array of peoples the ethnocentric still labels as "non-western." The heritage from the 1700s was upheld in the early 1800s, in part gently cultivated by a continuing spirit of humanitarianism which was to be institutionally realized in the abolition of slavery and verbally structured into the novels of exotic romance like Chateaubriand's *Atala* and Cooper's *Last of the Mohicans.* If much of this prose now seems redolent of a musty condescension, it was not yet sharply racist, and the thought supporting it had not yet been rigidly fixed in pseudoscientific ideas about human evolution and differentiation.

There is, however, no denying the categorizing tendencies of European observers throughout the century. With the partial secularization of the problem of genesis, the origins and varieties of the human species were no longer explained only by geographical effects or through extrapolation from biblical myth. A new geometry of race was elaborated, with measurement of facial angles, skull shape, and, later, cranial capacity arousing much attention. Eighteenth-century theorists like the German Blumenbach, the Dutchman Camper, and the Frenchman Daubenton had already stared intently and computed soberly in their determination to distinguish, to a certain degree, one human group from another.[1] Beauty was no longer in the eye of the beholder, but in the hand manipulating the calipers. And so each "race" was described and assigned a place on an imagined scale of physical attractiveness, personal sophistication, and intellectual refinement. By the middle of the nineteenth century, three, four, five, and even more fundamental races were defined, but in all such division, the well-formed numerator was the contemporary European, the Caucasian. He was allowed to enjoy not only the most finely proportioned geometric shape but also quickness of mind, temperateness of disposition, and capacity for leadership. The other peoples were shuffled about between the "primitive" and the culturally sophisticated but socially arrested. To the "Oriental," delicacy, intelligence, and cruelty were frequently attributed; to the Hindu, mildness, diffidence, and eroticism; to the Arab, sensualness, refinement, and deceitfulness; to the black African, licentiousness and superstition.[2]

All of these assigned attributes, appearing in an abundant literature of fiction, were reinforced by vivid descriptions inspired by the imagination or recounted from personal experience. The romantic interpretations of Algerian life that appeared in the painting of Delacroix suggested a world of unbridled force and lush indulgence. An emergent exotic literature, centered in the Far East, poetically depicted the land of the lotus-eater and that of the ivory-colored or porcelainlike maiden, exquisitely ornamental. More prosaically, John Ruskin, observing a visiting acrobatic team, described the Japanese as "human creatures of a partially inferior race, but not without great human gentleness, domestic affection, and ingenious intellect." The frequently sketched contemporary decadence of India was matched by accounts of its barbaric simplicity. Of the Punjabi populations, one English author stated: "Wild barbarians, indifferent to human life, they were yet free, simple as children, brave, faithful to their master, sincere toward their God." These same qualities, more harshly presented, were bestowed upon the black African who was most regularly

---

[1] See Jacques Barzun, *Race: A Study in Superstition* (New York: Harper & Row, 1965; first published, 1937), pp. 34–35; Philip Curtin, *The Image of Africa: British Ideas and Action, 1780–1850* (Madison: University of Wisconsin Press, 1964), pp. 38–40.

[2] On the varieties of caricature and stereotypes, see Christine Bolt, *Victorian Attitudes to Race* (London: Routledge, 1971), chapters 4 and 5; George D. Bearce, *British Attitudes toward India, 1784–1858* (Oxford: Oxford University Press, 1961), chapters 4 and 9; and H. Alan C. Cairns, *Prelude to Imperialism: British Reactions to Central African Society, 1840–90* (London: Routledge, 1965), chapters 2 and 3. Professor William B. Cohen's forthcoming study on French attitudes toward the African is rich in documentation.

presented as childlike by nineteenth-century European critics who placed him at the threshold of humanity. "The black mentality is somewhat like that of our first ancestors," asserted a French writer.[3]

The dimension along which all such imagined differences were measured was time. Indeed, the new appreciation that movement through time was as formative as movement through space was a major aspect of the nineteenth-century mentality which distinguished it from its predecessors. Mutability replaced immutability. The long abiding theory of the Great Chain of Being, that once-for-all act of divine forging in which every creature was assigned its fixed place in the grand scheme of things, was totally destroyed by mid-century, the victim of geological picks and biological scalpels.

It can be argued that the concept of growth, of change through time, has been a continuous one in western explanations of historical movement, an initial contribution of the Greeks and Lucretius.[4] But with the late eighteenth century the growth metaphor was modified by the soon popular concept of historical articulation, a theory of social development that described the giant steps up which mankind progressed to refinement and betterment. It was present in the writings of Voltaire and Condorcet and became clearly pronounced in Auguste Comte's three-stage theory whereby mankind proceeded from an age of religion through an age of philosophy to an age of positivism — the last, the rationally ordered, now technologically premised society of the modern European world.

Within this new time framework, nineteenth-century social and physical scientists tried to arrange the lines and span of human development in a manner not dissimilar to Comte's. Yet polygenesists still contended with monogenesists. Perhaps the great French paleontologist Georges Cuvier was correct when he defined three races of man descended from Noah; and perhaps he was wrong. By the moment Darwin was struggling to put his ideas on paper, the monogenesist point of view was gaining in acceptance: all men were descended from a common ancestor.[5]

[3] John Ruskin, *Time and Tide* (London: Longmans, Green, 1906; first published, 1890), p. 35; Henry Edwardes, *A Year on the Punjab Frontier*, quoted in Bearce, *British Attitudes*, p. 257; and Léon Pacquier, "Sur l'âme noire," *Dépêche coloniale*, June 3, 1902.

[4] This thesis is beautifully developed by Robert Nisbet, *Social Change and History: Aspects of the Western Theory of Development* (New York: Oxford University Press, 1972; first published, 1969).

[5] On the competition between these two theories, see Bolt, *Victorian Attitudes*, pp. 9–20.

Out of this chaos of thought would emerge, by mid-century, the discipline of anthropology, conditioned in its infancy by history — and
promptly thereafter by derivative Darwinian concepts. Man's passage
through time, unlike that of Bunyan's pilgrim, was seen as upward, culminating in the lofty station from which the European observed the physical world around him and the social world below him. It was, of course,
both tempting and flattering to so imagine the general history of mankind.
Yet such temporal differentiation soon was to have a perniciously con-
demning cultural effect. The French colonial theorist Paul Leroy-
Beaulieu, digesting the opinions so widely spread at the end of the century, asserted: "It has taken series of centuries for a savage people to pass
from a state of barbarism to a civilized state." Two other authors more
precisely stated that French civilization had been thirty centuries in the
making.[6] The inference was that a similar time-in-being would be required for other peoples. Three millennia was a long sentence for inferior
social status. And thus by an intellectual twist, which Darwin certainly
did not propose, the evolutionary process was charged with cultural
value, one which was bound to affect concepts of European colonial
supremacy.

In fact anthropological and biological theses were the basis for the
widely held belief in the European's ability and obligation to dominate
and lead the colored races. In the early years of the century it was generally assumed that the religious truths of Christianity conferred upon its
supplicants distinguishing qualities — and, in addition, the need to preach
and shepherd. Dr. Livingstone solemnly remarked of his efforts in
Africa: "The great thing in working with such people is to remember that
we are forwarding that great movement which God is carrying on for the
renovation of the world." Later on, divine inspiration was matched by
personal attributes, particularly those inhering in the civilized brain. The
early twentieth-century French novelist and critic of racist thought Pierre
Mille stated: "White men have believed and continue to believe in the
incontestable superiority of their brains. They have believed and continue to believe that this superiority gives to them an *imperium* over men
who are not white." And at the same time that such psychological variations were being discussed, so were the differences in national "spirit" or
"soul." The American Congregational minister Josiah Strong believed

[6] Paul Leroy-Beaulieu, *De la colonisation chez les peuples modernes* (6th ed.; Paris: Guillaumin, 1906), II, 621; F. J. Clozel and Robert Villaumin, *Les coutumes indigènes de la Côte
d'Ivoire* (Paris: A. Challamel, 1902), p. 69.

that the Anglo-Saxon had "an instinct or genius for colonizing." And many Frenchmen insisted upon their national genius for civilizing. As a summary of all degrees of this thought, the generalization offered by the British social psychologist Benjamin Kidd was perfectly acceptable in its time, 1898: "In dealing with the *natural* inhabitants of the tropics we are dealing with peoples who represent the same stage in the history of the development of the race that the child does in the history of the development of the individual."[7]

Supported by such concepts the European "took up the white man's burden" and ruled out of what he believed to be his right and responsibility. Although the greatest emphasis on this thought, like Kipling's words that expressed it succinctly, occurred at the end of the century, the general sentiment was older. However, colonial theory and opinion did not remain constantly fixed from the early years of the century to the late.

Between 1833, when humanitarianism had triumphed with the abolition of slavery in the British empire, and 1882, when Africa was being seriously partitioned by the British occupation of Egypt, attitudes toward peoples living outside of Europe — white colonists excepted — had changed dramatically. Benign condescension had already given way to haughty superiority. The effect on the consideration of colonial matters was significant.

There is a nice cluster of important events between 1857 and 1865 which the historian might try to squeeze together into a turning point in European thought about "native races." In 1857 the Sepoy Mutiny shocked English sensibilities, heretofore conditioned to Indian respect for the British effort and held by the illusion of the possible cultural assimilation of that subcontinent. In 1863 the emperor Napoleon III made a famous statement about Algeria as an "Arab Kingdom," which gave governmental expression to France's new concern with the political and social condition of the indigenous population. In 1865 the American Civil War ended in victory for the abolitionists, an outcome that interested as well as worried Europeans with colonies containing large, already freed black populations. And, finally, in 1865 the English were faced with

[7] David Livingstone, *African Journal, 1853–1856*, ed. I. Schapera, 2 vols. (Berkeley: University of California Press, 1963), II, 243–244; Pierre Mille, "La race supérieure," *Revue de Paris*, February 15, 1905, p. 821; Josiah Strong, *Our Country*, quoted by Louis L. Snyder, *The Imperialism Reader: Documents and Readings on Modern Expansionism* (New York: Van Nostrand, 1962), p. 122; Benjamin Kidd, *The Control of the Tropics* (New York: Macmillan, 1898), p. 52.

another disturbing rebellion of dominated persons, this in Jamaica which before then appeared to be a "model colony."[8]

Within this same run of years, the impact of Harriet Beecher Stowe's *Uncle Tom's Cabin* (1851), and Max Havelaar's *Multatuli* (1860) was being felt in Europe. Mrs. Stowe's novel needs only mention, for its plot and influence are universally appreciated. In a lesser sphere, Havelaar's work was equally significant. Written pseudonymously by a Dutch administrator named E. Douwes Dekker, it revealed the worst abuses of the Dutch colonial system in the East Indies: corruption and indifference of the colonial officials, ill-treatment of the Javanese, and crass exploitation of the land. The cynical mood of colonialism conveyed in the novel is captured in the ironic comment the preacher Caquet is asked to make: "Are not the Javanese poor? But yes. And why? They are pagans. Thus, the more the Dutch work among the Javanese the more our wealth prospers and their poverty increases. It's predestined."[9]

Political event, protest movement, and literary publication all converged into a turning point, or series of turning points in colonial thought and practice. Europeans were becoming aware of the dimensions of the "native problem" as they never had before. Local discontent and resistance might have been — and were — interpreted as expressions of ingratitude, but they also indicated that previously held assumptions about the cultural susceptibility or pliability of the indigenous populations needed reconsideration. Furthermore, revelations, such as those found in *Multatuli*, and vaguely sketched schemes, such as Napoleon III's "Arab Kingdom," argued for the need of a more serious "native policy," the creation of a science of colonization — to employ a contemporary expression. Yet the abolition of slavery and the recognition of cultural differences did not mean greater empathy or warmer feelings. As the law softened, sentiment seemed to harden. By the end of the century racism had become a formative factor in colonial thought and practice.

The "Colonial Situation" in Transition

In the vast majority of territories under European control before the

---

[8] A difference of opinion concerning the dating of the change in attitude exists. Curtin suggests the 1830s and 1840s as the period of alteration in British attitudes toward black Africa. See his *Image of Africa*, pp. 235 and 371–373. Bolt sees the turning point as the Jamaican Revolt of 1865, which idea forms the title of her chapter 3 in *Victorian Attitudes*.

[9] Max Havelaar, *Multatuli*, French trans. A. J. Nieuwenhuis and Henri Crisafulli (Rotterdam: Van Den Hoeven and Buys, 1878), p. 105.

nineteenth century, the colonial situation was essentially one of confrontation between the newly emigrated nationals and the colonial administration. What little "native policy" there was actually remained peripheral to metropolitan interests. The principal concern in the settlement colonies was not with social adjustment but with the repulsing or crushing of the indigenous populations. New frontiers were, in this manner, intermittent battle lines, as the general history of American westward expansion suggests. In the trade empires of the Indian Ocean and the eastern reaches of the South Atlantic, the situation was one of negotiation with the peoples of the littoral who performed the universally historical function of middlemen.

The only significant alteration in this pattern of social relationships was that caused by missionary activity. Here dominion of the soul paralleled and occasionally conflicted with dominion of the land and expulsion of the population. Moreover, such missionary effort frequently supported or modified the state's colonial efforts. Catholic missionary procedure in Latin America positively affected colonial principles, if it did not regularly mollify the harshness of colonial practice. And French Catholic endeavors to the north were in harmony with state policy during the days of Richelieu when converts were to be considered, the cardinal declared, "citizens and natural Frenchmen."

Overseas acquisitions in the nineteenth century forced changes in colonial policy, for the obvious reason that the social situation was drastically changed. Most of the new territory contained dense populations, as in India and Indochina, or was not deemed suitable for white settlement. According to many writers, the Europeans now had lands and peoples to control, not colonies to people. Even in the early years of the century, before vast "tropical estates" were made part of the national domain, European thought was occasionally directed toward the issue of "race relations": British involvement in India and French involvement in Algeria required some attention to the condition of the dominated populations. Yet at that time the major European social experience with other than colonists occurred in the region where European imperialism was least intrusive politically. Throughout the history of modern empire the black African populations were as much a subject of social concern as they were of cultural condescension. Edward Blyden, one of the first modern black writers extolling African culture, caught the temper of this ambivalence when he wrote that the well-meaning white "under a keen sense of the wrongs done the Negro, will work for him, will suffer for him, will fight for him, will even die for him, but cannot get rid of a secret contempt for him."[10] The history of European attitudes toward black Africa in the first half of the century is the story of these conflicting sentiments, but with a pronounced humanitarianism not so evident in the later years of the century.

From 1518, when the first shipment of African slaves went directly from the coast of Africa to the West Indian sugar plantations, until the end of the eighteenth century, when the movement against slavery gained momentum, the economy of the New World rested heavily on the shoulders of the oppressed blacks. As the trade intensified, the attitudes of the slavers tended to become routinely commercial: The traffic in ebony was that of a perishable commodity, but it paid exceptionally well. By the middle of the seventeenth century, a clear-cut pattern of intercontinental commerce developed, the famous "triangular trade" among Africa, the Americas, and Europe, which made the fortunes of many men and caused many, many more to suffer the cruel experience of the "middle passage."

To justify and rationalize this undertaking, an elaborate if unsophisticated literature developed which portrayed the black African as an unruly child of nature, a primitive dominated by the dual lusts of sex and violence, a heathen removed from the purifying light of the true faith. If some slavers expressed pity for the brutally uprooted African, others took comfort in the assertion that plantation conditions were better than indigenous African conditions. Most individuals involved in the trade were primarily concerned with its business aspects: their profit and, hence, the physical state of their human cargo.[11]

This rather large group of Europeans that touched upon Africa displayed little genuine interest in the social and cultural environment from which the black African emerged; however, such interest was provided by the increasing number of explorers who ventured into Africa at the end of the eighteenth and the beginning of the nineteenth centuries. Generally, their observations were devoid of contempt, not heavy in condescension, and full of detail. Yet their good intentions were frequently mitigated by the hazardous conditions under which they traveled and the depressing effects of the malaria they often contracted. Moreover, the

[10] Edward Blyden, *Christianity, Islam and the Negro Race* (Edinburgh: University Press, 1967; first published, 1887), p. 132.

[11] On the general subject, see Basil Davidson, *Black Mother: The African Slave Trade* (London: V. Gollancz, 1961).

audience to whom they addressed themselves wanted to learn of adventures, and their writing was directed toward that end. Thus the quality of the observations and the evidence which supported the generalizations were not always very refined.[12]

There was not, therefore, considerable scientifically based knowledge of the African in his native cultural surroundings, but there was nonetheless a substantial literature describing the lamentable condition of the slave. This literature prefaced and seriously influenced the political movement against slavery and forms an interesting aspect of both the religious and the secular thought of the eighteenth century that is called humanitarianism. As concepts of progress, of personal liberty, of social utility, and of *bienfaisance* — the desire to enhance human happiness — all gathered in the minds of polemicists, clergymen, and politicians, the reform of moral and social values occurred.[13]

Although slavery was not a dominant literary theme, it was of considerable significance, for it figured into the general thought about man's natural state, as loftily presented in the myth of the "noble savage." It also was an important institution in North America where the idle dreams and grand theories of the intellectuals of the age were, in reality, being tested. After American independence, the myth of the West became even more boldly defined, and interest in the institution of slavery was more sharply highlighted than it had been before. Slavery was most strongly criticized for being a violation of the basic natural right of man, a birthright that could be neither forcefully seized nor voluntarily surrendered. Socially, the institution was described as one that induced slothfulness and a subservient disposition; economically, it was proven — by Benjamin Franklin — to be less profitable than negotiated free labor.[14]

The real impetus for reform came, however, from religious circles. The new secularism of the eighteenth century infused Protestantism, particularly in Great Britain, with a sense of humanitarianism, a concern with the present as much as the future state of man, and a spirit of philanthropy which would liberate both slaver and slave. It was the Quakers who did the most as a group to force serious political consideration of the evils of the slave trade, but the dominant reformist element was that coterie of able evangelicals known as the "Clapham Sect," ded-

---

[12]Curtin, *Image of Africa*, p. 208.
[13]David Brian Davis, *The Problem of Slavery in Western Culture* (Ithaca, N.Y.: Cornell University Press, 1966), chapters 11, 12, and 13.
[14]*Ibid.*, p. 427.

icated to the lessons derived from biblical learning and hence convinced of the need and efficacy of education for spiritual and social reform. Their ideas were directed against the condition of slaves in the West Indies but were also soon to be found in plans to reform the administration of India.

Within that group the efforts of Granville Sharp and Thomas Clarkson were the most important. Both men wrote on the subject of slavery, and Sharp had the further distinction of initiating the famous Somersett Case of 1772, whereby Chief Justice Mansfield terminated the status of slavery within the British Isles. Clarkson, who avidly gathered in data and documents on slaving along the west coast of Africa, also won over the support of William Wilberforce, then doubly influential as a member of Parliament and as a close friend of the new prime minister William Pitt the Younger. The achievements of these men and many others were concerted in the Society for the Abolition of Slavery, founded in 1787. Success of its immediate objective was achieved in 1807 when the slave trade was abolished by the English government.

By comparison, organized French attempts at abolition were less impressive and much less successful. The Société des Amis des Noirs, rough counterpart of the Society for the Abolition of Slavery, lasted from 1788 to 1793, but neither enlisted popular support as great as that of the English group nor was able to mount as effective a campaign. The socially restricted nature of its membership, the fact that most of its leaders were of Girdonin political persuasion and thus arrested in the 1793 Jacobin Revolt, and the romantically intellectual attitude of its deliberations all tended to the diffusion, not the direction of its endeavors. Granted slavery was abolished in 1794, this was done hastily in face of a slave rebellion in St.-Domingue. That Napoleon was able to reinstitute slavery in 1804 is indicative of the minimal support which the antislavery cause aroused in France, for the revolt in St.-Domingue, like the uprising in British Jamaica a half-century later, engendered a persistent dissatisfaction with liberal policy. The French author Chateaubriand commented, "Who would dare plead the cause of the blacks after the crimes they have committed?"[15]

No humanitarian sentiment comparable to that in Great Britain swept across France in the first years of the nineteenth century. It was only at

[15] On the Société des Amis des Noirs, see Daniel P. Resnick, "The Société des Amis des Noirs and the Abolition of Slavery," *French Historical Studies*, 7:558–569 (1972). Chateaubriand quoted by Gaston Martin, *Histoire de l'esclavage dans les colonies françaises* (Paris: Presses Universitaires de France, 1948), p. 247.

British insistence that the French agreed to back the abolition of the slave trade, and this as part of the negotiations surrounding the return of the colonies to France after the fall of Napoleon. The Second Treaty of Paris, November 20, 1815, contained a statement that the powers would undertake those measures necessary for the swift end of the trade. However, French practice did not follow the official pronouncement, with shippers and merchants participating in the briskly continuing trade. Only in 1818 did the French monarchy pass an ordinance which made the trade illegal, although not a criminal act.

In the 1820s, nevertheless, domestic opinion in both countries was mobilizing in favor of more severe measures to curtail the trade, even to abolish the practice of slavery itself. In France there was a decidedly new expression of concern. Madame de Staël, Prosper Mérimée, and the young Victor Hugo were the most illustrious of a small number of authors who depicted the cruelties of slave existence; the French Academy bestowed official sanction on consideration of the problem by setting as the theme for a poetry contest in 1823, "The Abolition of the Slave Trade." And the Société de la Morale Chrétienne was founded on the principle of abolitionism, an objective to be reached by persuading public opinion through the publication of tracts, much as was then being done in Great Britain.[16]

The earlier active movement in Great Britain was given a new thrust when the foremost issue became the practice of slavery itself. Failure of the abolition of the trade to bring about a noticeable amelioration of slave conditions in the years after 1807 and the continuation of the illegal commerce in Africans by continental merchants convinced many in Great Britain that slavery itself must be frontally attacked. The Anti-Slavery Society was founded in 1823 and immediately centered its attention on possible parliamentary action, initially on the mitigation of slave conditions and then later on total abolition. In 1831, as an offshoot of this society, the Agency Committee emerged, which concentrated on bringing its antislavery message to the people, not the politicians, through the agency of paid public speakers.[17]

The national government was not unsympathetic to the abolitionist position, but it was quite cautious, proposing measures that the colonial

[16] See Gaston Martin, *Histoire de l'esclavage*, pp. 256–262; and Shelby T. McCloy, *The Negro in the French West Indies* (Lexington: University of Kentucky Press, 1966), chapter 8.
[17] Howard Temperley, *British Antislavery, 1833–1870* (London: Longman, 1972), chapter 1.

governments themselves should define as law and implement. However, the radically different perspective on the matter held by the colonial governments, which represented the interests of the plantation owners, led to complaints of metropolitan governmental interference. This reaction, in turn, further fueled the general movement toward abolition. Finally, the heady atmosphere of reform, generated around the Great Reform Bill of 1832, extended to the colonial issue as well. In 1833 an act of emancipation was approved, to be effective the following year. Nevertheless, emancipation was not then to be immediate, but contingent upon a period of apprenticeship lasting eleven years for field slaves and six years for house slaves. To ease their political discontent during the transition, the planters were given a large governmental loan.

The intended transitional period was one of some confusion and some abuse, about which abolitionist groups complained. But henceforth their greatest degree of attention was again directed toward the persistent illegal trade and its intercontinental implications. Here, as many had anticipated, other nations had picked up the activity abandoned by England in 1807. Although the Americans were notoriously in the forefront, French, Spanish, and Portuguese traders were stayed neither by humanitarian protest nor by governmental legislation. And they were willing to face the ever-present threat of the West African squadron, the naval unit Great Britain employed to search and seize ships engaged in the trade.

To some abolitionists the solution to the problem therefore lay far away, in Africa itself, not in the Caribbean colonies or in political arrangements made on the Continent. This redirected attention is no more clearly perceived than in the writings of Thomas Fowell Buxton, in effect Wilberforce's political heir in the abolitionist struggle and in fact a founder of both the Anti-Slavery Society and the Agency Committee. In the new edition of his *African Slave Trade*, published in 1840, Buxton added a section as long as the original text entitled *The Remedy*, which offered an argument soon to become one of the most popular and compelling: the slave trade could most efficiently be destroyed by the introduction of legitimate trade.

Convinced of the inherent wealth of the African continent and concerned about how it would be exploited by the indigenous populations, Buxton looked to European-stimulated commerce as the way to convince Africans to stop participating in the slave trade. "What we want is to

supplant the Slave Trade by another trade, which shall be more lucrative." The involvement of European agricultural instructors, the stimula-
tion of an export trade along the newly explored interior rivers, and the
introduction of financial aid to African chiefs were suggested by Buxton as
means to this end. Most of all he believed in the social power of Christianity. "This mighty lever, when properly applied, can alone overturn the
iniquitous systems which prevail throughout that continent."[18]

Like his contemporary Livingstone, Buxton proposed the combination
of Christianity and commerce. The empire they both desired to establish
in black Africa was not territorial, but of the spirit and in the market. "I
entirely disclaim any disposition to erect a new empire in Africa," Buxton
wrote — and with what he considered to be the bad experience of India in
mind. "What is the value to Great Britain of the sovereignty of a few
hundred square miles in Benin or Eboe, as compared with that of bringing forward into the market of the world millions of customers who may
be taught to grow the raw material which we require, and who require
the manufactured commodities which we produce?"[19]

The general thrust of such arguments was also felt in France where a
liberal spirit in politics and trade was affecting thought about the French
West Indian possessions. Men like the economist Hippolyte Passy, the
political theorist Alexis de Tocqueville, and the poet Alphonse de Lamar-
tine participated in what was a liberal protest against slavery. The year
before Buxton published *The African Slave Trade* in its original form,
1839, the French government entertained with much acrimonious debate
and no decision a proposal, sponsored by Passy, that would have allowed
the manumission of slaves by way of purchase and freedom at birth for all
children born of slave parents after the promulgation of the proposed law.
The Société pour l'Abolition de l'Esclavage, founded in 1834 and listing
the three figures mentioned above among its members, was the principal
driving force in the demands for reform, but some idea of the growing
pressure from the politically active portion of the French population can
be ascertained by a petition of 1844 that contained eleven thousand signa-
tures.[20]

Yet the institution of slavery persisted amid governmental investigation
and discussion until 1848, at which time the provisional government of

[18] Thomas F. Buxton, *The African Slave Trade and Its Remedy* (London: John Murray,
1840), p. 511.
[19] *Ibid.*, pp. 453–454.
[20] See Gaston Martin, *Histoire de l'esclavage*, pp. 281–291.

the Second Republic legally abolished it. This climactic event, dressed in the rhetoric of French republicanism, reiterated the principles of the French Revolution — sincerely believed in by many as the only basis for a viable colonial theory. The Alsatian minister Victor Schoelcher, who stood in the forefront of French abolitionist activities as Buxton had earlier in Great Britain, gave particular meaning to the word *fraternity*, as employed in the famous republican triadic verbal device, when he stated that "the republic no longer intends to make distinctions within the human family."[21]

The humanitarian pronouncements that gave the antislavery movement its nobility and inspired support in an increasingly liberal Europe were not unalloyed. The coincidence of the most intense activity of the antislavery movement with the advent of industrialization in Great Britain was indeed significant. Even at the time the slave trade was being abolished in Europe, English commercial considerations were suspected of being involved. The Duke of Wellington wrote to Wilberforce at the time of the Congress of Vienna: "It is not believed that we are earnest about it, or have abolished the trade on the score of inhumanity. It is thought to have been a commercial speculation. . . ."[22]

There is no doubt that the hue and cry over the plantation system as it existed in the West Indies intensified as that institution declined in profitability. The continental opponents of the planters were "not only the humanitarians but the capitalists. The reason for the attack was not only that the West Indian economic system was vicious but that it was also so unprofitable that for this reason alone its destruction was inevitable."[23] Men like Buxton did indeed combine commerce and humanitarianism, arguing that free labor in a self-regulating market system was a good in and of itself. However, such evidence does not severely discount the other motives that lay behind their desire to abolish slavery.

If industrialism made the slave system anachronistic, it did nothing to improve the condition of the black African in the colonial world. The economics of slavery persisted well into the nineteenth century, for the economic role forced upon the African for hundreds of years did not quickly change with emancipation. The history of continuing servitude in

---

[21] Schoelcher quoted by D. Bruce Marshall, *The French Colonial Myth and Constitution-Making in the Fourth Republic* (New Haven, Conn.: Yale University Press, 1973), p. 31.

[22] Letter dated September 15, 1814, quoted by Buxton, *African Slave Trade*, p. 442.

[23] Eric Williams, *Capitalism and Slavery* (New York: Capricorn, 1966; first published, 1944), p. 135.

the Caribbean colonies and in the American South is a familiar one. Furthermore, it should be remembered that the illicit slave trade continued on the west coast of Africa until Brazilian abolition in 1884. On the east coast the Arab-directed slave trade remained a major issue in European arguments for intervention and later domination, as witness the debates at the Brussels geographical conference called by King Leopold II in 1876. More significant, the black African was theoretically given only a slightly altered role once the new colonial era was initiated. The economic development of acquired territories depended on African labor, and thus a feudallike relationship was established with the European acting as lord over the African who was required to assume the function of serf. Yet such bifurcation of activity was defended, often sincerely if smugly, on the basis of the civilizing effect of regularized labor. About this aspect of colonial ideology, as will be indicated below, there hovered the claim that idle hands do the work of the devil.

The altering colonial situation, in which the social attitude of the black African was to be the most discussed, was already in evidence during the period of abolitionism in the Western world. At this moment when humanitarianism achieved its victory, political expansion and consequent European governmental involvement in the tropical world provoked new thought, as it necessitated new action, on the issue of racial relationships. The two regions where this concern was now most obvious were British India and French Algeria.

Although there is a variety of differences existing between the two areas as problems or paradigms of early nineteenth-century European imperialism, there is also a number of tempting analogies. It is important to remember that both India and Algeria remained the premium colonies, the oldest and most essential units of the new empire, and the regions in which doctrinal debate over colonial policy was initially the liveliest. Of course, British rule in India extended much further back in time than did French rule in Algeria, and India was never thought of as a colony of settlement, while Algeria rapidly acquired that status. However, in the early nineteenth century both possessions were the subject of similar considerations, relating to what today might be called modernization. If development was the broad concern, the cultural method by which it was to be achieved was the immediate issue. In British colonial history, this issue is defined as the Orientalist-Anglicist controversy; in the French, its counterpart centers on the argument of the Arabophiles. With the extension and intensification of British influence in India in the late eighteenth century, and seen against the previous history of the rapacious and self-serving activities of the East India Company, the need to improve local administration was evident. Whether the establishment of an effective civil service and of satisfactory cultural relations between the government and the indigenous governed would follow a policy of accommodation to local languages and culture or a policy of imposition of English customs was the major question underlying the Orientalist-Anglicist controversy. From the period of the governor-generalship of Warren Hastings (1774–85), the Orientalist approach was well defined, realized in the founding of schools that taught Indian classical languages, notably Sanskrit, and in the scholarly efforts to edit and publish the major works of Indian literature.[24]

Against this tradition, but nearly coeval with it, was the Anglicist approach, which began during the administration of Cornwallis (1786–93) with the assertion that English administrative and governmental institutions were necessary for good rule, but which later proceeded to a strong indictment of Hindu culture. Only by the introduction of English culture, it was now declared by the Anglicists, would there be any noticeable improvement in the condition of the indigenous populations. Based upon the thinking of evangelicals, liberals, and utilitarians, this argument stressed the need for order and reason in institutional organization and — depending on the particular beliefs of the proponent — the superiority of either the Christian religion or western science.

The antagonism between these two broad cultural positions was gathering for several decades and climaxed in the early 1830s when Thomas Babington Macaulay, future historian and then petulant Indian civil servant, wrote his famous "Minute" on Indian Education. Yet Macaulay's argument, however forceful, was neither original in thought nor sudden in impact; rather it rested on the ground prepared by two other men, James Mill and Charles Trevelyan. Mill had written the first major historical study of modern India, *The History of British India*, which appeared in 1818 and which — in considerable measure because of the author's eminence — was read and appreciated as were few works on India at that time or later. Even though Mill did not know any Indian language and

---

[24] On the subject see David Kopf, *British Orientalism and the Bengal Renaissance: The Dynamics of Indian Modernization, 1773–1835* (Berkeley: University of California Press, 1969).

had never visited the land, his comments were trenchant and fixed. Treating Hindu culture with contempt but accepting Mogul India with restrained respect, he saw little in the Indian past which was other than dismal and discouraging for the future. Mill was not an Anglicist in the sense that he demanded the introduction of English law and language, but he was a modernist who wished to discard as much of the indigenous past as possible in the name of utilitarianism: good government and economic prosperity.[25]

Charles Trevelyan, an employee of the East India Company and a remarkably outspoken young man who was to become Macaulay's brother-in-law, entered, indeed greatly aroused the controversy in 1833. Trevelyan's was also the utilitarian, the pragmatic approach to the problem. He denounced Oriental studies and the expenditure of money and effort on the dissemination of Indian classical languages and their literature. His chief desire was to bring to India the practical wisdom of the West, whether that be conveyed to the Indian mind in English or the vernacular. In a letter to the governor-general Lord Bentinck, Trevelyan remarked in 1833 that he wanted to dedicate himself to "the moral and intellectual regeneration of the people of India," which endeavor he expected to realize through a nationwide educational system.[26]

Macaulay presented the Anglicists' argument in its most trenchant form in his brief "Minute" on language instruction before the Supreme Council of India. Although personally unversed in either Arabic or Sanskrit, he unhesitatingly discarded these languages as vehicles of instruction in favor of English. His reasons supporting this position amounted to a total denunciation of Hindu civilization and unmitigated praise for European culture. What the English language contained and could best express, he maintained, was a literature "of greater value than all the literature which three hundred years ago was extant in all the languages of the world together." Not only was this extravagant statement obviously ethnocentric but it was also modern, a declaration of a post-Newtonian who saw in science and rationalism a kind of wisdom which paled all that preceded it and all yet untouched by it, like the Hindu, for example.[27]

[25] Bearce, *British Attitudes*, pp. 69–78.

[26] Quoted by John Clive, *Macaulay: The Shaping of the Historian* (New York: Alfred A. Knopf, 1973), p. 360.

[27] Macaulay's "Minute" on Education, dated February 2, 1835, in H. Sharp, ed., *Selections from the Educational Records of the Government of India*, pt. I, 1781–1839, reprinted in Philip Curtin, ed., *Imperialism* (New York: Harper & Row, 1971), p. 183.

Supporting his position by historical analogy, Macaulay first referred to the influence of Latin and of Roman literature on early England, and then he turned to a more recent instance of cultural transfer with the assertion that "the languages of Western Europe civilized Russia." Now, he thought, the same might be done for Hindu civilization, which he deprecated as a combination of "absurd history, absurd metaphysics, absurd physics, absurd theology. . . ." To the contention that only through instruction in Arabic and Sanskrit would Indian cooperation be acquired, Macaulay replied in terms echoing a common imperialist assumption: "I can by no means admit that, when a nation of high intellectual attainments undertakes to superintend the education of a nation comparatively ignorant, the learners are absolutely to prescribe the course which is to be taken by the teachers." But Macaulay totally dismissed this particular contention with the further statement: "We are forcing on them [the Indians] the mock learning which they nauseate."[28]

The proposed benefits of English were to be conferred upon a native elite, not broadcast to the majority of the population as Trevelyan desired. "We must at present," Macaulay insisted, "do our best to form a class who may be interpreters between us and the millions whom we govern; a class of persons, Indian in blood and colour, but English in tastes, in opinions, in morals and in intellect."[29] In this remark Macaulay gave full expression to the assimilationist ideal and suggested what was the most ever to be accomplished — the creation of a group of cultural middlemen, évolués, to employ a later French term, destined to assist in the colonial enterprise, yet later and unintended to be the first generation of a nationalist elite seeking greater control over the destiny of its land.

Macaulay's "Minute" has occupied an important place in modern colonial thought and academic commentary on it.[30] Few assimilationist statements exceeded it in directness and cultural assertiveness. In addition, it was a preface to frostier Victorian opinions: it bordered on arrogance in tone, racism in mood, and paternalism in purpose.[31] Yet it was never realized in any meaningful way as official policy, because the first Afghan War drained away the money that might have been channeled toward such reform. After the Sepoy Mutiny Englishmen in India were

[28] Ibid., pp. 191 and 185.
[29] Ibid., p. 190.
[30] See particularly the comments of Kopf, British Orientalism, chapter 14; Bearce, British Attitudes, chapter 6; and Clive, Macaulay, chapter 12.
[31] See the comments of Kopf, British Orientalism, pp. 245–247.

not so confident of their ability to make a world over in their image — nor did they ever again find it so desirable.

The French "native problem" in Algeria was, in its broad terms, not markedly different from the British in India. Whether to maintain and work through indigenous customs and institutions or to impose civilization *à la française* was the major and constant concern, but one seriously qualified by the presence of a substantial settler population. The first meaningful expression of a native policy did not occur until the Second Empire of Napoleon III.[32] Before that period the difficulties of military conquest and general administrative organization were all-consuming. Where thought was given to cultural matters, the French tended to rely on the policy of assimilation, a policy supported by the universalism so evident in the concepts of the French Enlightenment and in the principles of the great revolution. The belief in the common rationality of mankind and the political goal of establishing a "republic one and indivisible" were translated into colonial theory as cultural and administrative assimilation, the need to absorb the colonial possessions and their populations into the French system of ideas and things. Predominantly an element of French republican ideology, assimilation ran through French colonial theory and practice from the previous days of the Bourbon monarchy to the future moments of the Fourth Republic. It had a long history, this *idée force*.[33]

What first provoked serious consideration of the future of the indigenous Algerian population were the thoughts of the French utopian socialists and the sudden intentions of the emperor Napoleon III, inspired by a trip to Algeria. Here again, the problem can be loosely defined as one of modernization: what ought to be done to alter the Algerian social and cultural situation in order to assure what the Europeans believed to be the march toward progress.

The utopian socialist colonial view was not widely removed from the English utilitarian one. Where Trevelyan and Macaulay desired instruction in the useful and the reasonable, the utopian socialist looked to technological innovation and social rationalization as the catalysts for wondrous changes. For Père Enfantin, Saint-Simon's most influential follower, Algeria was to be a training center — a normal school, as he

---

[32] Hubert Deschamps, *Méthodes et doctrines coloniales de la France du XVIᵉ siècle à nos jours* (Paris: A. Colin, 1953), p. 113.

[33] See Raymond F. Betts, *Assimilation and Association in French Colonial Theory, 1890–1914* (New York: Columbia University Press, 1961), chapters 1 and 2.

called it — in which colonization would be "the achievement of labor, of agriculture, of industry." Already during the July Monarchy (Enfantin had himself resided in Algeria between 1838 and 1841) the Saint-Simonians were seeking reform, notably in the field of education, for the purpose of leading the Algerian population away from its traditional culture toward that of technological Europe. Enfantin employed the term *affamiliation* to describe the kindred relationship he wished to establish between the French and the Algerians.[34]

This furtherance of the assimilationist tendency was somewhat diverted a few years later by the early and influential ideas of Thomas Urbain, a Saint-Simonian in training and a member of the colonial administration. Urbain, born of a French father and a Guayanan mother, personally endured some of the problems caused by the racism that he tried to resolve in Algeria. His own involvement in Arab affairs began in 1833 when he traveled with Enfantin to the Near East, at which time he converted to the Islamic faith and took the name "Ismael." His colonial career began when he was made interpreter for the commanding general in Algeria, Thomas-Robert Bugeaud, but his real importance was achieved when he became counsellor on Arab affairs to Napoleon III. In fact, it was after reading Urbain's most recent work that Napoleon III issued his famous letter on the "Arab Kingdom" in 1863, a letter in which the language of Urbain was recapitulated along with the thought.[35]

Urbain was the outstanding exponent of the Arabophile position in Algerian colonization. He initially rejected the Saint-Simonian idea of assimilation and insisted that a policy of association be adopted. From his view the Arab peoples were distinct in culture, and therefore European colonization would necessarily have to be *contact à distance*, based on a policy of slow evolutionary change in customs and institutions. Urbain assumed that eventually a "new people" would emerge, "conserving its idioms, its customs and diverse beliefs," but sharing with the French the same general sentiments.[36]

As his ideas were elaborated, they revealed his desire for a joint colonial effort, an association of the two resident peoples in mutually support-

[34] Enfantin quoted by Marcel Merle, *L'anticolonialisme européen de Las Casas à Karl Marx* (Paris: A. Colin, 1969), pp. 348–349; on the idea of *affamiliation* and its role in French colonial theory, see René Maunier, *Sociologie coloniale*, 2 vols. (Paris: Éditions Domat-Montchrestien, F. Loviton, 1932–1949), I, 70.

[35] Charles-Robert Ageron, *Les Algériens musulmans et la France* (Paris: Presses Universitaires de France, 1968), I, 407.

[36] Quoted in *ibid.*, p. 404.

ing tasks, out of which would arise a "French Algeria," not an "African France." The French colonist would initially supply not only new techniques and methods of organization but also the knowledge and capital needed for industrial development. The Algerian, in turn, would be primarily responsible for the agricultural functions. In this arrangement Urbain expected equality under the law and eventually a cultural equality once Algerian society was modernized.[37]

Yet even though Urbain publicly denounced assimilation as being potentially more disastrous than advantageous to the Algerian population, he agreed with his Saint-Simonian peers and with the general argument of French colonial theory that the chief purpose of the colonial effort should be a civilizing one.[38] Urbain's ideas were anything but popular among the French civilians and the military in Algeria, but they did receive the enthusiastic endorsement of Napoleon III, with that ill-fated figure announcing in his famous letter that the French "would bring the benefits of civilization" to the Algerians. Yet nothing of substance came immediately, for colonial resistance was strong and the Second Empire collapsed in the Franco-Prussian War of 1870.

This brief survey of the major developments in English and French colonial thought suggests that general objectives were not dissimilar among any of the cultural interpretations; the process by which these objectives were to be attained did vary, however. Adherents to the Orientalist and the Anglicist schools in India were in agreement that the improvement of the condition of the Indian populations was a primary responsibility of the English; so were the French Arabophiles and the assimilationists with respect to Algeria. The conflicting approaches presented in their arguments, which would recur throughout the history of modern European imperialism, are most readily characterized by the words *assimilation* and *accommodation*. The Anglicist and French assimilationist schools generally considered their national language and educational process the only means by which the indigenous populations could be made to progress measurably; the Orientalist or accommodationist school — represented in Algeria by the earlier ideas of Urbain — believed that the local culture and languages were sufficiently adaptable to allow progress to occur within their native framework.

Still circulating through all this thought was a considerable spirit of

[37]*Ibid.*, p. 407.
[38]*Ibid.*, p. 412.

good will, an infusion of the humanitarian into the utilitarian. Most of the theorists were reformers of sorts, in no way shaken in their belief that the Europeanizing effort abroad was both noble and right. During the second half of the century, and particularly in the last two decades, this attitude was altered. *Civilisation oblige* still remained the continental imperative, but now, in both theory and practice, the primary imperial function was to establish control, or to dominate the peoples under European authority in order to lead them.

The general decline in Europe of the universalistic and liberal ideals so prominent in colonial thinking during the first decades of the century left its mark on theory, as did the effects of Social Darwinian thought. The new social emphasis in colonial ideology was on order and stability. "Efficiency," a favorite word of the Fabians, is perhaps most descriptive of professed colonial intentions; and this was to be achieved first by "protection," a popular colonial term employed by both the French and the English to define their basic political function abroad.

Before Social Darwinism provided a pseudoscientific justification for this new attitude, there was already a discernible disallowance of the supposedly mollifying effects of cultural assimilation. A series of insurrections and revolts in the colonial world raised doubts as well as fears about any harmonious society of the future. An insurrection in Algeria in 1845–46, the Sepoy Mutiny of 1857, and the Jamaican Revolt of 1865 all detracted from a socially liberal colonial policy. The Algerian insurrection dissuaded many resident French from any idea of association such as that just being proclaimed by Urbain, but the upheavals in the British empire, heavily commented on by the press, were much more important in results. The humanitarianism of the earlier period was berated as being unrealistic, while, conversely, the notion that barbarism and savagery were constant factors in African society was harshly emphasized. The *Times* editorialized on November 13, 1865, that the "signs and symbols of civilized society" must be constantly exhibited before the "barbarians" under British rule; such, repeated many critics, was the lesson of Jamaica.[39]

Strong rule, not compassion, was henceforth the watchword in colonial affairs; a spirit of imperialism was abroad, to be intensified by new theories of domination and authority derived from political interpretations of Darwinian thought. "I am out here to work," commented one

[39] *Times* quoted in Bolt, *Victorian Attitudes*, p. 92; also see her analysis, pp. 92–102.

of the main characters in E. M. Forster's *A Passage to India*, "to hold this wretched country by force. . . . We're not pleasant in India, and we don't intend to be pleasant. We've something more important to do."[40] The concept of guardianship, so effectively articulated here, was widely subscribed to even before World War I and the publication of Forster's novel.

Guardianship, or The New Paternalism

The attitude of cultural aloofness that is prescribed in so many colonial analyses of the late nineteenth century was most obviously conditioned by two factors: a shift in European ideas of social and sexual propriety and the acceptance of a scientific attitude. Neither the one nor the other can easily be dated or readily defined, but both immediately suggest a serious departure from the values of the eighteenth century.

If, as one critic has cleverly put it, this shift in behavior can be appreciated in English manners by comparing *Tom Jones* with *Pride and Prejudice*, so it might be extended in appreciation by comparing Molière's Monsieur Jourdain with Flaubert's Monsieur Bovary.[41] The English aristocrat was no longer to be a self-indulgent rake and the continental member of the middle class was no longer to be a *bourgeois gentilhomme*; they both were required to be more serious and austere now. Respectability seems the best word to use in describing the new social norm, with private behavior judged in the public domain, as unlike before, in matters of decorum and decency. To phrase it in a Victorian manner, one must act properly and maintain a personal deportment consonant with one's social station and expected sense of social responsibility. In this severely male-dominated society, one was obliged to strike a stern pose — as nearly every daguerreotype portrait still brings to sight.[42]

In an exaggerated and not always successful way — if later novelists are to be believed — this concept of social behavior was transported to the colonies, particularly the British, where it appeared in deeds of daring and self-abnegation, all encased in the harsh-sounding word *pluck*. "Good

---

[40] E. M. Forster, *A Passage to India* (New York: Harcourt, Brace, 1952; first published, 1924), p. 50.

[41] Philip Mason, *Patterns of Dominance* (London: Oxford University Press, 1970), p. 95.

[42] On this subject see the interpretation of Peter T. Cominos, "Late-Victorian Sexual Respectability and the Social System," *International Review of Social History*, 8:18–48; 216–250 (1963).

form" now demanded that the European stand apart from the local population: miscegenation was frowned upon where it had been countenanced before; personal respect was required for the sake of national pride and as an indication of racial superiority. Rectitude before the indigenous population was thus deemed necessary; "going native" was in the worst of taste. In what must be its classical form, this new social mood appeared chambered in Stanley's mind at the time of his famous meeting with Livingstone. "I must not let my face display my emotion," he thought, "lest it shall detract from the dignity of a white man appearing under such extraordinary circumstances."[43]

Socially and culturally two sets of individuals stood apart. Many Frenchmen admired the quality of the lesser Stanleys who did service in the British empire. "These island people," wrote one, "maintain wherever they are the rigidity of their manners which creates space around them, isolates them anew in an island."[44] As this statement suggests, the new hierarchy of ruler and ruled thus created a social distance which made, in Forster's wonderful line, bridge parties impossible. Once again "empire" became an active political word, describing despotism and domination. Such empire was declared an imperative: it had to be; it was a condition and a duty deriving from the responsibility of civilization.

Such cultural attitudes were reinforced by scientific judgments. Toward the end of the century the French spoke of a new "colonial sociology," which allowed for detached appreciation of the colonial situation and which dispelled any false sentimentalism. This sociology was Darwinian in mood; its first assumption was the law of evolution which forbade divine intervention and forced history to follow natural and therefore understandable patterns of development.[45]

Environmental influences played the most significant role in the thinking of late century theorists. Climate and topography had, of course, been factors in comparative cultural analysis for centuries, as witness the writings of Montesquieu, for instance. But with the natural scientific bent of the Darwinian age, the idea of social adaptation to physical and historical milieus suggested a slow and steady discriminating process which fixed cultures as firmly as it did races. Furthermore, the principle of

[43] How I Found Livingstone, quoted by Cairns, Prelude to Imperialism, p. 38. Chapter 2 of Cairns's work provides an excellent portrait of the Victorian Englishman in East Africa.

[44] Jules Blois, "Les Anglais dans l'Inde," Revue bleue, April 11, 1903, p. 477.

[45] On the ideas of "colonial sociology," see Leroy-Beaulieu, De la colonisation chez les peuples modernes, II, 619–621.

adaptation-to-environment was allowed to dictate the limitations of any proposed sociocultural change in the colonies. Gustave Le Bon, the most influential evolutionist in France at this time, told the International Colonial Congress of 1889: "Neither by education, institutions, religious beliefs, nor by any means at their disposal, will Europeans be able to exercise a civilizing action on the Orientals, and even less so on peoples who are completely inferior. The social institutions of these peoples are the consequences of a mental make-up which is the work of centuries and which centuries alone can transform."[46]

Although Le Bon did not in this case directly refer to cultural attributes as part of the individual's heredity process, he and others argued that such inheritance did occur. Psychological disposition, like biological characteristics, was acquired by way of inheritance and hence was not susceptible to rapid change. The "barbarism" of the black Africans was determined by environmental adaptation and the instinct to racial preservation, soberly commented a French colonial administrator. Therefore, he admonished, "Do not weigh down their infantile ideas, their limited brains with the mass of our hereditary aptitudes, our moral subtleties, our scientific speculations."[47]

That there was nothing novel or startling about these comments when they were offered in 1912 clearly suggests that the literate European public had by then accepted the idea of cultural heredity and social differentiation among the races as an unquestioned proposition of contemporary life. What particularly concerned many European theorists who addressed themselves to colonial problems was the possible effects of racial intermixture. Only a few saw any benefit deriving from interracial union in the colonies. Sir Harry Johnston, an English administrator in East Africa who was also a prolific writer, recommended sexual relations between the Indian and the African. "The mixture of the two races would give the Indian the physical development which he lacks," Johnston asserted, "and he in his turn would transmit to his half Negro offspring the industry, ambition, and aspiration towards a civilized life which the Negro so markedly lacks." Viewing the problem of miscegenation with a sense of greater inevitability, a French administrator in Algeria assumed that one day a new form of humanity would appear there, growing in

---

[46] Gustave Le Bon, address to the Première Séance Générale, *Congrès colonial international de Paris, 1889* (Paris: A. Challamel, 1889), p. 74.

[47] A. Cureau, *Les sociétés primitives de l'Afrique Equatoriale* (Paris: F. Alcan, 1912), pp. 24–25.

response to the law of sexual attraction and the "zootechnical" law which "requires every animal species imported into a new environment to mix gradually, even if remaining pure, with the similar native species."[48]

As if in accordance with Johnston's declaration, the French philosopher Alfred Fouillée, respected as a scientist in his day, saw racial mixture among near equal races, whether high or low on the evolutionary ladder, as one means, besides education, by which peoples might become civilized. However, he severely cautioned against miscegenation among widely separated peoples. "Unite a Bushman and a European woman," he ominously warned, "and the struggle of antagonistic elements, instead of taking place among diverse individuals, will be transported to the heart of the one and same individual. You will have a personality divided against itself. . . ." Le Bon also voiced such an opinion, but not so dramatically. For him such unions always worked to the disadvantage of the "superior" race.[49] And Lord James Bryce, as wise and temperate a man as the age produced, supported this general position in his 1902 Romanes Lecture:

Now for the future of mankind nothing is more vital than that some races should be maintained at the highest level of efficiency, because the work they can do for thought and art and letters, for scientific discovery, and for raising the standard of conduct, will determine the general progress of humanity. If therefore we were to suppose the blood of the races which are now most advanced to be diluted, so to speak, by that of those most backward, not only would more be lost to the former than would be gained to the latter, but there would be a loss, possibly an irreparable loss, to the world at large.[50]

The inescapable division of humanity, which all these racially imbued ideas affirmed, imposed an even more severe rigidity on colonial relationships. Under no acceptable conditions could the European be expected to be part of indigenous society, nor could he yet anticipate the day when that society would be sufficiently informed, according to his standards, so that it would thrive without his rule. The paradox arising out

---

[48] Sir Harry Johnston, *Report by Commissioner Johnston of the First Three Years' Administration of the Eastern Portion of British Central Africa*, quoted by Cairns, *Prelude to Imperialism*, p. 207; Auguste Billiard, *Politique et organisation coloniales* (Paris: Girard and Brière, 1899), p. 286.

[49] A. Fouillée, "Le caractère des races humaines et l'avenir de la race blanche," *Revue des deux mondes*, July 1, 1894, pp. 91–92; Gustave Le Bon, *Les premières civilisations* (Paris: Marzon and Flammarion, 1889), pp. 159–162.

[50] Lord James Bryce, *The Relations of the Advanced and Backward Races of Mankind: The Romanes Lecture of 1902* (Oxford: Clarendon Press, 1902), p. 36.

of imperialist practice by democratic states was thus dispelled in theory: good government meant continuation of their domination; self-rule only meant anarchy.[51] The colonial enterprise was therefore viewed as a long-range proposition, cautiously responding to evolutionary process and respectful of the obligation imposed on the ruler by his cultural maturity. "For the primitive, left to himself, does not always understand what conforms to his own interest properly understood, to his greater happiness. And this is why it is the duty of the civilized, the more enlightened and more experienced, to take those measures necessary for the defense of the best interests of the natives, despite the resistance which may arrive from their ignorance." These sober words were written in French, but they could in their day be matched many times over in most any European language.[52]

The qualities of European superiority listed by contemporaries were as much of the material as of the immaterial. Frequently, there was confu-

[51] Lord Cromer, *Ancient and Modern Imperialism* (London: John Murray, 1910), p. 118.
[52] G. Valmor, *Les problèmes de la colonisation* (Paris: Marcel Rivière, 1909), p. 92.

Coaling a royal mail packet in Jamaica, 1865. From *Illustrated London News*, November 25, 1865. (Reproduced by permission of *Illustrated London News*.)

THE ILLUSTRATED LONDON NEWS

REGISTERED AT THE GENERAL POST OFFICE AS A NEWSPAPER.

No. 2961.—VOL. CVIII.   SATURDAY, JANUARY 18, 1896.   WITH FOUR-PAGE SUPPLEMENT, GREAT BRITAIN'S NAVAL PREPARATIONS   SIXPENCE BY POST, 6½d.

Mining in Johannesburg, 1896. From *Illustrated London News*, January 18, 1896.
(Reproduced by permission of *Illustrated London News*.)

Porterage: Burton's march toward Central Africa, 1857–58. From James W. Buel,
Heroes of the Dark Continent (Philadelphia: Historical Publishing Co., 1890).

sion of the two or an ill-defined causal connection between them. In a
simple proposition, physical power seemed to generate metaphysical
Power. That adept and intrepid West African voyager Miss Mary H.
Kingsley summed up the issue in the following comment: "All I can say is,
that when I come back from a spell in Africa, the thing that makes me
proud of being one of the English is not the manners or customs up here,

Lipton's tea advertisement depicting a Ceylonese tea plantation, 1896.
From *Illustrated London News*, February 29, 1896.
(Reproduced by permission of *Illustrated London News*.)

certainly not the houses or the climate; but it is the thing embodied in a great railway engine."[53]

Even the relationship of Christianity to western civilization, a relationship often pondered by missionaries, was confounded by the assertion that European technological superiority was irrefutable proof of cultural superiority. The missionary might claim that such material progress was the result of the radiant guidance of the Christian God, while the secular rationalist might attribute it to the uniquely scientific bent of the western mind.[54]

As the described genius of the West was technological and organizational, so the lack of material innovation was considered proof of the inferior status of other peoples. In the sardonic words of the French colonial novelist Pierre Mille, "The Chinese, having no railroads, no mechanical textile machinery, no Napoleon and no Moltke, are extremely

[53] Mary H. Kingsley, *West African Studies* (London: Macmillan, 1899), p. 385.
[54] On this see Cairns, *Prelude to Imperialism*, notably pp. 199–201.

inferior to us."[55] Where seriously entertained, such a line of thought carried the corollary that the indigenous populations were all in need of regular work habits and material values like those which had made the West great. That most enterprising of European monarchs, Leopold II, gave simple structure to this general idea when he praised the Dutch use of forced labor in Java by stating that it was "the only means by which to civilize and moralize these indolent and corrupt peoples of the Far East."[56]

As a component of the social logic of the day regular work was made an obvious characteristic of civilized behavior and, consequently, a precondition of success in colonial development. Leopold was hardly the only commentator to describe the peoples of the Far East as irresponsible or corrupt in their work habits. But most attention was directed toward Africa where the parent-child metaphor was constantly employed and where, in Victorian mood, the need for discipline was deemed a categorical imperative. For every Albert Schweitzer given to romantic sketches of the black African as a child of nature who only had to reach about him to satisfy his basic needs, there was a troupe of critics who saw the African as primitive, to the point of lacking the westerners' organizational capacity.[57] Expressing the prevalent environmental thesis, one Belgian in the service of Leopold remarked: "The Congolese Negro is not just the indolent imagined. . . . He is in addition given to irregular work habits. His primitive customs have not allowed him to know the value of time. His easy existence has not imposed upon him punctuality. . . . His commercial instinct, when developed, will provide him with a sense of money which will incite him to work; his extraordinary aptitude for imitation will assure him rapid and numerous improvements."[58]

Because of the assumed incompetence of the non-European to superintend modern economic activities without guidance, there soon followed

---

[55] Pierre Mille, "La race supérieure," Revue de Paris, February 15, 1905, p. 821.

[56] Letter from the Duc de Brabant to Major Brialmont, dated July 26, 1863, quoted in Léon LeFebvre de Vivy, Documents d'histoire précoloniale belge, 1861–1865 (Brussels: Académie Royale des Sciences Coloniales, 1959), p. 20.

[57] See Albert Schweitzer, On the Edge of the Primeval Forest (New York: Macmillan, 1948; first published, 1923), p. 76.

[58] Ferdinand Gaffart, "Le main d'oeuvre," in Ferdinand Gaffart, ed., L'oeuvre coloniale du Roi en Afrique (Brussels: Imprimerie Veuve Monnom, 1898). In a similar vein, Cecil Rhodes remarked on the advantages of a money tax: "You will remove [the Africans] from that life of sloth and laziness: you will teach them the dignity of labor and make them contribute to the prosperity of the State: and make them give some return for our wise and good government." Quoted in Basil Davidson, The African Slave Trade: Precolonial History, 1450–1850 (Boston: Little, Brown, 1961), p. 110.

the argument that the European had to unearth the treasures still untouched and unappreciated by indigenous populations. Of the many expressions of this theme none was more widely appreciated in its time than that of Benjamin Kidd, self-taught English anthropologist, whose *Control of the Tropics* enjoyed enormous popularity. As the title of the book suggests, Kidd was concerned with who would control the economic resources of the tropics which he considered essential to European prosperity. Yet he believed that the development of such regions hitherto excluded from concourse with Europeans would assist the people resident there as well as the Europeans. The crux of Kidd's argument, however, is found in the following assertion: "Over a considerable proportion of these regions at present we have existing a state either of anarchy, or of primitive savagery, pure and simple, in which no attempt is made or can be made to develop the natural resources lying ready to hand."[59]

Supporting such an assertion of the need for all the world's regions to participate fully in the European-directed market system, many critics joined Kidd in anticipating Lord Lugard's famous "dual mandate," the provision of European civilization in return for the extraction of colonial resources. Of course, in the thinking of many imperialists this could and did necessitate an economic interdependence of unequals. The new colonial situation, defined by the laws of natural adaptation and those of the marketplace, suggested a modern-day variation of the old Pauline organic metaphor of social organization. "The civilized," a French author stated, "is the brain which thinks; the native is the arm which performs."[60]

In all this thought the older notion of *civilisation oblige* did not disappear; it was redefined. Not so much as schoolmaster but as taskmaster was the European immediately to benefit the indigenous populations. Assimilation as a cultural objective was everywhere discarded, and nowhere with more doctrinaire pronouncements than in France. Denounced as naive or idealistic in theory and as disruptive in practice, it was replaced by sterner theories of social relations. Justice, not indulgence, was the key word; its complement was respect for, not interference with local customs.[61]

More recently defined "native policy" thus traded the older humanistic

[59] Kidd, *The Control of the Tropics*, p. 15.
[60] Valmor, *Problèmes de la colonisation*, pp. 78–79. For a critical interpretation see Mille, "La race supérieure," p. 822.
[61] On this changing attitude, see, for instance, Betts, *Assimilation and Association*, chapter 6.

universalism for a stiff scientific acceptance of persistent and only slowly yielding cultural differences. Earlier hopes for grand imperial amalgams now faded, brightening again only rhetorically on glorious occasions such as "Empire Day." To the scientifically bent colonial theorist the new empires were destined to be temporary affairs, even though no one at the time anticipated the quick end that did indeed befall them. "Only one thing is possible," argued a French colonial administrator, "and that is to find the most effective means of making human beings accept a condition of temporary subordination from among the choice of affection, force or interest."[62]

In retrospect it can be seen that little affection was deeply generated, and mutual material interest was primarily restricted to only a few, a native elite introduced to and allowed to enjoy on a large scale the material benefits of the Western World. Force, however sparingly or symbolically displayed, was the ultimate cohesive, in fact as well as in the minds of many authors at the turn of the century. "The history of large empires formed of different races has always been the same," solemnly wrote Le Bon in 1899. "But with rare exceptions, all large empires uniting dissimilar peoples can only be created by force and are condemned to perish by violence."[63] These words were probably not considered prophetic in their day; they were probably not dimissed as outlandish either.

Even though Social Darwinian ideas of harsh domination in the world overseas were generally approved, few theorists who rejoiced in their nation's imperial undertaking were ever willing to deny the obligation they considered imposed by the high state of their civilization. Yet it was an obligation for which they anticipated respect from the colonial peoples rather than devotion.

[62] Billiard, *Politique et organisation coloniales*, pp. 275–276.
[63] Gustave Le Bon, *Les lois psychologiques de l'évolution des peuples* (Paris: F. Alcan, 1894).

PART III

Policies, Practices, and Protests

It is the largest Empire that now exists or that has ever existed. But numbers are not the main thing, excepting as indicating the scale of importance and responsibility; the test is not size, but the work done . . . the general impress left upon the well-being of mankind.

Lord Curzon, "The True Imperialism"

The civil service had a reputation, chiefly self-perpetuated, for efficiency. But it became evident that outside the narrow sphere of work to which they had been accustomed, they were helpless and incompetent.

Jawaharlal Nehru, *The Discovery of India*

Imperialism, it has been suggested, is a process, and empire is an administrative condition. The latter as a problem in constitutional organization has received the considered attention of many scholars and now occupies a more important place on library shelves than it did in the minds of the most ardent proponents of expansion. For the colonialist on the spot the essential matter was not structure but policy, and that was all too frequently a local and daily reaction.

In part this situation was the necessary result of geographic conditions. Until the latter part of the nineteenth century communication was a leisurely affair, still not universally wired. In 1828 the British undersecretary of state for colonies complained about the short-term legislation passed in Van Diemen's Land (Tasmania) which expired even before it reached London and possible judicial review.[1] And the dramatic death of Gordon by the dervishes at Khartoum, which occurred on January 25, 1885, was not known in London until February 5. Add to this time lag the

[1] See D. B. Swinfen, *Imperial Control of Legislation, 1813–1865: A Study of British Policy towards Colonial Legislative Powers* (Oxford: Clarendon Press, 1970), p. 3.

185

high ministerial officials' lack of firsthand knowledge of their colonial possessions, consider the prolonged period of "pacification" which allowed a high hand to military officers, and the gap between metropolitan intentions and colonial realities becomes as obvious as it was wide.

In effect, then, there were two colonial policies, sometimes in opposition and seldom well synchronized until the end of the century. This dichotomous situation actually meant that much of the inspiration and formulation of national colonial policy emanated from the colonies and was only structured in theory and in law at home. Given the generally authoritarian nature of colonial government, the governor ruled in the guise of a sovereign, as certainly did the viceroy of India at the end of the century, when he appeared with all the splendid trappings of an oriental despot.

Colonial administration was complicated by one other general feature worth mentioning, and this is contained in the word *discovery*. Regularly used at the time, the term essentially conveyed the meaning of physical encounter, not intellectual appreciation. If the average European was ignorant of the extent of the empire held under his nation's sway, the average administrator was ignorant of the culture and the language of the indigenous peoples he was supposed to serve. His attitude therefore was either arrogant or paternalistic, neither designed to enhance cooperation or mutual respect.

For a brief interlude colonial policy and practice were effective enough, or harsh enough, or brazen enough — for they variously appeared in all these poses — to assure a balance of local power. However, in that time few expansionists worrisomely sighed, as did Napoleon's mother for her son's imperial system, "If it only lasts."

CHAPTER 6

The Structures and Organization
of Empire

Few terms would strike contemporary ears with a more distant ring than "seat of empire," by which London was described in many nineteenth-century accounts. The settled concentration of power which the term suggests is almost a metaphorical contradiction of the reality that extended in so many directions from this and other imperial capitals. In fact, colonial empire was a diversified collection of territories, peoples, and administrative problems. The single common intention of the politicians and administrators involved in the management of these overseas units was order, a *pax colonia* which in a never clearly defined way was supposed to benefit all those who faced the colonial situation.

Only in the early years of the twentieth century can the historian find well-articulated administrative policies in most parts of the colonial world, attempts to balance theory and practice, and efforts to make intelligent accommodation to local needs. But the interwar years, the age of bureaucratic rule, constituted a brief, transitional period, which was totally unanticipated by any imperialist. The failure to perceive the imminence of decolonization may in part explain the slow installation of effective administrative organization, but a more important reason is found in the general lack of national interest. Neither great sums from the national treasury nor large numbers of the national reserve of human talent were channeled outward to the colonies. The entire enterprise was to be conducted "on the cheap," at minimal cost to the country and its citizenry. Given this condition no one should be surprised to find that the provisional, the ad hoc, the "make do" are the real elements of most colonial practice in the 1800s, elements often testing the ingenuity of the administrator on the spot and allowing for regular expression of his good will or ill humor.

Yet when fitted into the general mosaic of nineteenth-century European political and administrative history, imperial organization is not badly out of place. The age of directed development, of state planning, was certainly not the 1800s. Rather this was the era of the "night watchman state," as Ferdinand Lassalle so derisively yet aptly described it. The liberal stress on personal freedom and private property formed the philosophical base for the general middle-class belief that the state's social role should be to protect its citizens against disorder. The regulatory state did begin to emerge by mid-century, it is true, with the introduction of labor legislation. But the interventionist state dedicated to general social welfare is essentially a twentieth-century structure, a slow and rather confused undertaking, initially a response to World War I and the economic depression it provoked. Thus the administration of empire could not be expected to be more elaborate or socially motivated than that of the metropolitan state upon which it directly depended. When the French started speaking of *mise en valeur*, of economic development for their colonies, in the first years of the twentieth-century, their intention may have been selfish, but their outlook was quite far-ranging. Not until the interwar years did the first meaningful plans for development reach paper and receive governmental consideration; not until after World War II did colonial development — modernization — become the primary activity.

In historical contradistinction to this brief survey of nineteenth-century conditions stands a number of men who did speak and write in terms that would suit most contemporary definitions of modernization. A list of their suggested imperatives would include the following: the necessity to force capital formation; the requirement to develop education of a secular sort in order to train indigenous elites capable of participating in administration; and, above all, the urgency of providing the territory with an infrastructure, with ports and railroad systems. If the *broussard*, the "bush" officer, seldom rose above paternal considerations, higher placed administrators did at times have visions almost reaching forward to the developmental plans of their late twentieth-century descendants, who saw empire in its terminal decade as a problem in economic and social rationalization. These constructive imperialists found no one among their

Proposed statue commemorating Napoleon III's visit to Algiers, 1865.
From *L'Illustration*, September 16, 1865.

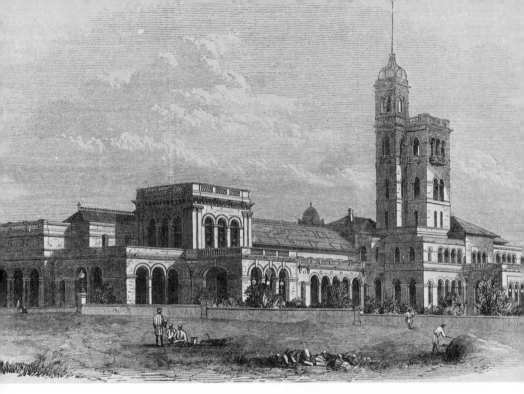

New government house, Poonah, Bombay, 1870. From *Illustrated London News*,
March 12, 1870. (Reproduced by permission of *Illustrated London News*.)

ranks more active than General Louis Hubert Lyautey, French resident-
general in Morocco, well known for his urban planning and priding himself with the self-assumed title of "builder."[1]

Persons like Lyautey could pretend to such a role because of the authority they enjoyed, which was guaranteed as much by national distance
and indifference as by the legal basis upon which they stood. Even with
the advances made in the technology of communication, imperial administration remained more a colonial than a national affair and, on that
level, more a personal than a collective operation. Discussing British
administration in mid-century, one historian has stated: "Much of the
business was transacted at Government House by the governor and his
private secretary alone, with little or no reference to any other administrative agency."[2] And speaking of his role in West Africa immediately after World War I, Robert Delavignette, who was to become
one of France's most influential colonialists, commented that he was less

[1] On Lyautey's role as "builder," see "Lyautey," special number of *L'officier de reserve*,
n.d., thirty-fourth year of publication.

[2] John Cell, *British Colonial Administration in the Mid-Nineteenth Century: The Policy-
Making Process* (New Haven, Conn.: Yale University Press, 1970), p. 63.

an administrator than a commander, in effect a surrogate "chief."[3] Such independence of action and extent of personal responsibility are indicators of the loose links in the colonial chain of command.

Influencing every evaluation of administrative conditions was one primal realization grasped by all: the new colonial experience was at considerable variance with the old because of the social situation it provoked. Earlier empire, of which the United States was the most significant decolonized unit, was principally settlement empire. The major administrative and political procedures involved the extension of metropolitan institutions to new regions inhabited by displaced nationals. Along with these settlement colonies, there were the "mixed" colonies, those in which European colonists and institutions subordinated or destroyed indigenous ones. Spanish America was the most obvious example.

The majority of the colonial territory acquired in the nineteenth century — Algeria and South Africa being the notable exceptions — did not fall into either of these two categories. What the English came to call their "dependent empire" provided a new experience for the European states. As late as 1882, Sir John R. Seeley wrote of India in his *Expansion of England*: "It is so different in kind from both England itself and from the Colonial Empire [the white-settlement colonies] that it requires wholly different principles of policy."[4] Granted India was an unusual instance because of its size and complexity, it was not unique; it did, however, become something of a colonial paradigm, offering instruction to the British in Egypt and West Africa, and causing the French to pause in reluctant admiration. What Seeley and his contemporaries observing India and other such possessions recognized was this: the colonial situation now meant the juxtaposition of two different, complex civilizations, whose interaction would not lead to "colonization" in its more pristine meaning.

The apparent newness of this relationship and its deviation from contemporary European political thought induced the colonial theorists to reach back to Rome in their search for historical reference. The fascination with Roman culture was a characteristic of nineteenth-century Europe which merits more historical consideration than it has yet received. Its impact, however, can easily be seen in a range of styles and

[3] Robert Delavignette, *Service africaine* (Paris: Gallimard, 1946; first published, 1940), p. 29.
[4] John R. Seeley, *The Expansion of England* (2nd ed.; London: Macmillan, 1911), p. 220.

mannerisms running from the wearing of clothes reminiscent of Republican Rome during the era of Napoleon's consular government to the late nineteenth-century construction of New York's Pennsylvania Station as a steam bath of Caracalla. Rome wended its metaphorical way through the century to be most generously received in imperialist thought. There Rome signified power, power heroically scaled: the mighty expansion of a small city state. And that earlier Latinization of so much of the Mediterranean world also suggested a proselytizing spirit pretending to moral goodness. The power of a highly formed civilization — this was the similarity that modern Europeans saw between their imperium and that of Rome's. The likely effects were best assessed by Lord James Bryce in his appreciation of conditions in British India: "The government of India by the English resembles that of her provinces by Rome in being virtually despotic. In both cases, whatever may have been done for the people, nothing was or is done by the people."[5]

Although the references to Rome were made for purposes of historical allusion, not contemporary emulation, they are particularly revealing of the awareness of the size and anticipated political significance of modern empire. As the nineteenth century closed, the nettlesome administrative problem was how to organize these empires so that they might both evoke the coherence and promise the endurance of that magnificent empire which had preceded them. Speaking of his own nation's effort, Lord Curzon remarked: "The Empire is still only in a fluid and transitional formation; it has to be welded into a great world state."[6] That objective was as grand as it proved to be unrealistic, but it suggests in extreme form the organizational problem that taxed, not the treasury, but the European imagination and institutions throughout the century.

Administration and Administrators

If, during the course of the nineteenth century, there was little reason for the structure of empire to be provided with the pyramidal definitions characteristic of metropolitan government, there was no more reason for it to be marked by any elaborate organization. Only late in the century was so much territory effectively occupied that administration became a

[5] Lord James Bryce, *The Ancient Roman Empire and the British in India* (London: Oxford University Press, 1914; first published, 1901 as part of *Studies in History and Jurisprudence*), p. 28.
[6] Lord George Curzon, "The True Imperialism," *Nineteenth Century*, 63:162 (1908).

problem sufficiently demanding to force home governments to the realization that centralization of the decision making process was necessary, as was decentralization of the means of enacting that policy. Then empire was so ordered that a meaningful bureaucratic form was achieved by the early twentieth century. At home a cabinet position was allotted to the colonies, with a minister usually assisted by a consultative council. Abroad the state delegated its authority to a governor who was less military commander than chief civilian administrator.

Yet the paper arrangements were not quickly matched by effectively altered political realities. The immensity of imperial holdings and the disparity of social relationships forced upon both permanent and temporary occupants were bound to cause a host of administrative problems and continued to do so well into the twentieth century. Earlier these problems were complicated by the fact that imperialism, as an aggressive act, involved the army and the navy and, hence, the state agencies from which their authority immediately derived.

The most significant official change in administrative structure at the turn of the century was the creation of separate colonial ministries. The small cluster of dates marking this change also stands as something of a turning point from the era of military conquest, "pacification," to that of bureaucratic rule, the so-called "colonial peace." Although Great Britain and Holland had such ministries before this time, France, Belgium, Germany, Italy, and Portugal established them between 1894 and 1911.[7] Most of the "dependent empire" fell directly under their jurisdiction, but it is interesting and important to note that not all possessions in all continents were so placed administratively. Both of the major imperial powers tolerated diverse modes of control. Within the French system, the "protectorates" of Tunisia and Morocco fell under the jurisdiction of the Foreign Office, while Algeria was, in the late nineteenth century, a direct responsibility of the Ministry of the Interior as the result of administrative assimilation. In the British system the "dependent empire" was under the supervision of the Colonial Office, India was the responsibility of a separate state secretary, and Egypt and the Anglo-Sudan Condominium were handled by the Foreign Office.[8]

An additional complication arose from the role of the military. As the

[7] The dates for the establishment of separate ministries of colonies are as follows: France, 1894; Germany, 1906; Italy, 1907; Belgium, 1910; and Portugal, 1911.
[8] On the various constitutional arrangements, see, n.a., *Organisation politique et administrative des colonies* (Brussels: Etablissements Généraux d'Imprimérie, 1936).

dominant agency in colonial acquisition the military continued to intrude into administrative matters during that long period of "pacification" which climaxed in the 1890s but continued in some cases well into the twentieth century. Instances of rivalry between civilian and military authorities are not hard to find, particularly among the French in Subsaharan Africa.[9]

Of more consequence was the military impress on the formation of an administrative pattern. Again the French, this time in Algeria, offer the most meaningful example. The colony was divided into military and civilian zones, a division which, like the Italian one in Libya, persisted well into the twentieth century. The Bureaux Arabes, established by General Bugeaud in 1841, were agencies that controlled areas under military domination and were staffed by officers trained in the language and culture of the region. From Algeria the military mode of organization was transported to West Africa through the person of Captain Louis Faidherbe, commandant of Senegal in the middle of the nineteenth century. The basic unit of administration he implanted there was the *cercle*, a military territorial division that retained its name even after the advent of civilian rule. In Portuguese Africa, the belated occupation of the hinterland after 1890 brought about fundamental reforms. Following their activities in Mozambique, a few soldier-administrators sought institutional renovation and realized that only through effective civilian control could Portuguese domination be assured. As a result of the suggestions offered by Eduardo da Costa, governor first of Mozambique and then of Angola at the turn of the twentieth century, the old military captaincies were replaced with civilian circumscriptions headed by civilian administrators. That this reform was embodied in a colonial act of 1907 gives some indication of the persistence of military influence.

At home jurisdictional divisions also reflected the importance of the military. Even in liberal England the combined secretaryship of war and colonies continued until 1854, although the Colonial Office had by then become a self-sufficient administrative unit. In France, the colonies were for long periods of time attached to the Ministry of the Marine, but, after being shunted about between that ministry and the Ministry of Commerce, were finally located in a separate ministry in 1894. In Germany, where a colonial division was first formed within the Foreign Office in

[9] See, for instance, the comments of Catherine Coquery-Vidrovitch, "French Colonization in Africa to 1920: Administration and Economic Development," in L. H. Gann and Peter Duignan, eds., *Colonialism in Africa, 1870–1960*, vol. I: *The History and Politics of Colonialism, 1870–1914* (Cambridge: At the University Press, 1969), p. 175.

1890, military affairs in the colonies retained a certain autonomy, for they continued under the administration of the Ministry of the Marine until 1896.

As the foregoing no doubt suggests, problems of colonial organization were many, but they aroused no great domestic interest and hardly inspired much parliamentary involvement. In this intensely political age, the issues of empire were seldom more than routinely considered by the parliaments, the running of the colonial machinery being left to the care of the bureaucrats in the colonial offices. Most frequently, the political responsibility for the governance and order of the empire rested with the executive branch, where it had arrived by way of legislative delegation or historical accident, the latter the result of constitutional crises and change during this revolutionary century.

Arranged on a scale of increasing legislative responsibility and administrative decentralization, the Dutch colonial system at the beginning of the century and the Belgian system at the end would appear first. In both Holland and Belgium the monarch exercised unusual control over colonial affairs for a considerable period of time. From the end of the Napoleonic era until the constitutional reforms of 1848, the king of Holland was held to no ministerial responsibility and was given further free rein between 1836 and 1848 when the Council of the Indies was reduced to the status of a consultative body. Thus, during this time span, the king ruled directly through his appointed minister at home and his appointed governor in the East Indies. The Belgian situation was unique, because the Congo Free State was Leopold II's personal possession, recognized at the Berlin West African Conference as a state and ruled over by a sovereign who was not constitutionally limited to one throne. Until he was forced to turn the Congo over to Belgium in 1908, Leopold II personally ruled like an absentee merchant-prince.

In the new parliamentary order that appeared in France, Germany, and Italy after 1870, executive authority over colonial matters was generally maintained. The French system was constitutionally the most curious, since it was essentially dependent on one piece of legislation left over from the Second Empire. The *Senatus-consulte* of 1854, which was primarily effected to regulate the constitutional structure of the then major colonies of Martinique, Guadeloupe, and Reunion, also asserted that the other colonies, at that time a minuscule cluster primarily on the west coast of Africa, would be governed by imperial decrees until they, too, were provided with particular *senatus-consultes*. This, however, did not happen, meaning that the act of 1854 imposed the requirement of special legislation for colonies acquired in the future — and these colonies were, of course, to become the immense portion of the French colonial empire. As the *Senatus-consulte* was never replaced or abrogated, it in effect became a colonial charter. Henceforth, most of the colonies had to be treated to special legislation; otherwise all laws in force in metropolitan France were effective in the colonies only if implemented by a ministerial decree.

In both Italy and Germany the domestic constitutional order had been completed in a precolonial epoch and therefore had included no provisions for an expanding state. Because parliamentary legislation provided the legal means for colonial annexation in Italy, parliamentary control was by and large accepted, but, as in France, the executive generally handled all administrative matters through royal decree. The German situation was quite different in its development, however. Although the kaiser was legally and effectively sovereign over the colonies and appointed the governors who were responsible directly to him, the Reichstag had an enormous, if unintended role. In the newly federated German nation, the Reichstag primarily controlled the finances of the federated state; the annual review of proposed colonial revenues occasioned extensive debate as well as allowed for considerable control of administrative policies through parliamentary funding of them. The centralized nature of the German colonial empire was a direct consequence of this political relationship.[10]

At the far end of the scale of increasing legislative responsibility would be Great Britain. The settler colonies had enjoyed representative government since the early days of the Virginia colony and in the nineteenth century would obtain responsible government. As the legislative function was in considerable measure transferred overseas, the arrangement did raise an important question of the possible inconsistency between laws passed in the particular colonies and those established for the empire as a whole. This issue was resolved in the most significant piece of imperial constitutional legislation passed in the century: the Colonial Laws Validity Act of 1865. Where local legislation was in disagreement with imperial

---

[10] See John Iliffe, "The Effects of the Maji-Maji Rebellion of 1905–1906 on German Occupation Policy in East Africa," in Prosser Gifford and William Roger Louis, eds., *Britain and Germany in Africa: Imperial Rivalry and Colonial Rule* (New Haven, Conn.: Yale University Press, 1967), pp. 564–565.

law such legislation, the act stated, would not be acceptable insofar as it was "repugnant" — in conflict with that imperial law. As for the growing "dependent empire," appointed governors were responsible to the Colonial Office, which in turn was officially responsible to Parliament through its secretary of state.

This similar relationship maintained between European parliaments and their nations' colonies, which can be described as casual except where budgetary matters were concerned, was matched in mood and method by the system of recruitment of personnel in the nineteenth century.

Seldom were administrators in the "heroic age" of empire well prepared by formal training or by previous experience for the tasks they were challenged to meet. The only service which stood out splendidly was the India Civil Service, effectively organized through the means of competitive examinations after changes were inaugurated in 1854. In that year the Northcote-Trevelyan Report appeared, the basis for general national administrative reform and a severe indictment of previous policies of recruitment and promotion which were denounced as a series of arrangements for assuring a "competence" to incompetents. Merit, not influence, intelligence, not endurance would be the new determinants of acceptance into and promotion within the system. In 1864, the Dutch also introduced an entrance examination for their candidates in the East India Service, thus adding a new qualification to the previous one of attendance at the colonial school in Delft. This institution was paralleled years later by the French Ecole Coloniale, which soon became the most significant European institution for colonial administrative training. Even before World War I, its impact was being felt in Africa, where its graduates were particularly directed. But the French colonial service obtained only part of its elite, not all its members, from this school before World War I.[11]

In every national colonial administration, the recruitment of personnel was both a difficult and an irregular process. Not infrequently the recruits at the lower echelons, particularly those in Africa, possessed less than satisfactory qualifications, educationally and socially. And at the higher levels their training and experience left much to be desired, whatever their degree of educational attainment and personal rectitude. Even the candidates obtained in the 1890s from the English and Irish universities

[11] See William B. Cohen, *Rulers of Empire: The French Colonial Service in Africa* (Stanford: Hoover Institution Press, 1967), chapter 1.

for administrative service in Egypt, men who were required to pursue a year's course of study in Arabic at Oxford or Cambridge, regularly arrived still functionally illiterate in the language and seldom proceeded to be well versed in it even after years of residence in the land.[12] Thus technical expertise and any particular cultural appreciation of the region served were neither the norm nor the practice with administrators.

Under this constellation of conditions colonial rule can best be seen as irregular, depending more on the mettle of the man and the nature of the social situation than on the structure of the system. Only the white-settled dominions and British India stand out as meaningful exceptions in the nineteenth century; elsewhere the improvisational usually had precedence over the institutional. However, this generalization needs some qualification when extended to the overall framework in which such colonial activity took place. For during the last decades of the nineteenth century colonial possessions were being defined as regional administrative units. This new structure imposed some restraints, as indeed it provided some order, both deficient, however, to the tasks defined in official ideology.

Modes of Colonial Administration

With the exception of the white-settler colonies of the British empire — those areas in the early twentieth century described as dominions and endowed with institutions of home rule — the vast tracts of territory incorporated into the European political system were ruled neither politically nor democratically, but administratively and autocratically almost to the end of the colonial era. This seeming dichotomy between the governmental trends at home and those abroad was as much the result of accident as it was of calculation, however grandly elaborate were the theories designed to explain and justify it.

Yet the general modes of colonial administration were discernible well before the "New Imperialism" enormously enlarged the problems of such rule. Indeed, the basic catalyst of change was the overseas war waged sporadically during the French Revolutionary and Napoleonic eras. By the successful outcome of this activity Great Britain found itself confronted with a new array of colonial territories and administrative prob-

[12] See Robert Tignor, *Modernization and British Colonial Rule in Egypt, 1882–1914* (Princeton, N.J.: Princeton University Press, 1966), pp. 187–190.

lems, the latter presaging what the rest of Europe would encounter in its imperialist involvement.[13]

For the first time the state — the East India Company had already been so involved — directly engaged populations that were not simply displaced nationals. In an enormous triangle stretching from the Caribbean to Cape Colony and then on to Ceylon and Java, British rule temporarily extended over alien peoples whose domination was assured only by the sword, not by transplanted institutions. The temporary expedient of rule by a military governor became, in those areas still retained by Great Britain after the Napoleonic era, the crown colony system, a type of autocratic control by a governor appointed by the crown and advised, but not bound, by an appointed colonial council. The issue of such rule was first joined in 1794 when the commander in chief of the West Indies Sir Charles Grey requested of the home government that civilian governors be placed over the territories newly conquered from the French. These governors were sent out and were provided with instructions which clearly stated that "all Powers of the Executive Government within the said Colony as well Civil as Military shall be invested in You our Governor. . . ."[14] This was the root clause of the crown colony system which, with but slight variation, became the dominant form of colonial government in the early nineteenth century.

At this time British policy exhibited tendencies toward both direct and indirect administration. The latter was most obvious in the former French colonies in the Caribbean and even Quebec, where French customs as well as institutions were allowed to continue regulating many aspects of the habitants' social and legal life. In a contrary manner, direct administration appeared most strikingly in Britain's brief, but influential control of the Dutch East Indies.

Although the history of the British occupation of Java is most remembered because of its economic effects, changes in administration were still significant, if unenduring. The efforts of Sir Stamford Raffles, who took over the administration of Java after the British defeated the Dutch-Napoleonic forces on the island, have been regularly praised in historical narrative, yet they are sequential to and constructed upon the

[13] Note the comments of W. D. McIntyre, *Colonies into Commonwealth* (New York: Walker, 1966), pp. 33–34; and David K. Fieldhouse, *The Colonial Empires: A Comparative Survey from the Eighteenth Century* (London: Weidenfeld and Nicolson, 1966), pp. 81–83.

[14] Quoted by Helen Taft Manning, *British Colonial Government after the American Revolution* (New Haven, Conn.: Yale University Press, 1933), p. 342.

policies introduced by the Dutch governor Herman Willem Daendels. During the three years of his rule, 1808–11, Daendels sought the administrative renovation of the colony. Its semifeudal form, which derived from the long rule of the East India Company, was replaced by newly defined administrative units. Called prefectures, they were assigned to prefects who acted as advisers to the Javanese regents, the semiautonomous officials selected by the company to handle its affairs in the provinces. In turn, the regents' position was redefined so that they became colonial administrators, enjoying the Dutch rank of lieutenant-colonel but no longer enjoying all the emoluments that stemmed from their earlier political condition.

These initial efforts, realized more on paper than in actuality by Daendels, were continued to greater effect by Raffles. Under his administration the regents were reduced even further in status and now were made directly responsible to the European residents, the name Raffles used in place of the French-inspired term *prefect*. Furthermore, he deprived the regents of their previous authority in matters relating to the magistrate and revenue collecting. Through these changes direct, centralized rule was instituted. "Salvation," wrote an outstanding Dutch colonial theorist, "was expected, mistakenly it proved, from direct contact between an enlightened European administration and the Javanese population."[15]

One other early attempt at direct administration merits consideration, that of France in Algeria. Here again the military experience determined the incipient action, although a soon installed settler population introduced political tensions not so boldly displayed elsewhere. The tendency toward bureaucratic and centralized control was stronger in French colonialism than in others, and Algeria, where the practice of administrative assimilation was most elaborate, stands out as the best, because the worst example of direct rule.

After the hesitations of the July Monarchy, which was initially confronted with the military situation left behind by Charles X, the Second Republic incorporated Algeria into the French body politic in 1848. This continuation of the earlier revolutionary objective of a "republic one and indivisible" was realized in Algeria by administrative reforms which eventually divided the colony into three regional departments, ad-

---

[15] A. D. A. de Kat Angelino, *Colonial Policy*, trans. G. J. Renier (Chicago: University of Chicago Press, 1931), II, 28. See also the comparison of Daendels and Raffles offered by J. S. Furnivall, *Netherlands India: A Study of Plural Economy* (New York: Macmillan, 1944), chapter 3.

ministered as were their metropolitan equivalents. The particular local services of the colony were controlled by the relevant metropolitan governmental agencies, and the French residents were allowed to participate directly in the national legislative elections.

These arrangements were as short-lived as the Second Republic which inaugurated them. However, after a round of experiments during the Second Empire of Napoleon III, the return to administrative assimilation was made by the Third Republic in 1879. Then the policy of *rattachement*, by which all Algerian administrative functions were "attached" to the appropriate metropolitan agencies, was pursued. In effect, Algeria became an overseas prolongation of France. Although this condition was modified by reforms initiated in 1890, at which time the governor of Algeria was invested with considerable powers, the tendency toward direct rule and centralized authority continued to remain, until the end of empire, the hallmark of French colonialism in Algeria.

With the rapid acquisition of tropical territories toward the end of the century, the enormity of the administrative task and the paucity of available administrators almost forced indirect supervision to be the more practiced one among all European colonial powers. In its most famous form this method was the "indirect rule" followed and doctrinized by Lord Frederick Lugard in northern Nigeria at the turn of the century. But as Lugard's biographer has argued, indirect administration is as old as colonial empire itself.[16] A cheap, convenient mode of alien control, it suggests domination through the use and manipulation of existing indigenous institutions. Most widely practiced in Subsaharan Africa between the world wars, it made its first appealing modern appearance in British India.

The admiration and zeal for emulation that British control of India aroused in the minds of imperialists of many nationalities were inspired by the observation of a few thousand Englishmen dominating a subcontinent of many tens of millions. When the government took over from the East India Company in 1858, it intensified more than altered the preceding policies of control which might best be described as mixed. Within "British India" itself, less than half of India at mid-century, the bureaucratic authority of the India Civil Service continued to provide what Lugard later called "a model of beneficent, bureaucratic rule."[17] In the

[16] Margery Perham, *Lugard*, vol. II: *The Years of Authority, 1898–1945* (London: Collins, 1960), pp. 141–142.

[17] Lord Frederick D. Lugard, *The Dual Mandate in British Tropical Africa* (3rd ed.; London: William Blackwood, 1926; first published, 1922), p. 46.

rest of the territory, scattered among some five hundred "protected states," the British controlled indirectly, using resident advisers to assure that local policy would be in keeping with British interests. It is this latter arrangement which had widespread appeal, although a Dutch shift to indirect rule in Java during the brief governorship of Johannes van den Bosch in the early 1830s was also respected.

These colonial experiences in the East were replicated in the West when North Africa fell under European control. Both the British in Egypt and the French in Tunisia and Morocco attempted to rule indirectly. Such an approach was no doubt partly the result of the hesitancy that first accompanied their invasion. As is well known, the British assumed that the occupation of Egypt would be temporary, the duration determined strictly by the amount of time needed to introduce administrative reforms, primarily to make the country fiscally responsible. The French official purpose for intrusion into Tunisia in 1881 was to chasten the government for its tolerance of raids into neighboring Algeria. But rapid military success converted military occupation into long-term political domination, just as delayed reform had the same effect on the British in Egypt.

In both cases, and later in Morocco, officially taken over in 1912, colonial control meant a form of administrative parallelism, with European advisers serving on all levels of indigenous government and all advisers responsible to the senior European officer — the consul-general in Egypt, the resident-general in Tunisia and Morocco. But it should be noted that the British position was initially the more tenuous because of international involvement in Egyptian finances and in the railroad system. This state of affairs required the English to count heavily on the willingness of the khedival government to cooperate with their reformist policy. However, largely through the determination of Evelyn Baring, later Lord Cromer, who was the major British figure in Egypt, control over the government was tightened, particularly in the 1890s when the ministries of justice and the interior fell under English sway. By the turn of the century Egypt was in fact ruled by the British who had set for themselves the objective of administrative efficiency.

The French administrative objectives in Tunisia and Morocco were not at severe variance with those of the British in Egypt, but the general political arrangement was cast in a "protectorate." Essentially this meant that the French government assumed all responsibility for foreign and military affairs, leaving to the indigenous regime the continuation of domestic policy, though under French guidance. The French-appointed resident-general was therefore automatically made minister of war and of foreign affairs; he exercised effective control over domestic affairs by being required to countersign any executive decree. Finally, it was his obligation to chair the state council of ministers, another activity assuring that he was the power behind the throne. Under the residency-general of Lyautey in Morocco the protectorate form of indirect rule was elevated to an impressive art, almost as resplendent in its trappings as its Indian predecessor.

By the end of the century all colonial theorists and most administrators were praising indirect administration as the means by which to secure imperial domination at minimum cost and with a maximum of local support. Yet the demands of political modernization allowed for no simple retention of the precolonial political-administrative system. Traditional offices were forced to new uses; new activities necessitated new services. However unintentionally, therefore, indirect rule gave way to bureaucratic rule; the dysfunction of indigenous institutions was thus begun.

As administration assumed some regularity toward the end of the nineteenth century, the overall structure of empire gained in consideration. From the metropolitan point of view, the issue was that of finding out how to organize the surrounding empire, if not into a coherent whole, then at least into large units guaranteeing both efficiency and profit. Even the French, who have been regularly labeled by historians as assimilationist and centralist in their colonial thinking and practice, argued against any "bloc" theory of empire.[18] On the contrary, they, like the English, were fascinated with the prospects of federation. Indeed, the tendency toward federation in the French and British empires is the most interesting administrative development in the last two decades of the nineteenth century.

Imperial Federations

In an opinion offered in 1892 by George R. Parkin, a Canadian who later became president of the Royal Geographical Society, "The aspect of the whole world irresistibly supports the thought that we are passing from a nation epoch to a federation epoch."[19] Among the major states of the

[18] For a strong French statement in opposition to the "bloc theory" of colonization, see Joseph Chailley-Bert, *Dix années de politique coloniale* (Paris: A. Colin, 1902), pp. 1–2.

[19] George R. Parkin, *Imperial Federation: The Problem of National Unity* (London: Macmillan, 1892), p. 27.

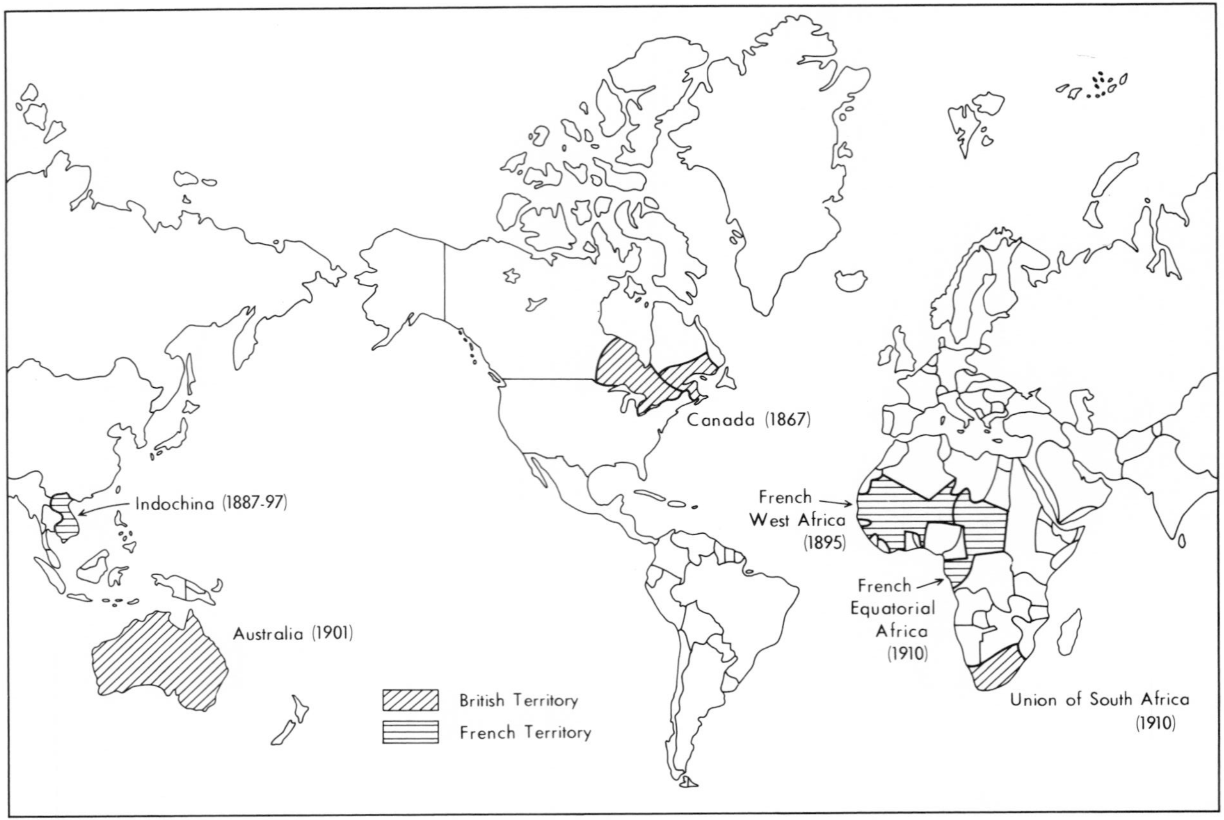

Union of South Africa (1910)

French Equatorial Africa (1910)

French West Africa (1895)

Canada (1867)

British Territory

French Territory

Indochina (1887-97)

Australia (1901)

Growth of federations in the colonial world before 1914

world, several varieties of such organization had already appeared: the United States of America, Imperial Germany, and the Dual Monarchy of Austria-Hungary can all be described as federal in some respect. And within the British empire itself, the successful federation of Canada in 1867 indicated a similar development.

There is no doubt that the changing factor of communication was most important in making large-scale federation seem both attractive and imperative. As one Canadian historian has said of the completion of the Grand Trunk Railroad in 1860: it was a "railway in search of a state."[20] In fact, a number of imperialists including Froude, Seeley, Milner, and Hanotaux all commented on the extensive binding qualities of the railroad.

The greater dimensions that federation suggested were desired not only for administrative efficiency but also for the effective pooling of resources. And along similar lines, federation promised the regional self-sufficiency that would help empire to guard against the international uncertainties of the day: economic competition and military rivalry. As a zollverein, or customs union, and as a *Kriegsverein*, or military league, a federated empire was theoretically attractive.

However, the generalizations just presented — which also were made by many imperialists of the time — will only lightly support an attempt to draw a comparison between French and British efforts at imperial federation. The British effort was primarily restricted to the white-settler colonies and was intimately connected with the movement toward local legislative control; the French examples of federation are found in the dependent empires of Indochina and black Africa, and they were closely tied with economic and administrative centralization. Because it was both more modest in scope and less significant in result, the French effort can be more readily considered.

Almost simultaneously in the late 1890s the French administrations of Indochina and West Africa were overhauled so that the disparate possessions in each region were brought under the unified administrative control of a governor-general who was supported by a set of federal institutions through which general economic and administrative policy was established. The more intrepid and individualized attempt by France at

---

[20] A. R. M. Lower, *Colony to Nation*, quoted by Nicholas Mansergh, *The Commonwealth Experience* (London: Weidenfeld and Nicolson, 1969), p. 50.

federation took place in Indochina, an achievement primarily of Paul Doumer, governor-general from 1897 to 1902.

Although the title and office of governor-general had been adopted in 1891, the position remained undeveloped and without supporting institutions until Doumer began his administrative renovation. At that time Indochina embraced four countries under various kinds and degrees of French control. Cochin-China at the tip of the peninsula was assimilated administratively, but Annam, Tonkin, and Cambodia were under a form of protectorate. With rapid decision Doumer moved to establish effective rule over the three nonassimilated territories where, it can be said, French policy was inchoate. In Cambodia he imitated British policy toward the princely states of India; in Annam and Tonkin he developed a modified form of indirect rule by allowing the French residents great executive power, channeled through the mandarins whom he retained in the provinces.

The most distinctive changes took place in the now centralized administration of the government through which Doumer personally intended "to govern everywhere and administer nowhere."[21] Henceforth policy decisions emanated from the governor-general and were to be implemented by the various regional residents. The governor-general would be advised on budgetary matters by a federal council, an administrative creation of Doumer but consonant with French practice elsewhere. This body represented French interests only, its membership derived from the chambers of commerce and agriculture already in existence in Tonkin and Cochin-China and thereafter founded expressly for this purpose in Cambodia and Annam. Despite initial opposition from a colonial council previously installed in Cochin-China and which rightly perceived the federal colonial council as a competitive institution, the arrangement was accepted and sustained by the French government at home.

In Indochina, and simultaneously in West Africa, the federal principle was introduced as an administrative device to stimulate economic growth. To make the colony prosper through federally sponsored and directed methods of modernization — from railroad building to unified tax systems — was Doumer's objective. Through a federal budget of sizable proportions, Doumer was able to implement the French idea of *mise en*

---

[21] Quoted by Stephen H. Roberts, *The History of French Colonial Policy, 1870–1925* (Hamden, Conn.: Archon Press, 1963; first published, 1929), p. 461.

valeur, of economic development, which was to be the motto of French colonial policy after World War I.

Less impressive in results but equally impressive in geographical size was the federation of French West Africa. In 1895 several of the colonies of that huge bulge of Africa which had fallen under French military control were organized into a federal administration, soon crowned with a governor-general's palace of grand dimensions and eclectic style which sat imposingly on a bluff overlooking the sea at Dakar, Senegal. The move toward federation was the French government's attempt to order the chaos primarily caused by the military occupation of the hinterland. Administrative rivalries, coupled with personal military ambitions, had created a condition not unlike that of the contemporary Balkan states. In the words of the minister of colonies Camille Chautemps, "The frontier violations which at times occur in Europe never occasion diplomatic correspondence as complicated and impassioned as that produced in those circumstances occurring between the three governors of the neighboring colonies. . . . "[22] This particular provocation to reorganization was also charged by the realization that the geographic contiguity of the colonies, like that of the units of Indochina, could be economically exploited if regulated by a unified administrative network.

The federation evolved rather slowly, over a ten-year period marked by decrees issued between 1895 and 1904.[23] Initially the governor-general's sole function was that of military control, but soon he had authority over such basic services as justice and public works as well as many of the administrative appointments, save the highest offices. The French political intention to subordinate the separate colonial governors to the governor-general was also achieved, with only the latter allowed direct communication with the minister of colonies. Armed with a federal budget essentially derived from indirect taxes accumulated in the separate colonies, granted the right to raise federal loans, and advised on budgetary matters by a colonial council, the governor-general became the chief agent of modernization which, as in Indochina, was realized primarily in the construction of railroads and ports.

As can be seen in this brief outline of French colonial policy, administrative centralization was considered a means by which to effect

[22] Quoted by Colin W. Newbury, "The Formation of the Government General of French West Africa," *Journal of African History*, 1:115 (1960).
[23] On this development, see *ibid.*, notably pp. 117–127.

economic rationalization. Similar efforts were made in French Equatorial Africa, which was federated in 1910, and in British Nigeria, which enjoyed a unified customs and communications system after 1912, even though it remained essentially two administrative units, north and south. In West Africa the administrative restructuring, which was dominated by the federal principle, led to the syphoning of raw materials from the hinterland out of the continent through the Atlantic seaports then being enlarged. For example, Dakar, Senegal, developed as an imperial port serving all the West African federation, and the Nigerian railroad system, based on similar purposes, followed a north-south axis, to the sea at Lagos. If, as American historians are wont to say, the transcontinental railroads made the United States one, then so did the incipient railroad systems of Africa and Asia join the disparate units of local empire administratively into larger units.

Traveling along a similar communications network but arriving at an entirely different political system was the process of imperial federation within the white-settler colonies of the British empire. There, the federal movement has been seen as the first stage in the historical growth of the Commonwealth idea. This aspect of modern European colonial history is at once the most told and the most heralded, one that fits well the Whig interpretation of English history and thus stimulates a type of historical analysis progressive in mood. Its theme is the evolution of self-government.[24]

There is, furthermore, a nicely formed chronological arch over it all, reaching across nearly a century, from the famous Durham Report of 1839 in which self-government was suggested for Canada to the Westminster Conference of 1931 when the Commonwealth was officially realized.

Despite historical qualifications recently accompanying interpretations of it, the Durham Report remains a grand and bold recommendation, a political turning point in Great Britain's imperial history. It was the first and one of the clearest justifications for what would become home rule in a colonial context; it was the prefatory statement to the institution of the dominions.

Enjoying the trappings of the high office of governor of Lower Canada and attended with great interest by Her Britannic Majesty's subjects in both English- and French-speaking Canada, Durham landed on Canadian

[24] On this general subject see the analysis of Mansergh, *Commonwealth Experience*, chapter 1.

soil in 1839 to undertake a governmental inquiry into the reasons for the revolts of Upper and Lower Canada in the previous year. His conclusion was that the revolt of Upper Canada arose out of grievances concerning the lack of locally responsible government, while that of Lower Canada arose out of racial antagonism between the earlier settled French and the newly arrived English. To correct the former condition, he suggested the first step toward self-government: ministerial responsibility on the nineteenth-century English model, that is, responsibility to the elected House of Commons. To correct the second condition, he suggested the union of the two Canadas, the result of which would assure an overwhelming English preponderance in numbers and would stifle any French hopes of national independence. In the Durham Report, therefore, are found the two elements that have molded the development of British imperial federation: the concept of responsible government and the ideal of provincial or colonial union. Although the former was not achieved until the momentous European year of 1848 when far-off Nova Scotia was so accommodated, the Act of Union did bind the two Canadas together in 1840 and was the first step toward the federal system legally inaugurated in 1867.

The British North America Act of 1867 really introduced the institution, if not the name of dominion as a form of colonial rule. Federal in principle, as many of the dominions were to be, Canada was a political amalgam of colonial territories previously administered separately, though each one was directly responsible to the crown. That the initiative for such action came from Canada itself, not from the home government, is indicative of a frequent occurrence in colonial administrative innovation, an occurrence no more distinctive to the British system than to the French, whatever the differences in resultant form. The Canadian precedent was repeated in the federal organization of Australia in 1901 and in the union of South Africa, forged in 1910 after the Boer War.

The initiation of a policy of federation with the British North America Act, as well as the examples of the United States and Germany, intimated at the larger possibility of an imperial federation within or of the British empire. Such a political structure was widely proclaimed by many British imperialists toward the end of the nineteenth century.

The imperial federation movement, as it is known, made its first appearance in the 1880s, then declined, only to reappear briefly in the thoughts and aspirations of Joseph Chamberlain a decade later. In its early, capitalized form, it implied a federated empire endowed with parliamentary institutions which would provide meaningful political cohesion of its sundry parts. The Imperial Federation League, founded in 1884 and the center of the movement, was an ideological response to the new political conditions evident on both sides of the Atlantic. If, as many critics now suggest, British imperialism of the late century was a fearful reaction to the expansionist tendencies of other states, then Imperial Federation was an attempt to reorder the empire so that it could measure up to the oppressive giantism of these other nations. At least one of its advocates coined the hybrid phrase "A United States of the Britannic Empire," and more than one enthusiast regarded the great republic across the ocean as historical proof of the possibilities of an effective federal system.[25]

The anticipated form of imperial federation was in some instances spelled out in detail, but the problem of representation within an extended imperial parliament was a knotty issue, never successfully unraveled in theory. One thing was certain, however: the federation would essentially be an Anglo-Saxon affair. "For the sake of consistency to a phrase," insisted a proponent, "no sane federal unionist would dream of advocating the admission of the Indian peoples into the Imperial Parliament."[26] This basic racial problem of imperial organization, suggested in the proposed distinction between the to-be and the not-to-be federated segments of the empire, was one that persisted well into the twentieth century. However, it did receive some preliminary resolution in the words of appreciation conveyed to the government of Australia by the president of the National Convention for a Union of South Africa. He wired: "We thank Commonwealth Australia (New Zealand) for its good wishes and sincerely hope the result may strengthen the wider commonwealth of states within the British Empire."[27] As a part of the whole, therefore, the commonwealth system modified the objectives of imperial federation.

Even if organizational problems had been wisely smoothed out, the federationists would have met with ill success. The federationists were

[25] Charles E. I. Stuart-Linton proposed the term and actually offered constitutional proposals to support it. See "The Problem of Empire Governance, VII: Draft of a Written Constitution for the Empire," British Empire Review, 13(no. 6):98–102 (1911).

[26] J. Stanley Little, Progress of the Empire in the Century, p. 105. One of the founders of the Imperial Federation League, Sir James Colombe, said much the same thing. See "Britannic Confederation: A Survey of Existing Conditions," Scottish Geographic Magazine, 7 (no 5):234 (1891).

[27] Quoted by Mansergh, Commonwealth Experience, p. 21.

Stylized representation of an incident during the Taiping Rebellion, 1862.
From James W. Buel, *Heroes of the Dark Continent* (Philadelphia:
Historical Publishing Co., 1890).

Indian frontier campaign, 1898. From *Illustrated London News*, January 8, 1898.
(Reproduced by permission of *Illustrated London News*.)

Napoleon III in Algeria, 1865. From *L'Illustration*, June 3, 1865.

The captive Emir Muhammad, paraded before Lord Kitchener during the Sudan campaign, 1898. From *Illustrated London News*, May 14, 1898, supplement. (Reproduced by permission of *Illustrated London News*.)

unappreciative of the localized nationalism emerging in the newly defined commonwealth states, a nationalism which was directed toward the idea of great autonomy within a loose imperial framework held together primarily by common loyalty to the crown. Under these circumstances, a transoceanic Greater Britain could not in any structured way replicate Imperial Germany or the United States of America, no matter how hopeful some of the imperial federationists may have been. What evolved was that unique and short-lived arrangement of the twentieth century, the British Commonwealth of Nations, which was flexible enough to include portions of the "dependent empire" and also to withstand the immediate political shock of colonial devolution.

Serious discussions of political federation were muted with the calling of the Colonial Conference of 1887, which clearly indicated that the major issues to be broached were imperial defense and imperial commercial relations. What these concepts suggested was less new structure and more cooperation. Lord Salisbury set the tone in his opening address before the conference delegates: "What we desire is that all parts of the Empire should be equally safe, equally prosperous, equally glorious. . . ."[28] Safety and prosperity remained the key words henceforth, although Chamberlain's hoped-for zollverein, proposed at the turn of the century, was doomed to failure. The notion of imperial defense, however, was given a particular patriotic fillip by the presence of dominions troops in the Boer War and was further realized by the generous effort of the dominions during World War I.

Cast in that political symmetry which almost mockingly characterizes the beginning and end of modern imperialistic activities, schemes for federation again appeared in abundance during the terminal colonial decade, at which time new states in Africa, Southeast Asia, and the Caribbean sought political amalgamation for purposes of economic modernization and administrative efficiency. These later efforts had less endurance than the earlier colonial ones, but both exposed the fundamental difficulties cached within the *pax colonia*: the new order desired had to assure a tax base and a market system large enough to provide the capital necessary for social and economic change. In effect, politics of scale was deemed the concomitant to any economy of scale. Thus the colonial world followed by a few centuries the historical process by which the European states of the seventeenth century had been organized.

[28]*Proceedings of the Colonial Conference, 1887*, vol. I; in *British Sessional Papers, House of Commons*, Vol. 65 (London: Her Majesty's Stationery Office, 1887), p. 6.

As for the particular mode of colonial rule within the new administrative structures, the differences were quite inconsequential in the long run. The greatest effect of indirect rule was found in the process of political devolution; it tended to allow the transfer of power to be conducted rapidly and smoothly. Conversely, the paternalistic administration imposed by Belgium and the political assimilation attempted by France are in large measure responsible for the civil strife in the Congo in 1960–61 and the drawn-out war in Algeria between 1954 and 1962.

What has endured as political reality and political problem is the general administrative structure that housed the governments of the newly independent states in the first decade of national freedom, the 1950s, and that still seriously conditions their political behavior. What has yet to be considered in this historical analysis is the "native policy" which both conditioned and was conditioned by these administrative structures. In the short run, which is to say in the imperialist era, it was "native policy" that counted the most.

CHAPTER 7

The Colonial Situation: Native Policy and Protest

Psychologists and novelists have often analyzed that moment of encounter when European and "native" found themselves in a situation which led one to become colonizer, the other to become colonized. The confrontation was frequently aggravated by the problem of mistaken identities, with neither party prepared to understand the other or to appreciate its cultural values. Both had a parochial view of the world, but as it was the European who aggressively extended his parochialism its effects were the more significant and disruptive.

From the plates of old travel accounts we can still clearly see that grandly heroic — but distorted — pose of a Columbus or a Pizzaro, setting foot on foreign soil and looking haughtily above the small assemblage of Indians drawn into attitudes of awestricken prostration. The gaze of the European at this moment, and for the next several centuries, was forward or upward, a vision of the future when the world at his feet would be reformed according to the moral dictates of his religion or the categorical imperatives of his technology. The artist's exaggeration was of no larger dimensions than that which usually filled the mind of the colonial theorist; it was, however, at severe variance with the thoughts of the colonist on the spot.

If in Europe the expression "native policy" frequently meant the fulfillment of a "civilizing mission," in the colonial situation it generally meant subordination, by direct or indirect means, of the local populations to immediate European purposes. These purposes were quite limited, usually clustering around two narrowly separated poles: administrative assistance, with elements of the population employed as auxiliaries, perhaps as minor clerks; economic development, to be realized in major part by the enlistment of indigenous labor. Employment and exploitation — there are the stark, alliterative complements of "native policy." But the race relations resulting from this practice were never so simple or so absolute in actuality. Therefore, before any discussion of official colonial and imperial activity, mention of the diverse factors at play in these relations is necessary.

The nineteenth-century European perception of the world was, as we are frequently reminded, ethnocentric. If colonialists were ready to distinguish among a limited variety of overseas possessions — triadically divided as settlement colonies, trade colonies, and plantation colonies — they seldom made refined distinctions among the indigenous populations encountered or the dialectical relationship any such abrupt cultural encounter was bound to involve. It is noteworthy that some Englishmen cast as far apart as India and New Zealand disparagingly referred to members of the resident populations in these lands as "niggers," a lamentable example of gross prejudice.[1]

Recently, in the era of decolonization, considerable academic attention has been directed to the problem of race relations and to the colonial encounter. A number of models has appeared and so have sets of variables.[2] From this increasingly sophisticated analysis, several dominant characteristics are now apparent. Besides the variations in the purpose of colonial possessions, briefly mentioned above, other factors that conditioned the type of colonial rule and "native policy" are the following: the territorial size and extensiveness of the preexisting governmental form; the intensity of resistance or receptiveness to accommodation by the "host" society; and the complementarity — or lack thereof — between the cultures in contact. With the "inside out" perspective that modern studies of im-

[1] See, for instance, Christine Bolt, *Victorian Attitudes toward Race* (London: Routledge, 1971), p. 210; and Keith Sinclair, *The Origins of the Maori Wars* (Wellington: New Zealand University Press, 1961), p. 9.

[2] Among the models, those which are now "classic" are the following: Albert Memmi, *The Colonizer and the Colonized*, trans. Howard Greenfield (Boston: Beacon Press, 1967; first published, 1957); Frantz Fanon, *The Wretched of the Earth*, trans. Constance Farrington (New York: Grove Press, 1966; first published, 1963); and Georges Balandier, "La situation coloniale: Approche théorique," *Cahiers internationaux de sociologie*, 11:44–79 (1959). Among the many analyses the most far-ranging and complete is Philip Mason, *Patterns of Dominance* (London: Oxford University Press, 1970).

perialism are taking, the monolithic interpretation of an all-imposing and regulating European political-economic expansion has been discarded.

Most obvious and significant of the local contributing factors was the one of geo-ecological dimensions: the extent and nature (economic value) of the land occupied. Just so long as the Europeans remained on the littoral of the continental landmasses and engaged in regional trade, or while and where the European pattern of internal occupation was one of the seizure and settlement of plateau grasslands, an effective "native policy" was nonexistent. In the first instance, the local populations were culturally ignored and civically absorbed into the simple, direct administrative arrangement. In the second instance, the indigenous populations were repelled or exterminated. However, with the new politics of penetration which were exhibited by the middle of the century as the hinterlands of the tropics, notably Africa, were annexed, a new set of administrative tactics and techniques emerged which did indeed constitute a "native policy" in which cooperation through forms of political accommodation was sought.

During the first half of the century, coastal politics, along with constitutional developments in the settler colonies, dominated the European overseas world. There was then little intention of occupying the interior of the continents of Asia and Africa and, consequently, little serious concern with the condition and possible importance of the indigenous population. This was the era in which the missionary effort was the most significant element in the formation of a meaningful "native policy," a policy that frequently preceded the arrival of European state influence and that occasionally depended upon avoiding such influence. For instance, agencies like the London Missionary Society and the Wesleyan Methodist Society endowed the local peoples of the "missionary kingdoms" of the Pacific Islands with new legal systems reflecting European codes of conduct and behavior. With influence unparalleled elsewhere the missionaries acted as surrogate legislators and as grey eminences whose advice was preponderant.[3]

On the African scene, where missionary influence was yet to have its most important effect, the small enclaves that were then the European colonies were generally submitted to a form of direct administration in

[3] On the missionary influence, see Stephen Neill, *Colonialism and Christian Missions* (New York: McGraw-Hill, 1966), particularly chapter 7.

which the indigenous populations were subordinated, yet at times modestly involved. In the British West African colonies, the governors in control appointed consultative councils that consisted of an "official membership," made up of colonial administrators, and an "unofficial membership," named from among local interest groups, such as merchants. By the end of the century, however, the "unofficial membership" included a few Africans, a first step — or so it is seen retrospectively — in the movement toward responsible government and the transportation of the "Westminster System" overseas to nonsettler colonies.

A more celebrated example, and one of obvious political assimilation, is that which the French developed in the four "old communes" of Senegal. Here, the notion of a "republic one and indivisible" was made official policy with the result that native-born residents enjoyed the status of French citizens. That the French never extended this ideological privilege to other territories later acquired in Africa may be taken as an indication that they earlier had no intention of constructing a large empire there.[4] But what remains important is the African factor in local politics, a factor whose significance was clearly measured in the election of 1914 when the first black African became a member of the French Chamber of Deputies. Blaise Diagne, whose honor this was, was a man of considerable political acumen. He had shrewdly galvanized the African voters into a strong block of support and thus had used the French parliamentary system to African advantage.

Such coastal politics were exceptional, far exceeded in scope and regularity of practice by the two major approaches toward the local peoples. The first was that of repulsion, even extermination of the population; the second was that of indirect administration through the use, in one of several forms, of existing indigenous authorities.

The method of repulsion has left behind a tragic and bloody history of war and deprivation, of which the occupation of the American West is the unbecoming paradigm. In the colonial world the drive to push back or even crush the resident population was much more a local — or colonial — affair than a national one. It was primarily an expression of acute "land hunger" and was most evident within those settlement colonies where pastoral economies were established. Its results, from Australia to South Africa, took shape in that institution of population relocation and concen-

---

[4]On the early French presence in Senegal, see John D. Hargreaves, "Assimilation in Eighteenth Century Senegal," *Journal of African History* 6:177–184 (1965).

tration known as the "native reserve." This movement of the indigenous peoples to land isolated within their former territories was not always the consequence of ruthless calculation, but sometimes the attempt of the imperial government to protect, however inadequately, the native population from the rapacious extremes of the settler population.[5]

In such areas colonial policy was most often a direct function of local — not imperial — economic policy. The profit-motivated agrarian or pastoral economy upon which colonial settlement was structured was directly opposed to the subsistence-based, localized economies of the indigenous populations. Local colonial activities therefore frequently contradicted imperial policy, for they were designed to assure the acquisition of large amounts of land while the home government was often trying to safeguard "native interests."

The history of English governmental involvement in New Zealand has thus just been summarized, but Australia, South Africa, and Algeria also lend themselves to such analysis. The "reluctant empire," as one historian has called British occupation of much of South Africa in the early nineteenth century, was essentially that of an expanding frontier resulting from the effort of the "imperial factor" to control or mediate Boer-Bantu relations, greatly aggravated by the land issue.[6] In New Zealand, the protection of the Maori people, who by treaty placed themselves under British sovereignty in 1840, was a major imperial consideration, but one turned to ill effect by the so-called Maori Wars of mid-century. According to J. E. FitzGerald, a sympathetic member of the New Zealand Assembly of that epoch: "At the point where his [the Maori's] possession of the land interferes with our industrial and commercial progress, there for the first time we trace antagonism between the two races."[7]

Even in a mixed colony, where trade and plantation settlement were in competition, the land issue was a provocative one. The Herero Wars of 1904–7 deeply punctuate the colonial history of German Southwest Africa and were waged with the intention, openly expressed by the German commander, of exterminating the Herero tribes. Although the land issue was only one cause here, the sum of causes was grouped together economically. In the words of the German governor Theodor Leutwein, a

[5] Examples of such attempts are to be found in German colonial policy in Southwest Africa and British colonial policy in South Africa.

[6] John S. Galbraith, *Reluctant Empire: British Policy on the South African Frontier, 1834–1854* (Berkeley: University of California Press, 1963).

[7] Quoted in Sinclair, *Origins of the Maori Wars*, p. 4.

man not unsympathetic to the African populations of the colony: "Let the native who will neither work nor do without worldly goods go to gradual ruin. The industrious whites can only profit from this."[8] And they did, as the remaining Hereros were placed in reserves.

A half-century later, Frantz Fanon remarked in his now classic work entitled *The Wretched of the Earth* that it was the settler who was the root-and-branch problem of the colonial system. "For it is the settler who has brought the native into existence and who perpetuates his existence. The settler owes the fact of his very existence, that is to say his property, to the colonial system."[9] Forced into a position of social and political subordination, victimized by a racism that had strong economic causes, expropriated of his lands, the indigenous resident was made the "native," a caricature of an existence that settler cupidity and insensitivity could not or would not understand. Exhibiting what might be called the frontier mentality of cultural arrogance, brutal force, roughhewn individualism, and disdain for the humanitarianism which at times permeated imperial policy, the settler provoked major political problems in his desire to stake out land for himself. War, therefore, became the immediate political response, if not the final solution.

In the growing "tropical dependencies" of the late nineteenth century, wars of "pacification" were also a major component of initial colonial policy, but they were directed more toward domination than toward repulsion. In contrast with so many earlier patterns of colonial development, the territory acquired here suggested a different set of administrative imperatives. Now it was realized that the so-called "empty spaces" and "wastelands of the world" were not to be filled with people cascading from Europe, that the vastness of the territory nominally under European control and the scarcity of colonial administrators available for local service necessitated some form of social accommodation, and that any effective utilization of the lands required some kind of mobilization of the indigenous populations. If much of the inspiration for a meaningful "native policy" as defined in Europe came from humanitarian and scientific considerations, exigency was the chief source of motivation on the local scene. In a simple procedure which affected the history of the nineteenth-

---

[8] Quoted in Helmut Bley, *South-West Africa under German Colonial Rule, 1894–1914*, trans. Hugh Ridley (Evanston, Ill.: Northwestern University Press, 1971; first published, 1968), p. 118.

[9] Fanon, *Wretched of the Earth*, p. 30.

century colonial world, political expansion forced indirect administration. The politics of scale demanded an administration which incorporated or cooperated with existing authorities.

Indirect Rule

By the time Sir Frederick Lugard, its most famous celebrant, had enshrined indirect rule in his famous study *The Dual Mandate in British Tropical Africa*, published in 1922, the principle had been recited in most European tongues. True, indirect rule supported a number of definitions, particularly as applied to Subsaharan Africa, but there was no dissent from the general opinion that some type of European-native administrative conjunction, however asymmetrical that might be with respect to political authority, was necessary. In general administrative terms, those through which "native policy" was to be effected, the most frequently discussed colonial method was that of the "protectorate." Particularly well suited to large territorial units already ruled by an extensive administration, this method required little more than that the indigenous ruler accept, willingly or coercively, the colonial presence. Widely used by the French and the English in Africa and Southeast Asia, the "protectorate" received two definitions worth repeating here.

Louis Hubert Lyautey, who was to become French resident-general in Morocco, but who was speaking of Madagascar at the time, provides the first:

To adopt the policy and administration of the protectorate signifies: to maintain as much as possible in their entirety native governmental machinery, institutions and customs: to use the traditional leaders . . . under the simple control of a single agent residing close to the chief.[10]

Lyautey's contemporary Captain A. B. Thruston, who was in the British colonial administration of Uganda, offers the second definition:

It has always been the practice of England to govern her distant dominions as apart from her colonies, whenever feasible by the system of Protectorate; by which system their administrators are placed under a native Prince who governs by the advice of a native Protector. The advantages are obvious; for the people through force or habit, love for the person, or the pres-

[10] Louis Hubert Lyautey, *Dans le sud de Madagascar* (Paris: H. Charles Lavauzelle, 1903), p. 362.

tige of his office, naturally submit to the orders of their Prince. The
Prince himself through the instinct of self-preservation if nothing else,
usually willingly obeys the orders of his protector, and these orders are further disguised under the name of advice, and are conveyed in such a
manner as to as little as possible destroy his prestige or wound his suscep-
tibilities.[11]

Such indirection found its most promising field, certainly insofar as doctrinal debate was concerned, in tropical Africa.[12] There the traditional
interpretation has it that the approaches undertaken by the British and
the French were dissimilar. In their "native policy," the British have
been seen as more pragmatic, allowing policy to fluctuate according to
local conditions; the French, however, have been seen as centralists, rep-
licating their national administrative policies everywhere overseas. In
broad terms such a contrast can be made, although both nations as colonial powers in Africa recognized the need for indigenous support of their
administrative effort. And what initially may have been distinctive between the two powers eventually became blurred as the demands for
change to accommodate the incipient modernizing process forced the
alteration and caused the disruption of existing institutions and authorities.

The "native policy" of France was derived in considerable measure
from the military character of so much of modern French colonialism.
From Senegal to Indochina and then back to West Africa and Dahomey,
the French military officer made his appearance as an individual happily
thrust into the colonial situation. Indeed, the outstanding triumvirate in
the second half of the nineteenth century was composed of military
officers: Louis Faidherbe, Joseph Gallieni, and Louis Hubert Lyautey.
Each exercised his talents as soldier-administrator; each was given to
making military policy an adjunct of "native policy." Faidherbe's was the
earliest effort, his in Senegal at mid-century. There he practiced what has
been called *colonisation-civilisation*, demonstrating respect for the Muslim faith, which he hoped to use as a support for the French colonial effort, and establishing the "School for the Sons of Chiefs," in which he
hoped an indigenous administrative elite might be trained.[13]

Lyautey, the most literary and philosophical of the three, explained his

[11] Quoted in J. A. Barnes, "Indigenous Politics and Colonial Administration, with Special
Reference to Australia," *Comparative Studies in Society and History*, 2:140 (1960).

[12] The main points in this debate are defined in Michael Crowder, "Indirect Rule —
French and British Style," *Africa*, 34:197–205 (1964).

[13] See George A. Hardy, *Histoire sociale de la colonisation française* (Paris: Larose, 1953),
pp. 124–125.

policy, which he acknowledged was derived from his service with Gallieni in Indochina and Madagascar, in an interesting article entitled "The Role of the Colonial Army." For him, Gallieni's technique combined military action and administrative control. In Lyautey's words, it was an *organisation qui marche*, an "administration on the march," simultaneously acquitting its responsibility of conqueror and of protector.[14] The troops that "pacified" the territory were also to be the occupation troops, those which would cast down the sword and seize the plowshare, which would cease being conquerors and would become colonists and administrators of sorts. Aware of this prescribed dual activity, the colonial forces would rebuild where they had just destroyed and cooperate with the indigenous populations they had only recently subdued. In rather elegiac terms Lyautey wrote: "And how easy it is for our dear French soldier, dispersed in ones and twos among the Malagasy villages, to become once again the worker of France, exhibiting all the qualities of order, foresight, ingenuity, endurance, cordiality and good humor that this term connotes."[15]

The military form of "native policy" imposed on the French possessions of Algeria, Tonkin, and Madagascar, and in those of West Africa, was one that subordinated local authorities directly to French purposes. The military *cercle* became the basic administrative unit in West Africa, an arrangement that was a major source of the criticism leveled against French methods: the indigenous authority was converted into a minor French functionary, controlled by the *commandant du cercle* and responsible to him, not to the resident populations, for he was now in effect a member of the French colonial bureaucracy. In the West African situation, this relationship was best summed up in the striking and frequently quoted statement made in 1917 by Governor-General Joost Van Vollenhoven. The local chiefs, he argued, "have no power of their own, for there are not two authorities in the *cercle* . . . there is only one! Only the *commandant du cercle* commands; only he is responsible. The native chief is but an instrument, an auxiliary."[16]

In practice, then, French administrative policy altered as much as it maintained indigenous administrative functions. New chieftaincies were created; chiefs were occasionally reposted to territorial units not tradi-

[14] Louis Hubert Lyautey, *Lettres de Tonkin et de Madagascar, 1894–1899* (Paris: A. Colin, 1921), p. 634.

[15] *Ibid.*, p. 614.

[16] Joost Van Vollenhoven, "Circulaire au sujet des chefs indigènes," in *Une âme de chef* (Paris: Dieval, 1920), p. 207.

tionally theirs. More in name than in form did the older office exist, particularly after World War I when administrative consolidation did make
the chief an auxiliary. Before the colonial era was to end, similar results
were to be exhibited in portions of British-dominated Subsaharan Africa,
but in the early years of the twentieth century indirect rule offered quite a
different appearance from French "native policy."

It was the administration of Captain Frederick Lugard in northern
Nigeria that gave British indirect rule its distinctive hallmark. As high
commissioner of that area when it passed from the authority of the Royal
Niger Company to the British crown in 1900, Lugard found himself with a
large-scale administrative system, deteriorated but capable of rehabilita-
tion. The rule of the Fulani emirs over the Hausa peoples had been most
effective earlier in the century and now suggested an inexpensive, indirect means of installing effective British control. Lugard had already
elaborated his approach during his previous service in Uganda; it was one
of respectful collaboration instead of disruptive subordination. He envisioned the "Native Authority," in this instance the emirate, as an au-
tonomous administrative unit, responsible for a native judicial system and
in no way overtly disturbed by the British presence.[17] The British "resident" was to be a persuasive and unobtrusive force, not an overlord. As
Lugard stated in his instructions to his officers in 1906, the arrangement
he desired was "a single Government in which the Native Chiefs have
clearly defined duties and an acknowledged status equally with the
British officials."[18] Lugard's intention, therefore, was to avoid any direct
interference with the existing indigenous system insofar as it appeared to
be compatible with general English purposes and mores. He wished to
work through it, not impose upon it. As his biographer commented, "The
great task of indirect rule is to hold the ring, to preserve a fair field within
which Africans can strike their own balance between conservatism and
adaptation."[19]

While both forms of rule were "indirect" in that they made use of local
authorities, the variation in practice was soon noticeable. The French
were far less respectful of existing administrative units than were the
British and tended to force a uniformity based initially on the military

[17] Later Sir William Temple, serving under Lugard, added the idea of a "native treasury" to
the arrangement, a treasury which would support the local administration.

[18] Frederick D. Lugard, *Instructions to Political and Other Officers on Subjects Chiefly
Political and Administrative* (1906), p. 191, quoted in Margery Perham, *Lugard, The Years
of Authority, 1898–1945* (London: Collins, 1960), p. 144.

[19] Margery Perham, "A Restatement of Indirect Rule," *Africa*, 7:331 (1934).

model mentioned above. On the contrary, Lugard and those of his "school" attempted to restrict the role of the local colonial administrator to that of adviser, not extend it to that of local executive. Van Vollenhoven's statement would, therefore, stand in diametric opposition to British intention. Lastly, the Lugardian approach was more appreciative of indigenous institutions than was the French.

Yet, whatever their differences in approach, the French and British were joined by other colonial powers that were moving toward methods of indirect rule. The Germans in East Africa, during the administration of Governor Albrecht von Rechenberg in the first decade of the twentieth century, started to give local chiefs greater authority in the administration of justice.[20] And so did the Italian officials in Somalia who approximated the Lugardian method in their use of local *cadi* who performed judicial functions according to the Moslem *shari'a*, or code of law. Even the Spanish in their portion of Morocco utilized the *cadi* in a manner not at all dissimilar to that employed by the Italians.

If, administratively, "native policy" was being provided with some definition in many parts of Africa as an expression of cultural appreciation, it was slowly formulated and only indifferently applied. The well-being of the indigenous population was more a cause and concern of humanitarians at home and missionaries abroad than of colonial administrators anywhere in the nineteenth century. The beginning of considerate "native policy" was interrupted by World War I and then somewhat inhibited by the effects of the Depression. Before the war, however, the persistent reason for this policy was economic, based primarily on the need for the effective enlistment of indigenous labor.

The Regulation of Labor

The prevalent nineteenth-century attitude toward colonial development in other than settlement areas is perhaps best captured in Joseph Chamberlain's phrase "tropical estates." To make the colonial territories as nearly self-sufficient as possible and to incorporate them as agricultural producers into the world economic system regulated from Europe were the objectives — even if never so clearly or directly stated — of all the colonial powers. The effort to raise cash crops led to a major and wide-

---

[20] See Prosser Gifford, "Indirect Rule: Touchstone or Tombstone for Colonial Policy?" in Professor Gifford and William Roger Louis, eds., *Britain and Germany in Africa: Imperial Rivalry and Colonial Rule* (New Haven, Conn.: Yale University Press, 1967), p. 373.

spread introduction of cotton growing, which was greeted with considerable lack of success. The French in Algeria and Senegal, the Germans in the Cameroons and East Africa, the English in Egypt and the Sudan all assumed that cotton, as in the American South, would be king. Along with such attempts to produce this and other cash crops went the search for raw materials, and thus the tapping of rubber or the extraction of copper was added to the agricultural activities that composed the colonial economic output.

These activities were what economists today call "labor intensive." The tempo of production, therefore, was principally determined by the European ability to enlist and regularize an indigenous labor force. The strategy pursued had the most immediate and far-reaching effects of any local aspect of colonial policy: forced labor and personal taxation, with the latter initially seen by some officials as a refined version of the former. Forced labor declined at the end of the century, replaced by the capitation or head tax which not only provided revenue for the colonial treasuries but also compelled the indigenous populations to become part of the money-oriented European economy.

An early and much criticized example of such economic mobilization in the nineteenth century was that introduced and developed by Johannes van den Bosch during his tenure as governor-general in Java. This was the "culture system." In 1830 when van den Bosch returned to Java, the Dutch economy at home and in the East Indies had been badly stricken by two wars, the one leading to the independence of Belgium, the other waged unsuccessfully by the prince of Jakarta. It was van den Bosch's intention to renovate the colonial economy, thereby assuring an export crop large enough to profit mother country and colony alike.

The essential feature of the system was its land-use arrangement which amounted to an indirect payment in kind, a substitute for a previous money tax computed in the amount of two-fifths of the crops produced on the land. Under this new plan, the people would put aside only about one-fifth of their land and devote one-fifth of their labor to its cultivation, raising export crops, usually indigo or sugar, for the government. A contractor, paid by the government, would see that the produce was refined — in the case of sugar — and shipped to Holland for sale, a contingent feature of the procedure and one called the consignment system.[21]

[21] On the "culture system," its organization and effects, see Bernard H. M. Viekke, *Nusantara: A History of Indonesia* (rev. ed.; Chicago: Quadrangle Books, 1960), chapter 13; and J. S. Furnivall, *Netherlands India: A Study of Plural Economy* (New York: Macmillan, 1944), chapter 5.

Originally voluntary in nature and open to private as well as state development, the "culture system" was extended in scope but restricted in use by individual Javanese so that the state became the chief agent both in the production and in the consignment aspects of the economy. The result was the conversion of the "culture system" into one of forced labor, with the state in effect owning one large plantation.[22] There is no doubt that economic production rose enormously, with benefits going primarily to the Dutch but to a lesser degree to the Javanese population which was, nonetheless, allowed little latitude in the growing of crops for other than state use. Holland's condition of bankruptcy was thus relieved, the Dutch merchant marine was greatly enlarged, and the colony thereupon became a vital element in the economic well-being of the mother country. This "net-profit" system continued until the 1870s when the governmental role was reduced and private entrepreneurs were again allowed to play in the economy on their own. The century ended, however, with the "Ethical Policy," in part a reaction to the laissez-faire arrangement of the 1870s and concerned with the encouragement of indigenous production, which was supported by such devices as better terms of credit for the Javanese and resettlement of the population on uncultivated lands in order to protect against the previously severe effects of an intrusive Dutch capitalism.

The "culture system" attracted others besides the Dutch. In fact, its influence was extensive. The French considered its possibilities in Indochina, as did the British in some of the Pacific Islands. Most interesting of all is the strong appeal the idea had to the Duke of Brabant, the future Leopold II, when he was turning his attention to colonial matters. What he admired in the "culture system" was its financial returns, "the immense revenue that these islands give the mother country," he declared.[23]

It was in the Africa of Leopold II's time that the worst offenses of labor exploitation for the profit of private company and state occurred. The economic problems confronting the Europeans in Africa were complicated beyond those encountered elsewhere. The lack of easily navigable rivers and the sparsely distributed populations placed a heavy emphasis on forced labor, in the first instance to find porters to carry goods

---

[22] See Furnivall, *Netherlands India*, p. 121.

[23] Letter of October 29, 1861, quoted in Jean Stengers, *Combien le Congo a-t-il coûté à la Bélgique?* (Brussels: Académie Royale des Sciences Coloniales, 1957), p. 146.

that could not feasibly be carried in any other way, in the second instance to concentrate a labor supply on plantations and in mines.

In the period of occupation, notably the years between 1880 and the outbreak of World War I, the use of porterage led to the impressment of thousands of Africans and to an exceptionally high incidence of death among them because of the dreadful conditions imposed by European economic imperatives. To supply French troops in Chad, for example, "we must transport more than 3,000 loads per month on men's heads," wrote an administrator.[24] And in the German Cameroons nearly 80,000 persons carried goods on one road alone in 1913.[25] In his *Heart of Darkness*, Joseph Conrad presents a hardly fictionalized version of his observations made a few years before in the Belgian Congo: "Day after day, with the stamp and shuffle of sixty bare feet behind me, each pair under a sixty-pound load. Camp, cook, sleep, strike camp, march. Now and then a carrier dead in harness, at rest in the long grass near the path, with an empty water gourd and his long staff lying by his path."[26] After the development of roads and railroads, the construction of which intensified porterage, the need for porters declined, but by then so had the population as a result of this practice.

The policy of forced labor was recognized by all the European powers having some hold on Africa, and it was a practice that continued in some colonies, despite severe criticism, until World War II.[27] After 1918, the policy was primarily restricted to state projects, to public works, but before then companies and state combined to use forced labor to develop cash crops and exploit natural resources. In some instances this led to the displacement of large numbers of peoples. The movement of seasonal laborers from the French colony of Upper Volta to the forests of the Ivory Coast is one example, but it hardly matches in ill effects that which occurred in Angola and is known as the São Tomé affair.

To provide the necessary labor for the cocoa plantations on the island of São Tomé, off the coast of Angola, the Portuguese authorities employed a system to recruit forced labor which was to be described by the British

---

[24] Georges Toqué quoted by Henri Brunschwig, *La colonisation française: Du pacte colonial à l'Union française* (Paris: Calmann-Lévy, 1949), p. 103.

[25] Harry Rudin, *Germans in the Cameroons, 1884–1914: A Case Study in Modern Imperialism* (New Haven, Conn.: Yale University Press, 1938), p. 316.

[26] Joseph Conrad, *Heart of Darkness* (New York: Signet, 1962; first published, 1910), p. 76.

[27] On this subject see Lord Hailey, *An African Survey: A Study of Problems Arising in Africa South of the Sahara* (rev. ed.; London: Oxford University Press, 1957), notably pp. 1362–75.

foreign minister Lord Granville as "simply a form of slave trade."[28] Africans seized inland were sold to the planters' purchasing agents and then shipped to the island under the worst of conditions. The practice, pursued throughout the last quarter of the century, caused little disturbance and aroused little concern either among the African populations or among European critics until the end of the century when cocoa production was increased. Then, about four thousand persons per year were being exported, a fact sharply brought to the attention of the West by a series of articles published in 1906 by an English journalist, Henry W. Nevinson. One of the largest chocolate manufacturers in the world, William Cadbury, had already protested to the Portuguese in Lisbon about these practices and later undertook a visit of inquiry to Angola. His investigation led to the publication in 1909 of *Labour in Portuguese West Africa*, a highly critical study which further intensified the growing sense of European indignation. Primarily because of this campaign of protest, which inspired the British to intervene diplomatically in Lisbon, the Portuguese authorities not only checked the practice but also began to send the workers back to the African mainland.[29]

Yet the extremes of the São Tomé affair pale in comparison with the labor exploitation found in the Congo of Leopold II. Similar to, but more intensive than the activities pursued in French Equatorial Africa where concessionary companies ruthlessly worked the population to obtain rubber and ivory, the Congo situation led to the decimation of millions of people who were forced to harvest wild rubber and extract ivory tusks for the profit of the king and the several concession companies to which he had granted the right of economic development. The population was burdened with an *impôt de cueillette*, a harvest tax, fixed in money but payable in kind. On the "vacant lands" he declared state property, Leopold required that all ivory and rubber obtained be sold directly to the state, a policy reminiscent of the "culture system" in Java.

The results of this labor exploitation were financially splendid, finally returning to the king the sum he had invested in the Congo as a private political-economic venture and allowing him to find sufficient quantities of additional money to indulge his tastes for constructing tourist resorts, both on the Riviera and in the city of Ostend. Leopold's gain was in in-

[28] Granville quoted in R. J. Hammond, *Portugal and Africa, 1815–1910: A Study in Uneconomic Imperialism* (Stanford, Calif.: Stanford University Press, 1966), p. 317.

[29] Good introductions to the São Tomé affair are found in *ibid.*, and James Diffy, *Portugal in Africa* (Baltimore, Md.: Penguin Books, 1963; first published, 1962).

verse ratio to the well-being of the Congolese people. Untolo numbers lost their lives, some murdered, others worked to death, still more starved because of their inability to work their own lands for food crops, so demanding was this crude form of the "culture system."[30]

In response, a protest movement of grander dimensions than that mounted by Cadbury and his colleagues against the Portuguese now aroused English public opinion. Beginning in the early 1890s when returning Protestant missionaries and the Aborigines Protection Society started expressing concern, the movement received its chief impetus from the publication of a report by Roger Casement, the British consul in the Congo. Casement joined forces with Edmund Morel, to whom the greatest credit for inciting the English people must be granted. An employee of the English steamship line Elder Dempster, Morel was avocationally a journalist, a muckraker of considerable skill in his protest against Leopold's policy, with which he first became concerned during his trips to Belgium for the steamship company.[31]

Morel was instrumental in the founding of the Congo Reform Association in 1904 which, with few finances, attempted to battle the impressive propaganda machine maintained by Leopold II. The association was essentially an English undertaking, though it had some support from groups in the United States. Because of its English origins, the movement aroused some suspicion on the Continent; moreover, the religious question also entered judgments of the association's purposes, since many of the protestors were Protestant missionaries in a state ruled by a Catholic monarch. But in the long run Morel's efforts yielded satisfactory results when the Belgian parliament, responding to public clamor, took over the Congo in 1908. Henceforth the Congo was ruled as a Belgian colony. Thus the most colorful and oppressive example of freebooting in the annals of imperialism came to a bitter end. Not that everyone was satisfied, certainly not Morel, for the concessionary practice continued under the aegis of the Belgian government, and effective reform, as indicated in the Colonial Charter of 1909, only began to yield significant results after World War I.

Forced labor was most pronounced in the Subsaharan African colonial

---

[30] On Leopold's policy see Ruth Slade, *King Leopold's Congo: Aspects of the Development of Race Relations in the Congo Independent State (1878–1908)* (London: Oxford University Press, 1962), and the lively account of Neal Ascherson, *The King Incorporated: Leopold II in the Age of Trusts* (London: Allen & Unwin, 1963).

[31] See particularly William Roger Louis and Jean Stengers, eds., *E. D. Morel's History of the Congo Reform Movement* (Oxford: Clarendon Press, 1968), pt. II.

possessions, but by the turn of the century it was everywhere decreasing, as the more efficient and less severe method of taxation was replacing it. To the system of indirect taxation by which the revenues for maintaining empire had long been collected — for instance, the salt tax in Annam — were added personal taxes, the head tax or capitation being the most prevalent; this was followed later by an income tax which, however, was of no great consequence to most of the indigenous populations until the terminal years of empire after World War II.

Tax policy, which varied in detail but not in general form from one colonial region to another, was seen as an essential element in native policy, the means by which to regularize labor and to "civilize" — make fiscally responsible and dependent — the indigenous populations. In the twentieth century its purpose was further and more regularly extended to that of making local colonial government fiscally responsible. Through such taxation the salaries of indigenous chiefs and administrators were frequently paid, thus including them as an integral part of the colonial machinery. In the words of Frederick Lugard: "The payment of taxes is in Africa, as elsewhere, an unwelcome concomitant of progress. It marks the recognition of the principle that each individual in proportion to his means has an obligation to the state. . . ."[32]

The economic needs that labor recruitment and taxation were designed to satisfy are a basic element in the extensive literature on modernization. According to this analysis, the industrial-market economy, which functions on the principle of monetary exchange, disrupted "traditional" societies and forced them along the upward slope of development. In the colonial setting this disruption provoked a number of social and cultural changes: population movements from countryside to colonial city; the replacement of cooperative communal life by competitive individualism; the institution of new social subgroups, such as the voluntary association that provided mutual aid or social solidarity to indigenous urban workers; the emergence of new elites as part of the colonial administration, which replaced the traditional political organization. If there was an obvious catalyst, it was the golden one of money. "It is money, not work," that brought him to the city, states an individual in Chinua Achebe's well-known novel of modern African life, *No Longer at Ease*. "We left plenty of work at home. . . . Anyone who likes work can return home, take up his machet and go into that bad bush between Umofia and Mbaino. It will

---

[32] Lord Frederick D. Lugard, *The Dual Mandate in British Tropical Africa* (3rd ed.; London: William Blackwood, 1926; first published, 1922), p. 232.

keep him occupied to his last days."[33] Regulated, routine work, induced and rewarded by cash, was the new primum mobile that set in motion quite a different social universe.

Although the extensiveness of European economic regimentation of the colonial world has often been exaggerated — for instance, in Subsaharan Africa of the 1950s only 8 million out of a total population of about 170 million worked at any time of the year for wages[34] — there is no doubt that the economic activity which formed such an important and active part of general "native policy" was soon to become one of the major causes of a most pronounced discontent among the indigenous peoples. The African author Joseph Casely Hayford, in a perceptive criticism of British colonial policy in the Gold Coast, put the issue in a caustic manner in which there was little room for dissent: "Again, take the labour question. It is dear to the heart of the European. Herein he shows his love for his black brother beyond all question. The black man fully understands that he has been expressly created by kind Providence to provide labour in the black man's country for the European."[35]

Signs and Forms of Resistance and Protest

The earlier European depiction of the colonial scene in which the indigenous populations appeared as quiescent, except for the occasional outbursts of renegades or fanatics, has been shattered in recent years by new scholarly investigations. The literature on protest and resistance movements has already reached impressive proportions and has been endowed with a triadic theory of development which nicely parallels the economic process of modernization. From initial accommodation to the colonial presence, indigenous attitudes proceeded to the reformation and reassertion of local institutions and values, and then were sharpened into expressions of open nationalist protest.[36] Heuristically valuable, such a

[33] Chinua Achebe, *No Longer at Ease* (Greenwich, Conn.: Fawcett, 1969; first published, 1960), p. 79.

[34] E. J. Berg, "Backward-Sloping Labor Supply Functions in Dual Economies," *Quarterly Journal of Economics*, 75:471 (1961).

[35] *Gold Coast Native Institutions with Thoughts upon a Healthy Imperial Policy for the Gold Coast Ashanti*, reprinted in Henry S. Wilson, ed., *Origins of West African Nationalism* (London: Macmillan, 1969), p. 320.

[36] Such stage theories appear in Georges Balandier, "Les mythes politiques de colonisation et de décolonisation en Afrique," *Cahiers internationaux de sociologie*, 33:85–96 (1962); and Edward Shils, "The Intellectuals in the Political Development of the New States," *World Politics*, 12:329–368 (1960).

stage theory denies the simultaneity with which such differences of cause and purpose occasionally occurred, as will be suggested below.

Scholars engaged in discussion of the matter have already engendered a historiographical debate on whether these protests were incipient forms of "national liberation," hence modern, or whether they were "romantic, reactionary struggles against the facts. . . ."[37] Whatever the sociological or historical perspective taken, every scholar agrees that these movements were significant, an attitude which has made the "inside out" interpretation of modern imperialism much more pointed. In addition, it has totally destroyed the myth of the passive and generously receptive "native" for whom western civilization was a welcome, if unanticipated blessing.

Yet all such analysis of popular protest invites distortion. In considering resistance and protest to be "native," to be a singular reaction against the colonial presence, the historian may be unconsciously excising from local or regional history social movements which had preceded as well as continued after the colonial experience.[38] Much of the history of Southeast Asia and Southeast Africa reveals that resistance was directed not only against the colonial invader, but also against the efforts of neighboring groups simultaneously trying to impose their political will. "Native protest" thus may be part of an indigenous sociopolitical pattern in which the colonial experience is one of several influences.

Yet there is no doubt that the colonial situation created new expressions of protest as well as provoked the reiteration of older ones. These expressions run across the pages of colonial history from an early date. The slave revolts of the eighteenth and nineteenth centuries are now being studied with greater appreciation in both their colonial and North American settings; and such research demonstrates that the plantation black was far from resigned to his fate. If this scholarly investigation suggests a new component of colonial history, the variety of outbursts that punctuated nineteenth-century colonial history has never been denied attention. Such occurrences as the Taiping Rebellion, the Sepoy

[37] On the "modernist" view, see A. B. Davidson, "African Resistance and Rebellion against the Imposition of Colonial Rule," in T. O. Ranger, ed., *Emerging Themes of African History* (Nairobi: East Africa Publishing House, 1968), pp. 177–188. The quotation on "romantic struggles" is from Ronald Robinson and John Gallagher, "The Partition of Africa," in *New Cambridge Modern History*, vol. XI: *Material Progress and World-Wide Problems, 1870–1898*, ed. F. H. Hinsley (Cambridge: At the University Press, 1968), p. 640.

[38] The idea is that of T. O. Ranger, *Revolt in Southern Rhodesia, 1896–1897: A Study in African Resistance* (Evanston, Ill.: Northwestern University Press, 1967), pp. 346–347.

Mutiny, and the Jamaican Revolt have been mentioned already in this study. To them should be added other signs of opposition to colonial rule.

Within the French sphere, the military was frequently very active. The aggressive reply of Abd-el-Kader, an Islamic leader who raised the banner of holy war against the French in Algeria, was sufficiently effective to catch the French off balance and tie up their forces there between the years 1839 and 1847, when Abd-el-Kader was captured. Across the world the French also encountered serious problems with the "Black Flag" movement in the Red River region of Indochina during the 1880s. Dismissed as "pirates" by the French, these marauders are today considered to have been more than that: Chinese supported by Vietnamese who in part were expressing their opposition to the western presence.[39] These two examples reveal that the reactions of indigenous resisters to the early aspects of imperialism not only were complex but also were motivated by many different factors.

Toward the end of the nineteenth century, particularly at the time of the "pacification" of Africa, popular protests were frequently caused by the economic aspects of colonial policy, again indicative of the problem of land, cash crops, and taxation. An obvious instance of political intrusion and tax imposition arousing violent protest is the "hut tax" war in Sierra Leone. Hostilities broke out in 1898 as the direct result of a five-shilling tax levied against each hut in territory just subsumed under a British protectorate. A local chief, Bai Bureh, rose in arms against the British. Although the revolt spread when the British retaliated militarily, it was soon contained.

More significant and historically complicated were the protests in East Africa, where the economic question essentially concerned land and crops, yet where the reaction was in part religiously inspired. The Maji-Maji Rebellion of 1904–6 in German East Africa began as a protest against the involuntary growing of cotton as a cash crop, an idea the Germans imported from the Cameroons. However, the revolt was soon expanded in scope and purpose as a religious element was added to it. The rebels were told that the application of a special holy water called "maji" would provide instant immunity to European bullets. Recent research suggests that much more than the economic factor was at play; ideological commitment, an attempt to thwart German colonialism by means different from

[39] On this interpretation, see David G. Marr, *Vietnamese Anticolonialism, 1885–1925* (Berkeley: University of California Press, 1971), p. 42.

and more extensive than tribal warfare, accounts for the virulence and intensity of the movement.[40]

Another outburst, motivated in some respects by the same conditions that spurred on the Maji-Maji Rebellion, was the double-faceted revolt in Matabeleland and Mashonaland — the future Southern Rhodesia — in 1896. The immediate causes were again economic, basically the land issue, which was manifested in European encroachment for both mining and grazing purposes. Cecil Rhodes's South African Company, pressing hard into Matabeleland, soon aggressively moved into Mashonaland as well. A series of grievances, resulting from the establishment of "native reserves," the loss of cattle by theft and disease, and severe measures taken by the British precipitated a violent upheaval. This was further inspired by a religious leadership which went beyond the traditional configurations of the local religious system. A prophetic leadership, as it has been labeled, it was "able to transform the appeal of the religious system into something more radical and revolutionary . . ."[41] The historian is therefore able to see the Ndebele and Shona revolts as pointing the way to future forms of protest. Like those later efforts in national liberation, they were movements of "mass commitment under the leadership most appropriate to the circumstances."[42]

Although such violent protests cannot be considered a regular aspect of colonial history during this period, they were part of an emerging pattern of defensive reaction against the West, which was already discernible everywhere before the outbreak of World War I. As new elites were formed and older ones began to take into account the European presence, a new cultural consciousness appeared. Perhaps it would be anachronistic to describe this consciousness as ideological, but it certainly was a first step in that direction. Political and cultural manifestations were the most common: the establishment of the Congress party in India in 1885 and the All-India Muslim League in 1906, the First Universal Races Conference bringing blacks from the United States and Africa together in London in 1911, and the formation of the African National Congress in South Africa in 1912 are well-known examples. Reform and political change in countries peripheral to the direct colonial experience also had a catalytic effect. The modernization of Japan and the subsequent defeat of Russia in

[40] John Iliffe, *Tanganyika under German Rule, 1905–1912* (Cambridge: At the University Press, 1969), pp. 26–27.
[41] Ranger, *Revolt in Southern Rhodesia*, p. 214.
[42] *Ibid.*, p. 353.

the War of 1904–5 went far to dispel the myth of white supremacy; and the Young Turk movement of 1896–1908 in which Mustapha Kemal, the "father" of modern Turkey, played a role attracted attention throughout the Mediterranean basin. Finally, the democratic nationalist regime that Sun Yat-sen proposed for China in 1912 was an early example of independent political modernization, even though Sun was not an effective president and China soon fell to the rule of warlords.

Educated voices were also raised singularly in verbal protest. A new proto-nationalist literature, one of cultural dissent as much as of nationalist assertion, emerged in most colonial regions. Schooled in the ways of the West, but often denied the opportunity to enjoy a befitting social role, a colonial intelligentsia began to determine ideologically the gap between colonial reality and imperial pretension. No one better captured in trenchant prose the mood which was to inform so much of this protest than Martin Robinson Delaney, a sometime explorer of the Niger, newspaper editor, and major in the American Civil War. In his *Condition, Elevation, Emigration and Destiny of the Colored People of the United States*, first published in 1852, he stated: "Every people should be the originators of their own designs, the projectors of their own schemes, and creators of the events that lead to their destiny — the consummation of their desires."[43]

The human element in the colonial experience has seized the attention of creative writer and social scientist alike. Yet whatever its importance, any measurement of the effects of the social disturbance caused by "native policy" is difficult to calculate. As part of a contrived socioeconomic policy, these effects were only extensively felt in the terminal decade of empire when financial and technological aid programs began to offer some realization of Lugard's "dual mandate." At no time before this did any of the colonial powers devote considerable sums of money or many personnel to the planned development of colonial human resources.

The population problem, both as a social and as a numerical issue, remained the most formidable, yet the most measurable in its consequences. Even if the money economy provided little increase in the per capita income of the colonial peoples, it did allow for some vertical mobility with the emergence of a colonial bourgeoisie, and it did induce an in-

[43] Martin Robinson Delaney, *The Condition, Elevation, Emigration, and Destiny of the Colored People of the United States* (New York: Arno Press, 1968; first published, 1852), p. 209.

credible amount of horizontal mobility, not only along a regional rural-urban axis but also along intercontinental axes. A cruel and ironic example which almost immediately appears to mind has as its geographical focal point Subsaharan Africa. Millions of Africans were forced to the New World to work on the sugar and cotton plantations. Hardly a half-century after this forced migration had crested, the colonization of Africa intensified the need for cheap labor to enhance economic production. The French played with the idea of importing Annamites to work on roads and farms in West Africa; the British, under Lord Milner, brought some fifty-one thousand Chinese between 1902 and 1906 to work the gold mines of South Africa. Economic development itself created a new sector composed of small businessmen, and before long much of the small-scale local commerce was in the hands of foreigners. During the interwar period East Africa received considerable numbers of Indians and West Africa considerable numbers of Syrio-Lebanese.

The disturbing effects of this dislocation on peoples in several continents are still being estimated, but their general significance has everywhere been recognized. Along with the administrative policies pursued by the imperialist nations, the demographic movement was an active agent in the modification of social and economic patterns of behavior throughout the colonial world. Such changes produced more anxiety and befuddlement among the indigenous populations than hope, but there were some persons within the newly emerging elites who did see some promise, however unintended by the conquerors, in the colonial presence. Jawaharlal Nehru, the former prime minister of India who was an intelligent, yet severe critic of imperialism, offered a comment indicative of this particular intellectual mood. "The impact of Western culture on India," he wrote in the 1940s when empire was waning, "was the impact of a dynamic society, of a 'modern' consciousness, on a static society wedded to medieval habits of thought, which however sophisticated and advanced in its own ways, could not progress because of its inherent limitations."[44]

The colonial situation and the "native policy" which in part defined it will remain one of the most significant cultural encounters that modern world history has recorded.

[44] Jawaharlal Nehru, *Discovery of India* (New York: Doubleday, 1959; first published, 1956), p. 201.

The False Dawn

"The sun rose without splendour," and to the disappointment of the English travelers escorted by their Indian hosts on a railway excursion into the mountains. This scene, found in E. M. Forster's *A Passage to India*, is depicted in symbols that appear to be almost crudely contrived; yet, they might be taken as a poetic synopsis of the imperialist enterprise. Despite the visible signs of technological progress that accompanied the Europeans abroad, and notwithstanding the outward social rapport so properly maintained between conqueror and conquered, empire fulfilled few of its promises. The throbbing colors soon languished into a vapid yellow; it was a false dawn which turned into an undistinguished day.

At one moment, enthusiastic spokesmen for both the parties forced into a colonial attitude had hopes for empire: two worlds would be regenerated, the one by reaching out and finding new national purpose, the other by being required to cast off its old ways. As late as 1945 a group of intellectuals, indigenous to several parts of the recently defeated French empire, could speak of a new harmony, based on humanism and mutual trust, rising on the morrow. Even in the 1950s European authors anticipated a Eurafrican community economically enriching its many participants.[1] Much earlier, of course, colonial protagonists spoke eloquently

---

[1] See Robert Lemaignen, Leopold Senghor, and Prince Sisowath Youtevong, *La communauté impériale française* (Paris: Éditions Alsatia, 1945). On the idea of "Eurafrica," see, for instance, Pierre Nord, *L'Eurafrique: Notre dernière chance* (Paris: A. Fayard, 1955), or Max Liniger-Goumaz, *Eurafrique: Bibliographie générale* (Geneva: Éditions du Temps, 1970).

of empire, a word then mystical in its resonance as it was sounded about a continent given to accounting-house pursuits, but occasionally taken with the heroic act.

It would be ungenerous to state that the only good that came out of imperialism was accidental. But there is no denying that empire did not live up to its expectations. Retrospectively, one can see that late nineteenth-century European assessments of the world order were both grand and gross. Colonial empires were indeed beyond the physical and moral capacities of the states that had created them; the very fragility of their structure was demonstrated by the rapidity with which they soon disintegrated.

Nonetheless, the possibility of such a sudden outcome was not widely entertained at the turn of the nineteenth century; the several activities which colonial administrators were then undertaking suggested some promise. The transformation of the land into patterns partly European, uniquely local, but strikingly different from what existed before was noticeable nearly everywhere, even if most evident in the white-settler colonies. Marshal Lyautey was unduly enthusiastic when he first remarked that boomtowns in the American fashion were popping up in Indochina or when he later announced that Morocco was the French "Far West," but an assertion of the need for and significance of physical change was often made.[2]

The crudely sketched grids that represented the introduction of modern European systems began to make their appearance in the late nineteenth century. Roads and railroads cut inland, wharves and piers extended out into ports. The compounds of schools and colleges occasionally dotted the countryside; aid stations and hospitals, with their regulated methods and orderly arrangement of beds and equipment, were as obvious. More imposing yet were the Eurasian and Eurafrican cities, which developed rectangularly and primarily along the coasts. In a few instances imperial pretensions were here given enduring physical shape. The buildings that Sir Edward Luytens designed for New Delhi were of the proper idiom; and so were the structures that marked the govenor-generalship of Ernest Roume and the site of Dakar in West Africa. Lyautey, this time in his most enjoyable role of builder, sought to harmonize European purposes with local architectural styles. Plans he was already adumbrating for

[2] Louis Hubert Lyautey, *Lettres de Tonkin et de Madagascar, 1894–1899* (Paris: A. Colin, 1921), p. 119; and *Paroles d'action* (Paris: A. Colin, 1927), p. 52.

Casablanca just before World War I were realized in the main squares
shortly thereafter.

All empires seem to reach an Augustan age, at which time monuments
are designed to translate into firm reality the ill-defined search after
grandeur and endurance. By the end of the nineteenth century some of
the many European colonial regents were hoping that just such an age
was about to begin; they were making an initial effort to ensure it, but
with little lasting political consequence.

In the vast reaches of empire in the tropics, the anticipated new order
was primarily evident in the presence of the European: the bush officer
and the missionary, each frequently ignorant of the language and the
mores of the people he was charged to serve. Taxes, military impressment, innoculations, these were the most significant marks of imperialism, to which was added a strange language expressing concepts and
concerns badly out of joint with the cosmos that encircled the local woods
or river. Even the European compound remained a strangely ordered
world. That singular British institution, the club, was widely implanted in
the colonies, where it was a source of contrived conviviality for the
whites, but of baffling discordance for the darker servants who prepared
the menu. As Forster remarked: "A dish might be added or subtracted as
one rose or fell in the official scale; the peas might rattle less or more, the
sardines and the vermouth be imported by a different firm, but the tradition remained; the food of exiles, cooked by servants who did not understand it."[3]

The local elites were, not surprisingly, somewhat hopeful at the outset.
With their children now being educated in European ways, and even occasionally in Europe — a rajah's son playing cricket on English turf was no
longer an event in late Victorian England — they could imagine a colonial
world in which they and their descendants might enjoy continuing or new
responsibility. Empire may have partly frozen the social order so that the
older leaders and their successors remained fixed in position, but the pro-
fessions tentatively beckoned to the younger members of a new elite.
Journalism, the law, the ministry made some accommodation — but at different scales of salary and social perquisite — for the educated "native."
And although the corporals and sergeants who helped staff the colonial
armies may not have been legion, they were sufficient in number to

[3] E. M. Forster, *A Passage to India* (New York: Harcourt, Brace, 1952; first published,
1924), p. 47.

suggest the military as one agency of social mobility. However, the officer corps were generally closed to colonials; the first black African to wear the *galons*, which signified a lieutenancy in the French army, did so only in 1918, and his command included no whites.

All such matters weighed, the colonial effort nevertheless did have some discernible influence. The copper mines of Rhodesia, the rubber plantations of Indochina, and the "bright lights" of the cities were beginning to force or attract populations into new patterns of social and economic activity. The effects on values and attitudes led to what some anthropologists have labeled "detribalization" and to what some sociologists have called an aspect of "modernization." Yet to argue that this was a widespread condition of the colonial world before the 1930s would be an exaggeration.

Neither European resources nor European intentions were such to make the slogan "the white man's burden" more than a responsibility easily shrugged off. In that the wealth amassed through industrialization was unequally divided among all strata of the European populations, a more generous use of it in the colonies would scarcely have been considered by the men who controlled it. However, belatedly, objectives were reversed; in a ratio of desperation capital investment increased as did colonial nationalist protest in the terminal decade of imperialism. "Too little, too late" is a pithy summation of the general results.

To this analysis must be added Lord Bryce's previously quoted appraisal of British activities in India: "whatever may have been done for the people, nothing was or is done by the people."[4] Collaboration was a limited affair between the two ruling elites — the imperial and the indigenous — and it never widely helped the local populations prepare for the adjustments necessary for effective participation in the "modern" world now being imposed. The European mental view of the colonial scene as "empty spaces" or "wastelands" rendered indigenous peoples "invisible," to use Ralph Ellison's apt term in a different cultural context.[5] They were undifferentiated masses to be assisted or manipulated, seldom to be considered or respected individually.

When seen from the nineteenth-century European perspective, modern imperialism suggests a theatrical aspect of considerable interest. The

[4] Lord James Bryce, *The Ancient Roman Empire and the British in India* (London: Oxford University Press, 1914), p. 28.
[5] Ralph Ellison, *Invisible Man* (New York: Random House, 1952).

graphic art displayed on the pages of the *Illustrated London News* and the French publication *Illustration* or in the commemorative brochures of international fairs and the popular geographies found in all private libraries has fixed this imperialist activity, as if in an imitative Greek frieze, for us to observe today. Does the word *tableau* serve better? For so much in that age was grandly staged. The naval procession and the glorious gala embellishing the opening of the Suez Canal, the Diamond Jubilee of Queen Victoria with its lavish parade through the streets of London, the contrived exoticism of the colonial displays at the Parisian Exhibition of 1889 — this is but to list only a few of the most spectacular of such scenes.

Indeed, the colonial situation was curiously stylized, with administrators acting not as themselves but as representatives or living images of the dominant cultural system. "Good form," a term favorably employed in Victorian accounts of public behavior, counted for much. Therefore, there was both acting and posing. When the Anglo-Indians in E. M. Forster's novel decide to put on a small production of the play *Cousin Kate* for their own amusement, "windows were barred, lest the servants see their mem-sahibs acting. . . ."[6] It seemed that one performance had to be hidden so that the other, the routinely colonial, could continue unaffected the following day. This matter of role playing, later to be probed as sensitively by the playwright Pirandello as by modern psychologists, is an intriguing but difficult piece of the colonial scene. A T. E. Lawrence and a Charles Gordon were complicated and confused men who donned masks to hide their real personae. Secluded and unimposing at home, they acquired dashing authority abroad, as if thrust into a milieu in which they could be themselves or become someone they long pretended to be. Even Lyautey, who strictly conformed to the social norms of his day, enjoyed acting the role of vicegerent.

All such personal performances were accompanied by elaborate collective ritual. The ritual of authority, of course, is often as impressive and frequently more effective than the brandishment of the force which ultimately maintains it. The history of western civilization abounds in examples that support this assertion. For instance, the medieval concern over who should wear the imperial diadem and the *phyrgium* was a significant issue in the political relationship between pope and emperor. And the fine act performed daily at Versailles as the *grande levée* of the Sun King helped to keep royal order among the nobles and glory around

---

[6] Forster, *A Passage to India*, p. 24.

the throne. The continuation of such ritual acts in the new colonial empires — consider the durbar of King George V in New Delhi in 1911 — may have been designed as a marvelous means by which to dazzle the local populations with the power transmitted from across the seas; however, these were also staged activities attended, if at great distance, by spectators at home. The religious ceremony of the medieval world was replaced by the national pageantry of the 1800s. In a reversal of values, European imperialism took on the trappings of the oriental despotism it was supposedly replacing.

The anachronistic nature of empire in the modern, democratizing, and industrializing world of nineteenth-century Europe was a source of its appeal. Overseas expansion was advertised as economic and political security against a menacing future, it is true, but it also provided a way of finding what Miniver Cheevy sighed for and thought was not: an age of the gallant and the heroic. From this perspective, imperialism may be considered a nonliterary form of romanticism, an expression of Byronic drama, a beau geste cast far away from and in defiance of the routine of the city office. Perhaps because of its formal stress on individualism and its gnawing realization that the exigencies of modern society severely restricted that individualism, the society of nineteenth-century Europe publicly adored its heroes. As the narrator in *Flashman*, that recent and remarkable parody of the colonial memoir, is allowed to remark: "Why, he had talked as though I was a hero, to be reverenced with that astonishing pussyfooting worship which, for some reason, my century extended to its idols." [7]

In historical retrospect imperialism can be seen as having occurred at two levels: that of the imagination, in which gallantry was frequently extolled; and that of real circumstance, in which crass exploitation all too often took place. A not unparalleled coincidence of these two states happened in 1903. In that year the French author Eugène-Melchior de Vogüé published his romantic novel entitled *Le maître de la mer*, in which the hero, Captain Louis Tournoel, is pitted against an American millionaire, when both, though for different reasons, express their interest in Central Africa. The American sees in empire booty, but Tournoel "was continuing the chivalrous follies of his ancestors who fought the Crusades and the Revolution, those liberators of the Holy Sepulchre and of man-

[7] George M. Fraser, *Flashman: From the Flashman Papers, 1839–1842* (New York: World Publishing, 1969), p. 272.

kind. . . ."[8] In the same year, and in the same geographical region selected by de Vogüé as the setting for his novel, a major colonial scandal was uncovered: the Gaud-Toqué affair. Gaud and Toqué, two junior French administrators, were accused of starving and murdering African porters; they were further accused of sadistic acts which would have taxed the imagination of the author of a Gothic novel. How far removed from de Vogüé's vision was the dreadful reality of colonial life at Fort Crampel in Central Africa.

The historian is provided with no fine instrument by which to measure the effects of European imperialism in the late nineteenth century or even in the twentieth century. As with all human endeavors, it was necessarily muddled. Pretentious in ideology, overbearing in political effect, condescending in social consideration, and exploitive in economic activity, modern imperialism fell short of every mark ascribed to it. Perhaps the final expression of that imperial idea which had extended westward from Rome to Aix-la-Chapelle and then on to the sea, modern European colonial empire was of brief duration, scarcely outliving its most fervent late nineteenth-century proponents. With promises unfulfilled and problems unresolved, imperialism disturbed the world, to the eventual disappointment of both those who supported it and those who endured it.

[8] Eugène-Melchior de Vogüé, *Le maître de la mer* (Paris: Plon, 1903), p. 63.

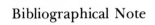

Bibliographical Note

Bibliographical Note

The end of colonial empire has been greeted by an increased academic interest in the causes and effects of European expansion. This development is the obvious result not only of the timeliness of the subject but also of the revision of historical interpretation brought about by the infusion of new ideas and concepts from the social sciences. No longer viewed as a basic problem in power politics, imperialism is now placed in a more complicated structure of economic and social change, and of institutional alteration and adaptation. The consequent historiographical debate which has been going on for the last twenty years has been marked by subtle differences as much as by the emergence of sharply opposing schools of interpretation.

The dominant element in the theoretical constructs upon which historical analysis of imperialism is now based is economic. Modified considerably from the forms given it by Hobson and by Lenin, this element gains purpose as part of that vast process gathered under the name of "modernization." (Since the two "classical" studies concerned with the causal pattern of European imperialism in the nineteenth century — J. A. Hobson, *Imperialism: A Study* (London: Allen & Unwin, 1902), and Vladimir I. Lenin, *Imperialism, the Highest Stage of Capitalism* (New York: International Publishers, 1939; first published, 1917) — have been mentioned in the text of this book, they are not discussed here.) The growth of European industry and trade, the social and political dislocation it caused, and the governmental reaction to the new set of seemingly pressing national

247

and international conditions at the end of the century are the background, as well as the motivating causes, for the most interesting theoretical interpretations of modern imperialism. Crucial to any appreciation of the range of this revisionist interpretation is a reading of that minor classic by Ronald Robinson and John Gallagher, "The Imperialism of Free Trade," *Economic History Review*, 2nd ser., 6:1–15 (1953). A speculative piece, based more on grand assumptions than detailed historical analysis, the article revolutionized the interpretations of British imperialist history in the nineteenth century. Furthermore, it has caused the interpretations of the imperialism of other European nations to be reexamined. Arguing for the primacy and constancy of trade in British expansion, the authors make political or "formal" empire a secondary characteristic and thus discard the older approach to imperialism as a function of power politics expressed only in the last decades of the nineteenth century. The most detailed examination of the debate which has spun around the theory is to be found in William Roger Louis, ed., *Robinson and Gallagher and Their Critics* (New York: Franklin Watts, 1975).

In its approach the Robinson and Gallagher thesis discounts the originality or even the sudden appearance of imperialism in the late nineteenth century, and thus attempts to destroy the long-held assumption of the "New Imperialism." But Robinson and Gallagher have been vigorously challenged by Donald C. M. Platt, *Finance, Trade and Politics in British Foreign Policy, 1815–1914* (Oxford: Clarendon Press, 1968), who denies any coordination between economic expansion and official foreign policy, hence any historical continuity of imperialism in the guise of "informal empire." Moreover, the introduction of a new set of causes has rehabilitated the notion of the "New Imperialism." The work of Hans-Ulrich Wehler, *Bismarck und der Imperialismus* (Cologne: Klepenheuer and Witsch, 1969), is highly innovative, suggesting that a set of social and political problems deriving from the uneven nature of German industrial development in the late century were important elements in Bismarck's acceptance of a policy of imperialism. This emphasis on a form of "social imperialism" was struck from a different continental perspective by Walter LaFeber, *The New Empire: An Interpretation of American Expansion, 1860–1898* (Ithaca, N.Y.: Cornell University Press, 1963), who argues that expansion was seen as a means of relieving the multiple social and economic pressures resulting from an onrushing industrialization.

The multiple facets of this newer socioeconomic approach and its relationship to the older Marxist interpretation were made the subjects of a seminar held at Oxford in 1969–70, the papers of which have been published in Roger Owen and Bob Sutcliffe, eds., *Studies in the Theory of Imperialism* (London: Longman, 1972). This slight volume offers the widest and most valuable introduction to the contemporary debate over the causal pattern of modern imperialism. However, the student desirous of dwelling on the subject longer will find several other studies of great interest. Tom Kemp, *Theories of Imperialism* (London: Dobson, 1967), offers the perceptive commentary of a young English scholar who has attempted to reaffirm the meaningfulness of the Marxist-Leninist approach. Earle M. Winslow, *The Pattern of Imperialism: A Study in the Theories of Power* (New York: Columbia University Press, 1948), written before the rage of revisionist interpretations, still provides a fine assessment of the more classical interpretations constructed in the first half of this century. One other study merits a prominent place in any introductory bibliography. This is Richard Koebner and Helmut Schmidt, *Imperialism: The Story and Significance of a Political Word, 1840–1960* (Cambridge: At the University Press, 1964), which traces the political history as well as the uses of that strategic word *imperialism*.

Despite the recent deviation from it, the political interpretation of imperialism has not been completely denied. All scholars still recognize the importance of the classic by William L. Langer, *The Diplomacy of Imperialism, 1890–1902*, 2 vols. (New York: Alfred A. Knopf, 1935), a finely wrought survey of European worldwide expansion and political involvement. And the chapters devoted to imperialism in A. J. P. Taylor's provocative *Struggle for Mastery in Europe, 1848–1918* (Oxford: Clarendon Press, 1954), offer a strong political interpretation, one in which the diplomatic rivalries on the European Continent are seen as being transported to new, external areas of contention. In his early reply to Robinson and Gallagher, David K. Fieldhouse, "'Imperialism': An Historiographical Revision," *Economic History Review*, 2nd ser., 14:187–209 (1961), argues that "imperialism may best be seen as the extension into the periphery of the political struggle in Europe." And, finally, Richard J. Hammond, "Economic Imperialism: Sidelights of a Stereotype," *Journal of Economic History*, 22:582–598 (1961), finds the major cause of imperialism in matters of national prestige. The most persuasive political arguments are, nonetheless, those nationally centered on French expansion.

In the historical analysis of that country's new empire, economic explanations are exceptional, not routine. The pivotal work around which the national argument revolves is Henri Brunschwig, *French Colonialism, 1817–1914: Myths and Realities*, trans. William G. Brown (New York: Praeger, 1966; first published, 1960). Herein the author insists that French expansion was a political reaction to the nation's ignominious defeat in the Franco-Prussian War. Empire was thus a form of nationalism extended overseas.

The Eurocentric bias of all these interpretations has been severely challenged of late. Indeed, some of the most striking new insights into the problem of imperialism have been derived from the "inside out" approach made by a number of scholars who have been examining imperialism on the scene or on the "periphery," to employ Fieldhouse's term. Fifteen years ago, John D. Hargreaves wisely argued for attention to the "missing element" in the history of the partition of Africa, namely, the role of African rulers and states. His "Towards a History of the Partition of Africa," *Journal of African History*, 1:96–109 (1960), is today very dated, clear proof of the article's timeliness and the academic response given it. Imperialism as a problem of interaction between competing cultures and political systems is now widely recognized. That such localized engagement may be the cause of expansion, for which imperialism — here defined as home governmental policy — is a response, is a historical proposition offered with considerable effect by Robinson and Gallagher, with Alice Denny, in their *Africa and the Victorians: The Climax of Imperialism in the Dark Continent* (New York: St. Martin's Press, 1961). It was what they call the "Egyptian crisis," essentially the nationalist revival directed by Colonel Arabi, which provoked British occupation; this, in turn, caused the scramble for Africa. This thesis is further elaborated and converted into a historical fact by the two authors in their chapter, "The Partition of Africa," in *New Cambridge Modern History*, vol. XI: *Material Progress and World-wide Problems, 1870–1898*, ed. F. H. Hinsley (Cambridge: At the University Press, 1968). The originality of the thesis has been heralded by Eric Stokes, "Late Nineteenth Century Colonial Expansion and the Attack on the Theory of Economic Imperialism: A Case of Mistaken Identity," *Historical Journal*, 12:285–301 (1969), who declares that the older Eurocentric interpretation of imperialism is a dead letter. Most recently, David K. Fieldhouse has attempted something of an interpretative reconciliation of the two competing geographical bases, the

European and the colonial, in his *Economics and Empire, 1830–1914* (Ithaca, N.Y.: Cornell University Press, 1973). He asserts that "positive action normally begins as a response to peripheral problems or opportunities rather than as the product of calculated imperialist policy." Something of a complicated and refined stimulus-and-response pattern is thus proffered.

These new historical appraisals have developed coincidentally with an impressive series of monographs on local expressions of imperialism. That a large number does exist and that the area most extensively considered is Subsaharan Africa is indicative of the movement away from older ethnocentric assumptions that colonized peoples passively accepted the imperial presence. Again, the monographs fall into two chronological categories: those concerned with the preconditions upon which imperialism was structured or by which it was later provoked, and those concerned with the immediate causes of the imperialist act.

In the former category, authors have expressed particular interest in local trade patterns and how, through change chiefly resulting from the impact of European industrialization, they developed into problems of national political concern and international rivalry. Kenneth Onwuka Dike, *Trade and Politics in the Niger Delta, 1830–1885* (Oxford: Clarendon Press, 1956), splendidly poses and solves this historical problem, as it surveys the deteriorating position of the African "middleman" and the littoral states he developed on the basis of the slave trade. A complement to this study is A. Adu Boahen, *Britain, the Sahara, and the Western Sudan, 1788–1861* (Oxford: Clarendon Press, 1964). More broadly based and detailed is the now indispensable study of John D. Hargreaves, *Prelude to the Partition of West Africa* (London: Macmillan, 1963), a clearly and judiciously written assessment of local Anglo-French trading factors and intensifying political rivalry. Across the world, John K. Fairbank has surveyed in elaborate detail the commercial, political patterns on the China coast in his *Trade and Diplomacy on the China Coast*, vol. I: *The Opening of the Treaty Ports, 1842–1854* (Cambridge, Mass.: Harvard University Press, 1953). And John F. Cady, *The Roots of French Imperialism in Eastern Asia* (Ithaca, N.Y.: Cornell University Press, 1954), has done likewise, but with greatest attention given to the all-important missionary factor.

Among those studies concerned with the immediate, local aspects in the outburst of imperialism, there is considerable range. John Galbraith has selected the "turbulent frontier" as provocation to military extension of territory in India, Malaya, and South Africa. Both in his seminal article, "The 'Turbulent Frontier' as a Factor in British Expansion," *Comparative Studies in Society and History*, 2:150–168 (1960), and in his *Reluctant Empire: British Policy on the South African Frontier, 1834–1854* (Berkeley: University of California Press, 1963), he effectively develops this idea. Also concerned with the military aspects of imperialism is A. S. Kanya-Forstner. In *The Conquest of the Western Sudan: A Study in French Military Imperialism* (Cambridge: At the University Press, 1969), he proposes that it was as much the ambitions of the *officier soudanais* as it was official policy at home which led to French territorial extension in this part of the world. And in a different historical situation, Damodar P. Singhal, *The Annexation of Upper Burma* (Singapore: Eastern Universities Press, 1960), sets out to show that local traders were chiefly responsible for inducing the British to annex this region.

Beyond the causal patterns now being reworked float the justifying ideology and the gossamerlike *Zeitgeist* which supported it. No appreciation of the contemporary meaning of imperialism can be obtained without some idea of the form it took in the minds of its proponents. Historians have long dwelt on the subject and therefore have written extensively about it. A very readable general introduction to the broad dimensions of this ideology is A. P. Thornton, *Doctrines of Imperialism* (New York: Wiley, 1965), which is something of an informal essay entertaining a number of contentious opinions. William L. Langer, "A Critique of Imperialism," *Foreign Affairs*, 14:102–120 (1935), is still singled out as a good attempt to capture the spirit that informed imperialism and that the author also asserted was a cause of it. Heinz Gollwitzer's little study, *Europe in the Age of Imperialism, 1880–1914*, trans. David Adam and Stanley Baron (New York: Harcourt, Brace and World, 1969), provides a good *tour d'horizon* of the intellectual and social forces which combined to make imperialism something of a popular activity. Among the particular treatments of national ideologies, the following are most commendable. Richard Faber, *The Vision and the Need: Late Victorian Imperialist Aims* (London: Faber & Faber, 1966), is an elegant little essay recapitulating the major lines of the most ardent proponents of imperialism in England at the time. Carl A. Bodelson, *Studies in Mid-Victorian Imperialism* (New York: Fertig, 1968; first published, 1924), is an early effort still useful for an appraisal of the thinking of men like Froude and Seeley. An important study which first analytically explored the arguments for "social imperialism" is Bernard Semmel, *Imperialism and Social Reform: English Social-Imperial Thought, 1895–1914* (London: Allen & Unwin, 1960). A. P. Thornton, *The Imperial Idea and Its Enemies: A Study in Power* (London: Macmillan, 1959), is most useful for an appreciation of the sense of duty which permeated the English upper classes and the concept generally defined as "muscular Christianity" which gave to British imperialism its haughty demeanor. For a review of the dissenters from imperialism, see Bernard Porter, *Critics of Empire: British Radical Attitudes to Colonialism in Africa, 1895–1914* (New York: St. Martin's Press, 1968), which offers valuable assessments of the thought of Hobson and Morel.

Crossing the Channel brings the reader to the even more rarefied ideological heights of France where national vocation and civilizing mission resided. Raoul Girardet, *L'idée coloniale en France de 1871 à 1914* (Paris: Table Ronde, 1972), is a magnificent survey of French attitudes toward the imperial endeavor and is nicely complemented by the introductory remarks of D. Bruce Marshall, *The French Colonial Myth and Constitution-Making in the Fourth Republic* (New Haven, Conn.: Yale University Press, 1973). Agnes Murphy, *The Ideology of French Imperialism* (Washington, D.C.: Catholic University Press, 1948), and Raymond F. Betts, *Assimilation and Association in French Colonial Theory, 1890–1914* (New York: Columbia University Press, 1961), provide good assessments of the doctrinal issues debated in the formative years of the Third Republic's overseas empire.

Related to the expressions of ideological concern are the premises upon which cultural contact was established and the effects of that contact. This subject is both a scientific and a controversial one, enlisting the support of sociology and cultural anthropology while engendering a debate over the oppressive psychological nature of European domination. Among the best known and most frequently commented on works are the major studies of Frantz Fanon, *Black Skin, White Masks*, trans. Charles L. Markmann (New York: Grove Press, 1967; first published, 1952), and *The Wretched of the Earth*, trans. Constance Farrington (New York: Grove Press, 1966; first published, 1961), and the brief essay — which complements Fanon's first study — Albert Memmi, *The Colonizer and the Colonized*, trans. Howard Greenfield (Boston: Beacon Press, 1967; first published, 1957). Both authors are concerned with the asymmetrical nature of the colonial situation: Fanon with its imposed violence and destructiveness;

Memmi with the problem of role playing between the dominator and dominated. As Fanon's work has had considerable influence in the ideologies accompanying decolonization, it merits close reading.

One of the best general introductions to the issue of social domination in the colonial world is Philip Mason, *Patterns of Dominance* (London: Oxford University Press, 1970), in which the general literature on the subject is given close consideration and a number of case studies are thoughtfully presented. With respect to particular colonial situations, several works should be examined. Philip D. Curtin, *The Image of Africa: British Ideas and Action, 1780–1850* (Madison: University of Wisconsin Press, 1964), is a splendid survey of British observations and perceptions of black Africa. It is complemented by H. Alan C. Cairns, *Prelude to Imperialism: British Reactions to Central African Society, 1840–1890* (London: Routledge, 1965). More theoretical and quite indispensable is Georges Balandier, *The Sociology of Black Africa: Social Dynamic in Central Africa*, trans. Douglas Garman (New York: Praeger, 1970; first published, 1955). For a wider historical appreciation, Immanuel Wallerstein, *Social Change: The Colonial Situation* (New York: Wiley, 1966), has carefully amassed some of the most significant writings on the myriad of problems, such as urbanization, education, labor, which the colonial situation provoked. For those readers who would have an olympian perspective on the vast effects of the forced cultural contact which was the nature of modern imperialism, two studies in particular will stimulate the historical imagination. K. M. Panikkar, *Asia and Western Dominance* (London: Allen & Unwin, 1959), traces the European presence and its effects from Vasco da Gama to the end of the colonial era, with stress on the thalassocracy maintained for so long by the British. Still more ambitious is William H. McNeill, *The Rise of the West: A History of the Human Community* (Chicago: University of Chicago Press, 1963), in which part III provides a grand historical explanation for European dominance in the world from 1500 to the near present.

Related to this subject, of course, are the administrative structures and colonial policies which were designed to form empire into units of meaningful organization. This part of colonial history is one of the oldest, initially an adjunct of the constitutional history which so held European attention in the late nineteenth and early twentieth centuries. Between the wars, when the common problems of imperial rule were widely discussed, a large number of studies appeared, some yielded from international conferences held for the express purpose of arriving at a comparative approach to the colonial situation. The Royal Institute of International Affairs produced such a study entitled *The Colonial Problem* (London: Oxford University Press, 1937), and the International Colonial Institute published the findings of its conference in *Organisation politique et administrative des colonies* (Brussels: Etablissements Généraux d'Imprimérie, 1936). Both studies are favorable to the colonial enterprise, expressive of the then prevalent view that colonial empire had a long future. Although they are therefore very dated, these two volumes do illuminate the problems and aspirations that motivated the European nations in the halycon years of colonial administration. More historically analytical and generally more encompassing are the following studies of particular national colonial development. E. M. Walker, *The British Empire: Its Structure and Spirit, 1497–1953* (London: Oxford University Press, 1954), is a standard introduction to the subject. Nicholas Mansergh, *The Commonwealth Experience* (London: Weidenfeld and Nicolson, 1969), a study of the evolving general form of the British empire and the thought which guided it, is particularly recommended. Then, a reading of the following three excellent monographs, in order of the chronological periods with which they are concerned, will provide a good understanding of the relationship of British home policy to colonial developments: Helen Taft Manning, *British Colonial Government after the American Revolution, 1782–1820* (New Haven, Conn.: Yale University Press, 1933); Paul Knaplund, *James Stephen and the British Colonial System, 1813–1847* (Madison: University of Wisconsin Press, 1953); and John W. Cell, *British Colonial Administration in the Mid-Nineteenth Century: The Policy-Making Process* (New Haven, Conn.: Yale University Press, 1970). For France, the best brief introductory study is Hubert Deschamps, *Méthodes et doctrines coloniales de la France du XVe siècle à nos jours* (Paris: A. Colin, 1953). An exceptionally detailed study which has weathered the years quite well is Arthur Girault, *Principes de colonisation et de legislation coloniale*, 3 vols. (Paris: Recueil Sirey, 1930), which first appeared in 1895 and ran a course of several editions to 1927. Stephen H. Roberts, *The History of French Colonial Policy, 1870–1925*, 2 vols. (London: P. S. King, 1929), still serves as the standard text in English, to which might be added the sympathetic treatment found in Georges Hardy, *Histoire sociale de la colonisation française* (Paris: Larose, 1953). On the other colonial administrations a few standard studies will be mentioned. A. D. A. de Kat Angelino, *Colonial Policy*, 2 vols., trans. G. J. Renier (Chicago: University of Chicago Press, 1931), provides close analysis of the Dutch system; John S. Furnivall, *Colonial Policy and Practice: A Comparative Study of Burma and Netherlands India* (Cambridge: At the University Press, 1948), does well what its subtitle suggests. On Belgian policy, Roger Anstey, *King Leopold's Legacy: The Congo under Belgian Rule, 1908–1960* (London: Oxford University Press, 1966), offers some trenchant introductory comments. And Jean Sohier, "Du dynamisme Léopoldien à l'immobilisme belge," *Problèmes sociaux congolais*, 73:39–71 (1966), provides a clear outline of Congo administration. German rule in Africa is covered in three particular monographs. Harry R. Rudin, *Germans in the Cameroons, 1884–1914: A Case Study in Modern Imperialism* (New Haven, Conn.: Yale University Press, 1938), was a pacesetter, now complemented by two other regional studies of importance: Helmut Bley, *Southwest Africa under German Rule, 1894–1914*, trans. Hugh Ridley (Evanston, Ill.: Northwestern University Press, 1971; first published, 1968), and John Iliffe, *Tanganyika under German Rule, 1905–1912* (Cambridge: At the University Press, 1969), both of which merit close attention.

The men who managed empire on its many fronts have recently enlisted the efforts of historians who have assessed their role in terms of individual biography, institutional development, and social profiles. Philip Woodruff (Philip Mason), *The Men Who Ruled India* (New York: St. Martin's Press, 1954), stresses the personalities and functions of the viceroys. Robert Heussler, *Yesterday's Rulers: The Making of the British Colonial Service* (Syracuse, N.Y.: Syracuse University Press, 1963), is particularly concerned with the methods of recruitment which, in fact, were essentially the personal decisions of Sir Ralph Furse who, between the wars, ran this service. And William B. Cohen, *Rulers of Empire: The French Colonial Service in Africa* (Stanford, Calif.: Hoover Institution Press, 1971), provides a social profile of the men who entered this service and an analysis of the role of the famous Ecole Coloniale in their training. Rupert Wilkinson, *The Prefects: British Leadership and the Public School Tradition. A Comparative Study in the Making of Rulers* (London: Oxford University Press, 1964), analyzes the values and attitudes which formed part of the Victorian public mentality and offers some useful comments on the servant of empire. Finally, a most indispensable reference work is David P. Henige, *Colonial Governors from the Fifteenth Century to the*

Present: A Comprehensive List (Madison: University of Wisconsin Press, 1970).

Whether the calculated efforts of administrators and home governments yielded attractive monetary returns to the nation as a whole is a question which has been raised since empire became a reality. Against the theoretical studies that made an expansionist capitalism the motor force of imperialism, there is a number of studies treating in detail and with dispassion trade and monetary patterns in the nineteenth century. The classic is Herbert W. Feis, *Europe the World's Banker, 1870–1914: An Account of Foreign Investment and the Connection of World Finance with Diplomacy before the War* (New Haven, Conn.: Yale University Press, 1930), a detailed assessment of European national banking habits and investment patterns. The author concludes capital went abroad for many reasons, but often its location was determined by the "calculations of national advantage." Grover Clark, *The Balance Sheets of Empire: Facts and Figures on Colonies* (New York: Columbia University Press, 1936), offers an impressive array of statistical charts and the general conclusion that empire did not pay. As might be expected, most of the studies concentrate on the British experience, and a few of the major ones will here be mentioned. Leland H. Jenks, *The Migration of British Capital to 1875* (New York: Alfred A. Knopf, 1938), is a general study in which empire is but one component. The author argues that British investment in the dependent empire, notably India, returned an "income of imponderables." S. B. Saul, *Studies in British Overseas Trade, 1870–1914* (Liverpool: Liverpool University Press, 1960), specifically concentrates on the economic purposes of empire; he concludes that the British empire was a political, not an economic creation, which was of economic value in indirect ways. A. K. Cairncross, *Home and Foreign Investment, 1870–1913: Studies in Capital Accumulation* (Cambridge: At the University Press, 1953), is particularly valuable for the correlation it makes between British migration to the English-speaking colonies and the migration of capital.

Proceeding from the topical monograph to the general study defined along national or chronological lines, the reader will soon encounter a general *embarras de richesses* in almost any good library. But equally noticeable will be the dirth of good recent syntheses which treat of the activities of competing empires over any long period of time. The best recent introduction is David K. Fieldhouse, *The Colonial Empires: A Comparative Survey from the Eighteenth Century* (London: Weidenfeld and

Nicolson, 1966), which is chronologically arranged and subdivided according to national effort. More restricted in scope and sociological in its treatment of British, French, and German imperialism is the work of G. W. Hallgarten, *Imperialismus vor 1914*, 2 vols. (Munich: Beck, 1963). Also European-centered is Wolfgang J. Mommsen, *Das Zeitalter des Imperialismus* (Frankfurt: Fischer, 1968). That older works like Parker T. Moon, *Imperialism and World Politics* (New York: Macmillan, 1926), are still cited in most bibliographies gives some indication of the paucity of studies at this level.

In contrast stands the long list of recent histories devoted to particular national empires. Among the ample collection on the British empire, a readable, if slightly sentimental introductory work is Charles E. Carrington, *The British Empire Overseas: Exploits of a Nation of Shopkeepers* (Cambridge: At the University Press, 1950). William D. McIntyre, *Colonies into Commonwealth* (New York: Walker, 1967), has the virtue of conciseness and the persistence of a theme. And A. L. Burt, *The Evolution of the British Empire and Commonwealth from the American Revolution* (Boston: D. C. Heath, 1956), has long enjoyed the reputation of being a standard text. The most useful recent analysis of the French empire is Jean Ganiage, *L'expansion coloniale de la France sous la Troisième République, 1871–1914* (Paris: Payot, 1968). Still serviceable and the only major works available in English are Stephen H. Roberts, *The History of French Colonial Policy, 1870–1925*, 2 vols. (London: P. S. King, 1929), and Herbert I. Priestley, *France Overseas: A Study of Modern Imperialism* (Berkeley: University of California Press, 1938). Henri Brunschwig, *La colonisation française: Du pacte colonial à l'union française* (Paris: Calmann-Levy, 1949), provides a brief colony-by-colony assessment, as does at greater length Henri Blet, *France d'outre-mer*, vol. III: *L'oeuvre coloniale de la Troisième République* (Grenoble: Arthaud, 1950). Of particular note is Jean Suret-Canale, *French Colonialism in Tropical Africa, 1900–1945*, trans. Till Gottheimer (New York: Pica Press, 1971; first published, 1964), the second volume of a severely critical assessment by a Marxist author of the French effort in this part of the world.

The lesser colonial empires have not been ignored by recent historians. German colonial activities are receiving considerable attention, as the reception of the work by Wehler, *Bismarck und der Imperialismus*, cited above, has already demonstrated. An interpretation stressing the economic factors at work in German expansion is Henri Brunschwig, *L'expansion allemande outre-mer* (Paris: Presses Universitaires de France, 1957), in conjunction with which the slight volume of brief essays, W. O. Henderson, *Studies in German Colonial History* (Chicago: Quadrangle Books, 1962), might also be read. A. J. P. Taylor, *Germany's First Bid for Colonies, 1884–1885* (London: Macmillan, 1938), attributes Bismarck's colonial policy to considerations of European policy, a means by which to draw close to France by irritating Great Britain. Mary E. Townsend, *The Rise and Fall of Germany's Colonial Empire, 1848–1918* (New York: Macmillan, 1930), still is of use, although its supporting interpretation is outdated.

Research on Belgium's sole colony has also been brisk. Ruth T. Slade, *King Leopold's Congo* (London: Oxford University Press, 1962), is a clearly written introductory study, the best available in English. The Belgian historian Père A. Roeykens, who has long explored the motives behind Leopold's actions — and sees these of long gestation — provides a synthesis of this thought in *Léopold II et l'Afrique, 1880–1885: Essai de synthèse et de mise au point* (Brussels: Académie Royale des Sciences Coloniales, 1955). On the financial manipulations of Leopold, see Jean Stengers, *Combien le Congo a-t-il couté à la Bélgique?* (Brussels: Académie Royale des Sciences Coloniales, 1957). The Dutch in the East Indies have been considered in Bernard H. M. Vlekke, *Nusantara: A History of Indonesia* (rev. ed.; Chicago: Quadrangle Books, 1960), and in John S. Furnivall, *Netherlands India: A Study of a Plural Economy* (New York: Macmillan, 1939). The standard treatment of Portugal is James Duffy, *Portugal in Africa* (Baltimore, Md.: Penguin Books, 1963; first published, 1962), to which should be joined Eric V. Axelson, *Portugal and the Scramble for Africa, 1875–1891* (Johannesburg: University of Witwatersrand Press, 1967). On Italian efforts, see Robert Hess, *Italian Colonialism in Somalia* (Chicago: University of Chicago Press, 1966), and, as a convenient introduction, Jean-Louis Miège, *L'impérialisme colonial italien de 1870 à nos jours* (Paris: Société d'Édition d'Enseignement Supérieur, 1968).

Since an introductory bibliographical essay of this sort can only include the most significant of the historical works on this general subject, the student wishing to probe further should turn to some of the more recent bibliographical studies. John P. Halstead and Serafino Porcari, *Modern European Imperialism: A Bibliography of Books and Articles*, 2 vols. (Boston: Hall, 1974), is the most comprehensive, but it is not annotated. It supersedes Lowell J. Ragatz, *The Literature of European Imperialism: A Bibliography, 1815–1939* (3rd ed.; Washington, D.C.: Pearlman, 1947). Robin W. Winks, ed., *The Historiography of the British Empire-Commonwealth: Trends, Interpretations and Resources* (Durham, N.C.: Duke University Press, 1966), is a fine, critical review made by eminent scholars in the field. The bibliographical essays found in the two volumes edited by Prosser Gifford and William Roger Louis, *Britain and Germany in Africa: Imperial Rivalry and Colonial Rule* (New Haven, Conn.: Yale University Press, 1967), and *France and Britain in Africa: Imperial Rivalry and Colonial Rule* (New Haven, Conn.: Yale University Press, 1971), are outstanding.

Index

Index

263

28; emergence as European power, 75, 77; Tirpitz plan, 78; imperialism after *1870*, 79–81, 91; interests in Far East, 106, 111–114; economic ideologies of imperialism, 130–132; political administration of colonies, 194–196; federation of Imperial Germany, 205; native policy, 225. *See also* East Africa, German Southwest Africa

Girault, Alfred, 26

Godeffroy, J. C., and Son, 111–112, 114

Goldie, George Taubman, 28, 93

Gordon, Sir Charles, 24, 61n28, 92, 98, 185

Grand Trunk Railroad, 205

Granville, Lord, 88, 228–229

Great Britain: imperialist thought, 11–18, 123–127, 130–135 *passim*; support for imperialism, 23–30 *passim*, 146–147; relations with Germany, 26, 75, 77, 103, 104, 117; "informal empire," 37–38, 41, 46, 48–49, 70, 124, 148–149; Pax Britannica, 38–39, 75; overview of imperial politics, 38–39, 75, 77–79, 81–83, 116–117; relations with France, 38–54 *passim*, 75, 76, 79, 81, 83, 86–89, 98–101, 116; relations with Holland, 58; abolitionist movement, 159–163 *passim*
    Structure and policy of imperial administration, 41, 193, 194: colonial administrators, 26, 197–198; federation movement, 78, 203, 205, 208–210, 213; decentralization, 196–197; crown colony system, 198–199; direct/indirect administration, 199–202; native policy, 222, 224, 227

Great Reform Bill (*1832*), 162

Green, Thomas H., 27

Grey, Sir Charles, 199

Grey, Sir Edward, 99, 135

Guadeloupe, 42–44, 195

Guiana, 44

Guizot, François, 61

Haggard, Rider, 24

Hangchow Bay, 107

Hanotaux, Gabriel, 20, 99, 205

Harmand, Jules, 12–13

Hastings, Warren, 166

Havelaar, Max, 156

Hawaii, 105

Hay, John, 107–108

Hayford, Joseph Casely, 232

Heligoland, 97

Henty, G. A., 24

Herero Wars (*1904–7*), 219

Hilferding, Rudolph, 140–141

Hobson, J. A., 121, 122, 125, 142: economic imperialist theories, 136–138, 145

Hohenlohe, Prince, 80

Holland, 56, 113: loss of colonial empire, 39, 58, 64; occupation by French in *1795*, 45; political administration of colonies, 195, 197; employs "culture system" in Java, 226–227

Holy Alliance, 46

Hong Kong, 60, 107

Hottentots, 64

Hugo, Victor, 161

Ibrahim Pasha, 92

Iloo, king of Congo, 24, 90

Imperial administration, structure and policy of: colonial administrators, 25–26, 197–198; autocratic control, 40, 198–199; imperial federations, 127, 203–214; general features of colonial administration, 185–192; colonial ministries, 193; role of military, 193–195; responsibilities of executive branch, 195–196; responsibilities of legislative branch, 196–197; direct administration, 199–201, 204; indirect administration, 199, 201–203, 214. *See also* Imperial native policy

Imperial Conference (*1897*), 134

Imperial Federation League, 23, 210

Imperial native policy: factors influencing, 215–218; subordination of indigenous peoples, 218–221; under system of indirect rule, 221–225; forced labor, 225–231; taxation, 225, 231; modernization, 231–232; resistance to, 232–236; effects of, 236–237. *See also* Imperial administration

Imperialism: causal patterns of, 33–36, 69–72; effects of, 238–244

Imperialist thought, 18–19, 22–31, 50, 119–120: prestige, 11–12, 19–21, 26–27
    Socioeconomic, 12–18
    Economic, 21–22, 40, 121–123, 225–226: in England, 123–127, 130–135 *passim*; in France, 127–130; in Germany, 130–132; anti-imperialist, 135–142; gap between theory and practice, 143–149
    Social, 20–21: impact of racial theories, 150–156; social factors influencing racial theories, 156–159; humanitarianism and emergence of abolitionist movement,